DATE DUE

MILITARY OCCUPATION
AND NATIONAL SECURITY

MILITARY OCCUPATION
AND NATIONAL SECURITY

By Martin and Joan Kyre

Public Affairs Press, Washington, D. C.

TO EDGAR AND SARAH RANDOLPH

PREFACE

In conceiving this book we intended to focus our attention chiefly on the U.S. Army's record of successes and failures in governing conquered territories. As research progressed, however, it became clear that the military's function in foreign administration was influenced by many unanticipated facets of American life. National interest, national principles, and national mood emerged as forces which could not be overlooked or minimized. Political interest groups, Congress, and international law also demanded exploration and inclusion. Hence it became evident that it was necessary to broaden our inquiry to encompass much of what has come to be known as national security policy.

Techniques of occupation control have varied greatly according to the locale, social background of the population, and nature of the U.S. military involvement undertaken. Their range has included belligerent occupations stemming from major wars, civil assistance programs associated with small undeclared wars such as in Korea and Vietnam, and random civic action projects in friendly, underdeveloped countries. Moreover, increasingly frequent use of the more unconventional forms such as police actions and pacification efforts has intensified the average voter's interest in the Pentagon's civil programs overseas.

Unlike the Army commander in the field who often must act intuitively when solving day-to-day problems, or the Washington official who must of necessity deal with compartmentalized segments of the question, the detached observer freed from decision-making responsibilities has the opportunity to assess the overall implications of civil-military policy. That is the perspective adopted in this book. Conclusions reached here are in some instances quite speculative, but hopefully they will be considered by those officials and laymen who are trying to foresee America's role in future international conflicts.

Although the authors hold a deep respect for the professional military establishment, some of the incidents described here are unavoidably tragicomic. Certainly it is not our intent to question the integrity of individual officials, but, instead, to scrutinize the Army's control of civilian life abroad.

As in all books thanks must be expressed to those people who went beyond normal expectation in furnishing assistance. Colonels Leroy

Wade, Tom H. Barratt, William R. Swarm and William P. Wainsboro — consecutive Commandants of the U.S. Army Civil Affairs School since its inception — were most helpful. Throughout a decade of association we benefited from their personal insights. We also profited from the views of numerous civilian officials, particularly Anthony J. Auletta and Loyal Swick, who are among the few persons in active service who have remained concerned with military occupation matters since World War II. Former Chief of the Army Civil Affairs Section in Washington, Colonel Norman D. King (Ret.), has contributed as much as any single individual to further the efforts of researchers in this field. Recently he donated his extensive collection of U.S. and foreign documents and personal papers to Syracuse University's Library in order to insure their continuing availability.

Political scientists and historians representing varied specialities were called upon frequently for advice and assistance. We wish to thank especially professors Jacqueline Collins for editorial and substantive criticisms, James V. Reese for reading the Civil War sections, Shirley Chapman for commenting on references to political interest groups and American governmental institutions, Metin Tamkoc for offering advice on the international law of war and for reading the entire work from the standpoint of a European scholar, and, finally, Lynwood M. Holland, Chairman of the Department of Governmnt at Texas Tech, for insisting that the time had arrived to submit the manuscript to a publisher.

Needless to say, each of the academicians and Army officials who gave us their time naturally saw military occupation problems from widely divergent backgrounds, and cannot be held accountable for the ideas and judgments in these pages.

Appreciation is also owed Lynn Collins, Shirley Reese, Diana Collins and Bobbie Perry for typing and proofreading assistance.

MARTIN AND JOAN KYRE

Lubbock, Texas

CONTENTS

ABOUT THE AUTHORS

Both members of this husband and wife team hold degrees from Ohio Wesleyan University. Martin T. Kyre (Ph.D. in political science, University of Washington) is currently an Associate Professor of Government at Texas Technological College. His firsthand experience with Army civil affairs encompasses civic action work during the Korean conflict, a variety of assignments with USAR military government units, and Mobilization Designation status with the U.S. Army Civil Affairs School and the Civil Affairs Division in the Pentagon. In a university capacity he organized and was the initial Director of the Peace Corps Training Center at Texas Tech.

Joan Randolph Kyre's academic field is sociology. In preparing this book she has been a full-time research and writing collaborator with a special concern for the problems of social and political theory connected with Army management of civilian institutions.

As this book goes to press, Mr. and Mrs. Kyre have just returned from the Far East where Professor Kyre was on leave under a research grant studying the nation-building implications of the American administration of Okinawa.

Chapter I

INTRODUCTION

America gained its initial experience in conducting a major military occupation during the Mexican War. However, the idea of occupation was already a familiar one. Britain, France, Spain, Russia, and Mexico had each employed armies to enforce policies upon the territory which later became the United States. And during the early years of its existence, the new republic itself engaged in several conflicts to retain or extend its national boundaries. Because of historic experiences, the United States began early to develop a negative attitude toward occupations. This was a logical outgrowth of the unsavory incidents which occurred under British rule and which were still vivid in the memory of those who had lived during the Revolutionary period. Later generations perpetuated this heritage as they feared a military tyranny as the very antithesis of American freedom.

Another habit of thought can be traced to the prolonged Indian Wars. Following the Revolutionary War and the War of 1812, important campaigns were undertaken against the Indians in the West and the South. Because military problems for the settlers ended with victory, the belief took root that winning the battle itself was the ultimate goal of war. The Indian Wars did not necessitate occupations. Since the red men were considered savages ineligible to claim sovereign statehood for the territories which historically had been theirs, it was impossible for them to demand the rights which international law and custom bestowed upon the citizens of defeated nations. The tribes were eliminated, pushed farther west, or relegated to reservations in undesirable regions. There were too many other pressing problems connected with the building of the new nation for people to worry much about what happened to the Indians.

Through the unfolding of these events the U.S. acquired considerable practical knowledge of warfare, but gained little understanding of the problems of belligerent occupation. However, two basic precepts became evident which were often afterwards applied in governing enemy civilians during and following conflicts. The first and readiest approach to the problem was simply to ignore it. Hopefully, it would disappear. Moreover, the concept of formal occupation could be dismissed as merely another undesirable facet of the militarism

1

belonging to the perpetually fighting nations of Europe. If, on the other hand, the persistence of the quandary prevented its being ignored, the second axiom came into play. This was that though occupation might be necessary it was still contemptuous and unclean by the standards of democratic men. It must be recognized, of course, that as new problems arose and traditions evolved these original assumptions were incorporated into a broader context of national views. Nevertheless, America continued to disregard the difficulties of occupation rather than to prepare for them as a necessary aspect of military policy.

The strength and durability of this factor in our heritage has influenced our foreign operations in many respects. It has resulted in a failure to recognize the full significance of the perennial weakness in American policy for governing civilian populations. For example, at the turn of the century the United States fought bravely and won the Spanish-American War. But the new Caribbean holdings were governed so ineptly that the eventual establishment of a communist regime in Cuba was almost inevitable. Two major wars were fought with Germany. One wonders if the second war would have been necessary if the U.S. had followed a different course in dealing with the German problem in the first instance. The American people detest war, but somehow they find the moral strength to destroy cities and kill enemies in combat. But rebuilding towns and rehabilitating conquered populations have proved to be much more uninteresting and distasteful.

These attitudes also have permeated the American academic community. Most of the relatively few books dealing with occupations were written during or soon after the conclusion of hostilities by scholars who had witnessed or participated in military government. Whether admitted or not, many of their works exhibited a viewpoint stemming from intense personal involvement and offered little more than pretense at objectivity. They frequently concentrated upon particular situations and were generally restricted to recording events which took place in a single occupied country or even a single city. The impression left, usually without intent, is that each operation has been such a unique and isolated venture that the problem of occupation policy itself is rather minor when weighed against the backdrop of overall foreign policy.

Few of the personal narratives have attempted to integrate local happenings into a more inclusive picture. In fact, not a single satisfactory study of a general nature has ever been completed, let alone a comprehensive policy analysis. Therefore, our objective in preparing this book is to attempt to draw together the major policy threads which have consistently been important in determining the approach adopted in handling foreign civilians. No attempt has been made here to record the details surrounding each and every past undertaking. This book is not a history of events and personalities; it is confined to an analysis of only those factors which reflect the persistent ingredients of policy.

Another impression gained from the literature is that policy planning involves a seemingly endless array of confused and insoluable diplomatic and military questions. With few exceptions, Army officials who subsequently wrote about their experiences emphasized the difficulties they had individually faced rather than exploring the significance of the overall effort. It is also true that occupation officials generally had only enough time and energy to deal with their assigned duties and could not be expected to evaluate alternate patterns of action. As a result, they usually came away from their assignment with frustration arising out of the small progress made during their tenure. Often they looked back with genuine disgust and seemed to wonder how the area survived the occupation at all. Such attitudes of pessimism and futility, though not always justified, have in fact tended to mar the thinking of those who plan future occupations.

Journalists have also contributed numerous accounts describing the actions of military governors. Unfortunately, such narratives typically focused upon and sensationalized instances of corruption, inefficiency, and lack of adequate planning. While the essential truth of many of these sordid tales can hardly be denied, they nevertheless tend to cast an irrational stigma over the total effort. After the journalists had capitalized upon the situation by writing a series of devastating articles or, in several cases, books, they too wanted nothing further to do with military occupation.

These criticisms should not be misinterpreted. There have been significant though rare writings which reflect serious thought, and even the most biased personal accounts are of value. Rather than censuring previous efforts because of their omissions, it is only fair to give them credit for having made an invaluable step in the right direction.

Perhaps the most important reason for the lack of systematic, objective treatment of this aspect of policy is the private disposition of those who know most about the field. Individuals who can speak with authority, either because of active participation or scholarly research, are frequently the very ones who are most appalled by war and everything connected with it. Included here are the academic specialists who after studying the records are prone to write books advocating disarmament or urging fuller participation in international organizations such as the United Nations. This attitude is understandable and certainly should not be condemned. As thoughtful human beings who have a keen awareness of war and its aftereffects and who argue that the only answer is permanent peace, they deserve our respect, gratitude, and sincere agreement.

Any American who has seen first hand the full magnitude of war upon civilians appreciates this. If war is hell, military occupation is a severe form of purgatory. Malcolm S. MacLean has captured the sense of the awesome human, social, and political responsibility of the occupier in a classic description: "Military government runs the gamut of human affairs. It finds a chaotic welter of dazed human beings of all ages; of animals; of smashed buildings; shattered communications; hospitals in rubble; empty court rooms; broken water lines; pocked roads; burned food warehouses; shelled churches; destroyed schools; pillaged libraries and looted galleries and museums. Out of this physical and human debris of war it must speedily bring order; establish law; get a government going; provide food, water, shelter, and medical care and carry off wastes; organize and supply labor to itself and the combat forces."[1]

LEGAL STATUS

The war law codes, manuals of the American Army, and international law publicists are in general agreement on the definition of military government (MG). It is the "form of administration by which an occupying power exercises governmental authority over occupied territory."[2] This concept was embodied as a principle of international law in Article 42 of the Fourth Hague Convention of 1907. Current American military manuals elaborate upon that definition by adding the phrase, "by which an occupying power exercises executive, legislative, and judicial authority over occupied territory."[3]

International law has sought to establish criteria for controlling the behavior of armies engaged in military government activities. These criteria become applicable when troops exercise jurisdiction over (1) occupied enemy territory, (2) occupied domestic territory recovered from rebels who had been classified legally as belligerents, and (3) friendly foreign territory recovered from an enemy but territory which has not been covered by a civil affairs agreement.' In each of these situations world law sanctions the use of necessary military pressure to coerce the civilian population into obeying the occupation directives. Presumably, both the directives and the implementing actions of officers are in line with international law.

The law of belligerent occupation is derived from the branch of international law known as the law of war. It is designed to take into account situations wherein an army, by the fact of present or past hostilities, assumes a degree of responsibility for governmental functions. And it sets forth the liberties and obligations of both occupier and occupied in the critical areas of human rights and political freedom.

Invading armies can invoke specific provisos when dealing with civilians. One of these is the principle of military necessity, designed to insure that the local people will not interfere with the effectiveness of combat units.⁵ Using this justification the commander may enforce extraordinary restrictions on the non-combatants, but he is expressly forbidden to impose demands prohibited by the law of war. Even in the combat zone, he must insist that, to the best of his ability, the standards of humanity and common decency be applied to enemy and friend alike.

Technically, the law of military occupation becomes effective when the actual battle line has passed and the enemy population is clearly within the territory belonging to the invading army. The precise moment at which legal occupation replaces the former law of the country may be difficult to determine because the attacking army must have "firm possession of enemy territory for the purpose of holding it."⁶ Customarily, a proclamation will be issued by the invader signaling the suspension of local laws and the substitution of occupation statutes. However, it is meaningless unless it is possible to continue to enforce control over the specific region involved.⁷

Since the war is still in progress, the invading army should expect a minimum of trouble from the cities and countryside located to the rear of the front lines. People within the conquered territory must not, theoretically, interefere with the movement of the invader's combat units destined for the front, nor should they attempt to harass the supply and support units stationed there. The logic behind this assumption is that these areas have been lost to the defending army and local resistance will only multiply the miseries of war.

However, the legal conduct of a belligerent occupation imposes definite obligations upon the victor as well as providing that the inhabitants submit to the new law without resistance. The humane treatment of enemy civilians under these circumstances is protected under Article 55 of the 1949 Geneva Conventions which stipulates that: "To the fullest extent of the means available to it, the Occupying Power has the duty of ensuring the food and medical supplies of the population; it should, in particular, bring in the necessary foodstuffs, medical stores and other articles if the resources of the occupied territory are inadequate."[8]

Gerhard von Glahn suggests that there is present a marked trend to impose increasingly strict obligations on the conqueror and that Article 55 is a drastic regulation which places the responsibility for local welfare squarely upon the shoulders of the field commander.[9] Legally, acts of omission constitute violations of the law as much as the deliberate imposition of inhumane directives.

When the armistice or formal surrender is negotiated, or when opposing forces have been weakened to the point where the entire state has been conquered, the combat phase of the occupation ends. With the cessation of organized warfare the process of return to normal peacetime international relations begins. The departure of occupation troops might not take place for years after the last battle was fought, or withdrawal might occur immediately. This will depend upon the speed with which the victorious and defeated nations can agree upon a peace treaty.

After a military government has functioned in excess of one year a harsh or formal belligerent occupation is supposed to be terminated. Beyond that point the occupier is primarily bound for the duration of his presence to adhere to the general provisions of Article 6 of the Geneva Convention governing humane conduct.[10] Under any circumstances being caught up as a civilian who is subject to military rule is unpleasant. But the prospect is especially uninviting during the first year when the foreign army can so easily invoke legal justification for many cruel forms of behavior. After one year passes and a semblance of order and calm has at least started to return, the military government may respect the admonition of international law calling for less severe restrictions. It might not happen, however, as witnessed by the conduct of German forces which overran Western Europe at the beginning of World War II.

Modern international law makes a clear distinction between military occupation and subjugation. The former is inherently a temporary status reflecting the fact that territory of one state has been brought under the military domination of another state. Sovereignty and the legal rights which are a part of sovereignty are not claimed by the occupier. In the case of subjugation leading to annexation, however, the invader assumes the prerogatives of sovereignty over the conquered territory.[11] The signing of a peace treaty providing for annexation terminates the status of legal occupation, though military agencies may remain for an indefinite period to administer the new municipal law. This situation occurred, for example, in the areas of Eastern Poland incorporated into the Soviet Union after World War II.

Occupation may legally be terminated by means other than a formal peace treaty providing for withdrawal or annexation. Obviously, if the defending army ejects the invader the legal state of occupation automatically ceases. However, a small-scale rebellion or guerrilla action within an area already under the general control of the invader which can be put down has no effect upon the law of occupation.

International law permits military government to suspend local laws, to halt the operation of governmental agencies, and to assume all executive, legislative, and judicial functions within the conquered territory.[12] Morris Greenspan has noted that the occupant suspends or amends local laws which are "essentially political or constitutional in nature, as well as laws which adversely affect the welfare and safety of his command."[13]

In establishing military government, the invader has a choice of two administrative patterns. On the one hand Army officers may take over the role of dealing directly with the civilians of the defeated state. For example, during combat operations and during initial periods of belligerent occupation some civilian services often must be provided by military units. On the other hand, military government can work through the civilian structures of the local government, and assume indirect rule. Typically, the longer the belligerent and peaceful occupations continue the more indirect will become the role played by military government. It is assumed that each operation will require administrative machinery which is tailor-made to the particular circumstances.

Whenever it becomes necessary to establish a military government administration in a friendly or neutral state, the immediate problems at hand will dictate its precise character. If the recognized government of the nation, which may be a government in exile, has negotiated a specific agreement with the country whose army is operating in its territory, the functions of military government will be subject to both that agreement and the provisions of international law.[14] If an agreement does not exist, military government may be created unilaterally by the nation whose army is in the field. It must, of course, operate in accordance with pertinent codes of war and belligerent occupation.

Definitions of both occupation and martial administration under the historic pattern of international law may be insufficient to cover the current strategic responsibilities of the United States. In a practical sense, though not in a legal one, enemy states have in modern times surrendered their sovereignty when they capitulated. Edward H. Litchfield points out that in post-World War II Germany, for example, "occupation in the traditional meaning of international law was impossible."[15] He further suggests that a contradiction between political policy and the concepts of law arose because "international law had not developed as rapidly as the problems with which the victors . . . were faced."[16]

Litchfield's point is further clarified by recognizing that the Second World War was the harbinger of the large-scale ideological and military struggles between competing systems, and the new reality of international relations has characterized world affairs since that time. Traditional definitions associated with the law of war were products of the Western European states system, wherein a presumption existed that the only significant conflicts would be those waged by nations which belonged to the same states system. However, the war against fascism and the ensuing cold war with communism ushered in a new era. Consequently, in this new struggle the ideological foundations as well as the political structures of countries are at stake.

These and other developments lead to the conclusion that the standard definitions of military occupation and government are no longer wholly adequate. The existence of nuclear weapons also produced drastic changes, and there is a serious question as to whether either the United States or the Soviet Union would be capable of launching or conducting a traditional occupation in the aftermath of a full-scale nuclear war between them. Guerrilla warfare has assumed a new respectability which is a practical concern to both Western and communist policy makers.

The free world response to this strategy in Asia, Africa, the Near East, and Latin America has resulted in the sending of substantial numbers of soldiers as "advisors" to unstable countries. This has created a situation wherein the intent of international law may be clear, but its practical application in these extraordinary circumstances is not defined adequately in the statutes. Military civic action, formerly a minor task of combat units stationed abroad, has gained the proportions of a major policy. While its immediate avowed goal is the betterment of the economic and social conditions of civilians, it operates as a part of national security policy.

When acting as advisors and engaging in insurgency, counter-insurgency, or civic action, forces from the major democracies and the major communist states are in reality waging a low-level military conflict without enjoying the security of a clearly defined legal status. And what is equally significant, the civilian populations caught up in such overt and covert operations are left in a legal limbo. It can be argued that the international law of peace furnishes safeguards against wanton acts of terrorism perpetrated by foreign troops since it provides that during a legal state of peace outside forces possess only the specific rights conferred under terms of an agreement negotiated between the foreign power and the host government. And, after all, international agreements are enforceable legal instruments. However, such a formal pact, should it exist, is subject to a wide latitude of interpretation by a weak and threatened regime. Further complicating factors arise when attempts are made to invoke the treaty as a meaningful legal curb. For example, during wars of national liberation a foreign power may extend formal recognition to an insurgent regime and enter into an accord with it which provides that its troops aiding the insurgents have almost a free hand in dealing with civilians. Thus, the plight of the civilians is made more desperate because, in the absence of a legal war or occupation, there is no internationally authorized agency to which they may directly appeal.

While it can be contended that existing conventions and customary law cover this type of small war situation, the scope of coverage seems inadequate. The Hague Conventions held that a legal state of hostilities might begin prior to a formal declaration of war between governments. Traditional international law has presumed, however, that sooner or later both sides would show their true colors and formally declare war on one another.[17] The Geneva Conventions of 1949 broadened these definitions to include civil war and "armed conflict not of an international character occurring in the territory of one of the High Contracting Parties"[18] (nations signatory to the conventions). A military action sponsored directly by an international agency, such as the United Nations, would bring the provisions of these conventions immediately into effect. But the void continues in instances where a nation, whether one of the High Contracting Parties or a major power which is not a party to the conventions, uses its army indirectly to support large-scale insurgency. The customary law of war becomes operative in a civil war when the rebels are classified as belligerents. However, under the strategy of insurgency the besieged regime may for political reasons refuse to grant this status of recognition. This leaves both the civilians and the army in a precarious position during a conflict that defies precise definition in the traditional legal sense.

Government leaders and international law publicists have recognized the need for modernization, and some concrete steps have been taken to develop a new policy reflecting strategic innovations. While international lawyers have shown little interest, military officials because of the urgency of their responsibilities were forced to restate and redefine their terminology. They recast the traditionally narrow concepts of belligerent occupation and military government into a more inclusive framework. The term *civil affairs* (CA) was adopted as a broad definition to encompass the spectrum of situations, including military government, faced by a commander dealing directly with a civilian population.

Historically, the term civil affairs became popular during World War II. During its early stages planners realized that driving the enemy from the Allied countries overrun by the Axis would later present serious political and legal problems. The term civil affairs was used to describe the relations between the liberating army and the local population and the legal rights and obligations of both. Since the territories involved were recognized as friendly and sovereign, policy had to be couched in terminology which avoided the implication that this type of administration would be as harsh as that which was to be imposed upon the enemy. For example, in France, the Low Countries, and Scandinavia, the term civil affairs was used because these were friendly areas, while in Germany and Italy the traditional term military government was applied. If it was impossible for the Allies to negotiate an agreement in advance, the invading commanders based their civil activities upon the inherent rights conferred under the law of war, and adopted a form of military government.

A need for distinguishing administration in friendly territory from pure military government was even more obvious from the standpoint of political wisdom than from that of legal necessity. Harry L. Coles and Albert K. Weinberg reported that the agreements, "which contained the basic policy guidance for all planning and civil affairs operations, originated in considerations of policy rather than legality."[19] Though the liberating army might be forced to resort to strict regulations and impose drastic penalties for disobedience, just as military government did, these actions had to be described in softer language.

Hardy C. Dillard believed that the distinction between military government and civil affairs was "purposely blurred in the Army Field Manual, but it was well known and applied in the Second World War."[20] To him, "the distinction is that military government is the power to tell people what is law and what is not law and put them in jail if they do not obey," while civil affairs is the way people are treated in friendly areas occupied for one reason or another.[21]

As Allied armies brought North Africa, the Mediterranean countries, and finally Western Europe under their control, their task became increasingly complex. Initially, most political leaders exhibited little concern for the difficulties which were later encountered. This oversight can be attributed in part to the gravity of the situation and the need to reverse the depressing trend of the war. Progressively, however, manuals and policy directives were redrawn to meet the new difficulties which were being encountered by the MG units in the field.

The trend toward expanding the scope of policy definitions can be seen by comparing the different approaches embodied in the field manuals and policy statements published between 1943 and 1959. In 1943 the *Manual of Military Government and Civil Affairs* was keyed to the immediate needs of the Allied invading armies. Its definition of military government was consistent with the traditional pattern and stressed reliance upon the interpretations of the law of war and belligerent occupation.*

Superseding the earlier version, the next manual, published in 1947, contained an obvious shift in terminology as was evidenced by the

---

* Manual of *Military Government and Civil Affairs,* Field Manual 27-5, U.S. Army, 1943, Section I, page 1:

1. Military Government-Civil Affairs
   a. Military Government. The term "military government" is used in this manual to describe the supreme authority exercised by an armed force over the lands, property, and inhabitants of enemy territory, or allied or domestic territory recovered from enemy occupation, or from rebels treated as belligerents . . .

   b. Occupied Territory . . .

   c. The term "civil affairs" is used to describe the activities of the government of the occupied area and of the inhabitants of such an area except those of an organized military character. "Civil Affairs Control" describes the supervision of the activities of civilians by an armed force, by military government or otherwise . . .

title itself: *Civil Affairs Military Government* (CAMG). The new emphasis was the product of considerations over and above a review of World War II experiences. Soon after the close of hostilities the possibility of future aggression began to receive attention. Actions by the Soviet Union in Eastern Europe, the Balkans, and the Near East were viewed as signaling the advent of renewed international strife. Should American combat units become engaged in these areas in support of friendly governments or populations, the development of an adequate policy for dealing with local inhabitants would be critically important.[†] While the 1947 definitions were somewhat ambiguous and confusing, they did provide a wider latitude in framing a policy which could be more politically practicable than one based exclusively upon the Hague Regulations and customary international law.

Direct military confrontation between the Western and communist forces did not occur in Europe. Korea became the battleground instead, though combat strategy was not a radical departure from past wars. Massed troops still faced each other across a reasonably well defined front line.

But the Korean Conflict represented a strategic turning point for

---

[†] Manual of *Civil Affairs Military Government*, Field Manual 27-5, U.S. Army, 1947, pages 2-3:

    b. Definitions. (1) Civil Affairs/military government (CA/MG). CA/MG encompasses all powers exercised and responsibilities assumed by the military commander in an occupied or liberated area . . . whether such administration be in enemy, allied, or domestic territory. The type of occupation, whether CA or MG, is determined by the highest policy making authority. Normally, the type of occupation is dependent upon the degree of control exercised by the responsible military commander.

    (2) Military Government. The term "military government" as used in this manual is limited to and defined as supreme authority exercised by an armed occupying force over the land, properties, and inhabitants of an enemy, allied, or domestic territory. Military government is exercised when an armed force has occupied such territory, whether by force or agreement, and has substituted its authority for that of the sovereign or previous government . . .

    (3) Civil Affairs. The term "civil affairs" as used in this manual is defined as the assumption by the responsible commander of an occupying force of a degree of authority less than the supreme authority assumed under military government, over enemy, allied, or domestic territory. The indigenous governments would be recognized by treaty, agreement, or otherwise as having certain authority independent of the military commander.

the planners of American long-range military policy. It created a new awareness of the problems of waging war in underdeveloped countries. Though the South Korean people were solidly behind the anti-communist forces which fought on their soil, in other Far Eastern nations, especially in Malaya and Indo-China, Western troops did not always have this advantage. The rapid spread of Peking's doctrine of mass insurgency could not be ignored by Washington.

When the Korean War was finally settled, the Pentagon again took stock of its policy on military government and civil affairs. The need for greater flexibility in dealing with civilians had to be balanced against the binding commitment to international law. One result of this re-evaluation was the writing of a new manual. The 1958 statement of policy superseded the earlier, 1947 version and was titled: *Joint Manual of Civil Affairs/Military Government.* It was to apply equally to the Army, Navy, Air Force, and the Marine Corps.‡

Progress toward a more inclusive policy definition had reached the stage where the discussion of civil affairs took precedence in the official field manual over that of military government. Remaining, however, was the implication that civil affairs and military government had a co-equal status. "Civil affairs/military government" was described as a "combined term." Presumably this meant that they

---

‡ *Joint Manual of Civil Affairs/Military Government,* Field Manual 41-5, Depts. of the Army, Navy, and the Air Force, 1958, pages 2-5:

2. Definitions

   a. Civil Affairs/Military Government (CAMG). A grouping of terms employed for convenience to refer to either Civil Affairs or Military Government, depending upon the context. . . . In this manual, the combined term refers to the functions, activities ,and common mission of these operations and will be used when referring to either or both civil affairs and military government.

   b. Civil Affairs. Matters concerning the relationship between military forces located in a friendly country or area and the civil authorities and people of that country or area usually involving performance by the military forces of certain functions or the exercise of certain authority normally the responsibility of the local government. This relationship may occur prior to, during, or subsequent to military action in time of hostilities or other emergency and normally is covered by a treaty or other agreement express or implied. . . .

   c. Military Government. The form of administration by which an occupying power exercises executive, legislative, and judicial authority over occupied territory. . . . In the practice of the United States, military government describes a situation where armed forces assume complete governmental responsibilities normally exercised by local authorities. . . .

were indivisible yet distinguishable elements within a combined policy.

In 1959 the military assumed an important role in furthering foreign policy goals by working directly with foreign civilians. The legal considerations which had dominated occupation and military government now fit side by side with political ingredients such as civic action; and the overall policy was regarded as primarily political and only secondarily legal.

The Draper Report, especially Annex D which was written by Brigadier General Donald G. Shingler, revealed the new position. Conducted by the President's Committee to Study the United States Military Assistance Program, it represented the findings of an extensive policy review. Annex D was titled the "Contribution of Military Resources to Economic and Social Progress." It examined "the extent to which the military has contributed, and can in the future continue to contribute, to economic and social progress" in the emerging nations.[22]

Annex D reported that several military agencies have this capability and at the top of their list was the "Civil Affairs/Military Government Department [sic] of the Army." It concluded that: "The work of CAMG in occupation duties and in performance of civil affairs and military government work in time of combat is well known. CAMG training includes instruction in dealing with and assisting civilian agencies and the people themselves in dealing with public administration, health, communications, transportation, food, supply, etc. Such functions have obvious peacetime application in underdeveloped and newly emerging countries." [23] The Committee Report then examined the doctrine, pioneered by the Army Civil Affairs School, whereby other military agencies, such as the Corps of Engineers, could also assist in military civic action.

Because the Committee's findings confirmed the popular belief that American military policy was proving inadequate under the impact of the new type of international challenge they were highly significant. In the civil affairs field, the need was for a long-range peacetime approach which could better guide the relations of U.S. military personnel with foreign populations. This had to be sufficiently flexible to incorporate the techniques which Western Powers had found successful in defeating the communist insurgents in Malaya and the Philippines.

Simultaneously, the Committee, while not advocating the alteration or elimination of the traditional Army function of CAMG, did sanction the civil affairs mission of the armed forces. The Army could now expect authorization to conduct programs for actively influencing civilians within the periphery threatened by communist actions. This was a function which the Army had consistently been reluctant to assume except in emergency situations growing out of open warfare.

The Draper Report apparently had an immediate impact upon the Joint Chiefs of Staff since shortly after it was completed the JCS issued a basic "Statement of Current Policy on Civil Affairs, Civil Affairs Operations." ** While defining the concepts in the 1958 manual, there was one critical difference; this was the elimination of the co-equal status of civil affairs and military government. Henceforth, civil affairs would be the official designation of the overall policy, within which military government was rated as a subordinate ingredient. A wide spectrum of functions was included in the definition of civil affairs operations, and additional assignments could be given should the demand arise. Emphasizing broader political goals of foreign policy, civil affairs' status was elevated from the Department of the Army, Navy, and Air Force to the higher level of the Joint Chiefs and recognized as a major and permanent element of military policy. It was probably hoped that the new definitions would also end the confusion in terminology and interpretation which had persisted since 1943. Military government, with its traditional legal implications, was to be recast into a broader and more political context. Being outdated, it was no longer the Army's primary civilian mission.

** The Joint Chiefs of Staff, *Unified Action Armed Forces*, JCS Publication 2, Washington, 1959, page 97:

Definitions:

Civil Affairs. Those phases of the activities of a commander which embrace the relationship between the military forces and civil authorities and people in a friendly country or area, or occupied country or area when military forces are present. Civil Affairs include, among other things:

   a. Matters concerning the relationship between military forces located in a country or area and the civil authorities and people of that country or area, usually involving performance by the military forces of certain functions or the exercise of certain authority normally the responsibility of the local government. This relationship may occur prior to, during, or subsequent to military action in time of hostilities or other emergency, and is normally covered by a treaty or other agreement, express or implied.

   b. Military government. The form of administration by which an occupying power exercises executive, legislative, and judicial authority over occupied territory.

Forces had been at work since 1943 which brought about this evolution in terminology. For example, the connotation of military government is negative, while that of civil affairs has a positive meaning. In the modern world the idea of military government implies the imposing of ideological "reconstruction," opening itself to the charge of "militarism." On the other hand, civil affairs suggests the physical reconstruction and rehabilitation of areas devastated by war or natural disaster.

Considering that the two concepts, civil affairs and military government, are basically distinct and different, it can be seen that one takes over where the other leaves off. The intended result is a continuous and uninterrupted policy endeavor. Military government, by itself, is viewed as obsolete because of the new strategic requirements and limitations imposed by international law. But when the new elements of civil affairs are added, the total concept which emerges is a politically realistic military policy for the nuclear age.

Unfortunately, the gap in legal protections described earlier has not been alleviated. The need for meaningful provisions in international law to cover the total range of functions anticipated in the new policy still remains. Hopefully, a next step will be the adoption of a full-fledged international civil-military relations code which will be both politically workable and legally enforceable for all nations. This should be given high priority if states continue to expect their armed forces to play under the new rules of military strategy.

CIVIL-MILITARY DEBATE

Difficulties over and above international law were also behind the American decision to break new ground in the historic and almost sacrosanct domain of military government. The charge has often been made that such government should be avoided because the use of army personnel as civilian governors is unnecessary and inefficient. In theory as well as in actual practice, a technically advanced and democratically oriented nation such as the U.S. is relying upon a weak crutch when it charges its military establishment with major responsibilities for dealing with foreign populations. Many thoughtful observers believe that in cases where a temporary government must be established, *civilian* rather than Army officials should perform this work.

The most frequently cited reason is that the Army does not even pretend to be a democratic organization.[24] Since military institutions are designed to operate on a hierarchical basis, their *modus operandi* stresses that the most desirable relationship between leaders and rank and file is an authoritarian one. In contrast, democracy centers on a polyarchical arrangement wherein non-leaders are able to control the actions of those in authority, at least in principle if not in every detail. Therefore, it is inappropriate to use the Army as an agency for setting the example of democracy among people in a military occupation or counterinsurgency operation.

Further, there is the impact of the particular type of organization upon the behavior of the individual official. In this regard, Hanson W. Baldwin makes some pointed remarks concerning the so-called "military mind." He sees the danger of lower ranking officers developing into "yes men" and those of higher rank becoming petty tyrants. Though he admits this happens in a minority of cases, the idea is still disturbing. Baldwin contends that the "military mind" is "accustomed to the habit of command, taught to think fundamentally in terms of physical power. It can grapple with tangibles but not too well with intangibles." And frequently it is an "insulated mind." [25] As such, it is not pleasant to imagine the "military mind" governing civilians and teaching them to appreciate democracy.

In the light of these historic and devastating accusations, are there any justifiable reasons why the Army should be permitted to exercise a major role in administering foreign civilian populations? A case can be made that CAMG control, though undemocratic, can still perform a function consistent with democratic principles and goals. [26] These officers can start the local people on the path to democratic government through the establishment of free institutions. And presumably, fair elections, local self-government, and a free press can be initiated as effectively by them as by civilian administrators.

This argument, logical as it might be in theory, is not however the primary reason why the military plays a commanding role. The actual explanation is much more practical. When a traditional military government is established or when instability in a friendly country reaches the point of counterinsurgency operations, the Army is invariably the first agency on the scene. Following a major war it must remain after formal hostilities cease primarily to enforce the terms of the surrender. Other difficulties exist: a state of near anarchy may grip the conquered territory; the threat of organized guerrillas must be met and random acts of terrorism against Americans prevented. The Army is trained and paid to accept such risks, civilians are not.

It is imperative that some form of local governmental administration be established and law and order restored as quickly as possible; the logical first step is the creation of a military government. Local institutions cannot be held in abeyance until the safety of incoming civilian administrators can be guaranteed. Unfortunately, this period may extend over many months or perhaps years.

Another practical reason for Army control is the need for providing civilian and military supplies. Because of America's influence over the area, this country assumes a commitment for the physical well-being of the local population. Disease, starvation, and similar calamities must be alleviated if the respect and confidence of the inhabitants is to be gained. Furnishing even a minimum level of civilian supplies is difficult, and evidence indicates that the military's control over this function is generally desirable. Normally, substantial numbers of occupation troops are stationed in the area and their supply and transport remain an Army responsibility. Consequently, it seems practical to leave the logistical needs of conquered civilians in the hands of the military and thereby avoid unnecessary duplication. In commenting upon the World War II European situation, Hajo Holborn suggests that since Army commands must retain ultimate control over supply channels to insure their own security, perhaps they should also control the other elements of the civil affairs program.[27]

A further justification for favoring Army management over Washington civilian control is the maintenance of continuity within the organizational structure of the occupation regime. Since the efficiency of civil affairs administration depends largely upon an uninterrupted personnel policy, a sudden shift from uniformed officers to civilian counterparts can seriously disrupt relationships which have developed between the military governors and the defeated citizens.[28] Besides, there exists no automatic assurance that the civilian replacements would be better qualified. This was demonstrated after the Second World War when a number of Washington agencies disbanded and many of their employees were reassigned to overseas posts. These men were frequently unsuitable for their new chores.[29]

One more reason for the choice of the military to operate the World War II CAMG programs was the unreadiness of the civilian authorities to accept the responsibility.[30] Washington bureaus lacked the necessary experience for the effective management of masses of foreign people. Of course, the State Department and other cabinet offices contain talented professionals, and the arguments advanced here should not be misinterpreted as a blanket assertion that all Army officials are better prepared than their civilian counterparts. Available evidence merely demonstrates that recruiting qualified civilians is extremely difficult. For example, in Vietnam both the Agency for International Development (AID) and the Army sponsored civic action projects. Each conducted a nation-wide search to locate skilled people, seeking volunteers especially from universities and military reserve groups. These drives achieved a less than enthusiastic response, presumably because pacification is a hazardous and a thankless task.

While the training of Army officers for civil affairs assignments has been less than ideal, preparation of civilians for this duty has been until recently nonexistent. The Army, at least, established a semblance of a training program and in addition prearranged pilot CA units. In further moves, the Civil Affairs Branch was created within the Army Reserve, a permanent CA School was placed in operation, and a research library was opened for the use of interested officials and scholars.[31] These actions by the Pentagon imply that pressures were exerted on the highest levels to examine more carefully the cold war potential of CA organizations.[32]

Much of the civilian-military debate has revolved around the qualifications of officials. Three distinct personnel problems have existed in all major occupations, and each difficulty reduced the effectiveness of the policy being administered. They were, first, the training and placement of civil affairs officers, second, the obtaining of satisfactory replacements, and third, the antagonism between officers working with local populations and those assigned to Army tactical units. Some of the personnel issues are unique with civil affairs because it has stood as a stepchild within the overall Army structure.

However, the entire Army has had difficulty in the areas of training and selection, and these problems for civil affairs were reflections of the general predicament. A number of CA officers have been incompetent in their posts. For them it made little difference where they had happened to be assigned, to CAMG units or elsewhere. They were ineffectual due to a variety of professional and personal deficiencies over which the Army had little control; their selection was a mistake.

Some classic stories describe incompetents who through comic circumstances became military governors. Often men were dumped into CAMG teams because they were in trouble in their former posts; rarely did commanders of combat or support units who were ordered to supply a quota of officers for civil affairs send their best men. In an extreme illustration, Marshall M. Knappen cites the words of one Major as to how and why he found his way into occupation duty: "I was a supply officer in Hawaii, and you know how those jobs go after you've been on them a while. They pulled a snap inspection on me, and I was two thousand blankets short. They gave me my choice of standing court-martial or transferring to military government, and here I am. I know how these transfers are arranged." [33]

Harold Zink recounts another example of the ludicrous way in which an officer received his assignment. It seems that he had failed to appear at the port of embarkation on the day his ship was to sail because he could not tear himself away from his "sweetie." Instead of being court-martialed and punished in the usual manner, this former pugilist with little formal education was made deputy commander of the first available military government company. [34]

In cases such as these, it was immaterial whether the officers were Reservists or members of the Regular Army. There were instances, however, where careerists who had established records of failure in their basic branches were given military government assignments. Openly exhibiting displeasure with their new duties, they habitually absented themselves from their offices on the slightest pretexts. When they were present they often refused to be bothered about making decisions, preferring instead to sit-it-out awaiting reassignment to a more popular branch. Thomas R. Fisher reports that this problem was chronic in postwar Italy, and that mismanagement caused by unqualified people assigned to the Allied Control Commission and other bodies impeded the occupation effort. [35] Robert B. Textor encountered a similar problem in the Kinki region of Japan. He found in 1947 that two of the four careerists assigned to the U. S. headquarters there had previously been passed over for promotion to higher rank within their parent branches. While the Army apparently did not consider these men sufficiently fit for normal advancement, it was acceptable for them to exercise authority over hundreds of thousands of Japanese civilians. [36]

Inexperience, poor placement, and inadequate training were also responsible for many of the Army's personnel problems. The men considered here as falling within this area were often professionally qualified in their own branches, but for one reason or another they were shuffled into military government. Textor makes the blanket indictment that many of the highest positions in Japan were filled by general officers who lacked background in civil affairs. He relates an incident where a Regular Army Major General, who had spent his entire career in the Infantry, was placed in charge of the Civil Affairs Section of General MacArthur's Headquarters (SCAP) in 1951. Another Major General, after a lifelong association with the Artillery Branch, was chosen to manage the scientific and economic phases of the entire occupation. In each of these cases the generals were unquestionably qualified within their own specialties, but much time was lost and effort wasted because they came to their posts lacking a clear idea of the tasks entailed in governing civilians.[37]

Instances of the same problem in postwar Europe are cited by Zink, who, though more lenient toward the Army and its training policy, still saw serious consequences which resulted from the assignment of inexperienced officers to MG units. One instance involved a former manager of a five-and-ten cent store, who was given command of older and more experienced governmental experts. The resultant friction was eventually overcome, but in the meantime the unit's efficiency dropped.[38] Ironically, this young officer became so impressed with the potential of civil affairs that he decided upon a career in the area. And when as a full colonel he retired from active duty in the middle 1960's, he had become one of the most knowledgeable, and controversial, authorities in the field.

After World War II additional problems occurred because of inadequate training and selection. Many of the most flagrant failures on the part of individuals in the history of American occupation efforts came about through the actions of the older officers, especially those coming from the defunct horse Cavalry and Coast Artillery, which were clearly obsolete by 1945. After devoting a lifetime of service to one of the most historic and proud of all branches, they must have thought it a bitter fate to await retirement in a "second rate" activity such as military government. Even with high rank and influential friends, their repeated appeals for transfer were usually disapproved because the Pentagon did not know what else to do with them.

Constantly lecturing upon the pride and traditions symbolized by their riding breeches and Sam Browne belt, these officers ignored or downgraded suggestions made by the trained CAMG people. Their tendency toward obstructionism and detachment from the realities at hand only served to make them the butt of cruel personal jokes. As a result, a climate of cliquism, suspicion, and open feuding partially paralyzed several military government headquarters.

Such personal tragedies in assignment grew out of the larger problem of the Army's inability to locate adequate replacements for the specialists who were being relieved. In postwar Germany, the difficulty was on the policy level, where improper assumptions and lack of planning can be blamed upon Army chiefs,[39] who habitually operated on the premise that occupation was of temporary and secondary importance and therefore made little provision for the turnover of personnel. These authorities seem to have had the unrealistic belief that the bulk of the CA experts would remain at their posts for the duration of the World War II occupations. And the generals often thought that career combat veterans, though lacking specialized training and experience, could quite ably step in and fill the shoes of the departing experts. Such reasoning revealed an unwarranted level of overconfidence, for as age and completion of overseas tours caught up with the Reservists, units lost their most qualified people at the very time their services were most valuable.[40]

The result in Europe was a succession of MG unit commanders and staff officers whose actions, based upon inexperience, served to hamper rather than further the implementation of policy. And further aggrevating the problem, the Army decided to close its military government training schools too soon after the end of the war.

Selection of the best qualified officers for occupation duty was complicated by the constant friction existing between commanders of combat units and commanders of CA organizations. Combat forces must understand and execute the tactics of battle in a manner akin to the working of a mathematical formula. In planning, the aim is to create a set of methodically exact diagrams and timetables which show the commanding general precisely how he will defeat the enemy. Quantities of men, material, and information are balanced and counterbalanced with attention to minute detail. Impersonality in weighing the human impact of the battle upon the individuals involved is the key to the staff officer and combat officer retaining his own mental balance in the face of the misery and suffering caused by the war. If the soldier did not view himself as an engineer dealing with inanimate objects, it is likely that modern war would be so repugnant that it would be impossible.

The CAMG forces, in contrast, must work with the enemy people on a highly personal basis. While overall plans for military government can be laid well in advance, they can never anticipate with the precision of the engineer the reaction of the local population. Officers selected to deal with civilian problems must appreciate the delicacy of their task; they cannot ignore the individual human being but must establish a working rapport with him.

It is not surprising then that occupation specialists experienced great difficulty in having their ideas accepted by the invasion forces which were often still in control of the geographic region when they arrived. The aims and approaches of the two were so different that serious communication barriers often occurred. From experience the career general knew that he could expect little besides criticism for any CA actions undertaken, and his instinct was to avoid becoming involved. This attitude was further reflected in combat leaders who frequently expressed lack of respect for the motives and judgment of the governmental experts and sometimes openly questioned their professional competence. These doubts of the combat officers were strengthened by the hesitancy of CA people to make the type of unqualified decision characteristic of the Regular Army officer.[41]

The difficulty in establishing satisfactory relations between the combat forces and the officials responsible for formulating civilian policy has been a recurring theme throughout military history. As early as the era of Caesar, home governments have suspected that military commanders were making improper political decisions in the field.[42] In American history a similar pattern was visible during the Mexican War and subsequent conflicts.[43] The nation's most extensive occupations were conducted during and immediately following World War II and reportedly, "To Roosevelt and many of his administration, military government was . . . a repulsive notion, associated . . . with imperalism, dollar diplomacy, and other aspects of our behavior we had abandoned." [44]

POLICY RESPONSIBILITY

Previous neglect in exploiting fully the capability of the Army in civil affairs may have been shortsighted, yet it is understandable. All aspects of foreign policy, including the various phases of military policy, respond slowly to changing events. Patterns which emerged from the initial postwar world could be assessed only on a daily basis without the advantage of historical perspective. A new military-diplomatic policy framework evolved gradually while the occupations were in progress and only when they were drawing to a close was it apparent that the occupations themselves had formed a critical bridge between the defeated regimes and the new governments. Increasingly, foreign policy experts realized that a new era in the final resolution of international conflicts had been inaugurated. Military administration and occupation programs had replaced the traditional armistice and peace treaty as the prime vehicles for returning to peace.

The aversion of the Army to accept what were often policy-making responsibilities in the diplomatic field is understandable since this is the function of the State Department and the highest civilian levels of government. However, when all of the arguments, pro and con, are added up regarding the desirability of the Army playing a policy role in the field of foreign civil-military relations, one conclusion emerges. In the past neither the State Department nor the military has sought or wanted the task, but some agency had to step forward and assume the burden. The Army was on the spot, the lot fell to it, and this will probably continue to be the case in the future.

Advances in missiles and nuclear weapons may mean that occupation experiences of the past will never be repeated. Yet the problem of who should frame policy for the Army's relations with foreign civilians and set the goals of that policy still remains. The policy question has been the source of perhaps the sharpest criticisms of American occupations and civil affairs operations. This is proper because it is the core of the whole issue of military occupation. Therefore it is the subject to which we now turn our attention. Thomas R. Fisher found that the number one reason for failures during the Italian phase of World War II was the lack of a clear cut policy.[45] James P. Pappas condemned the too frequent instances where major guidelines were decided in haste at the very last moment and as a result were often amended or revoked even before being distributed in the field.[46] Robert W. Komer reported that in Sicily the aims and purposes of civil affairs were misunderstood by the combat commanders, whose units consequently tended to hinder or undo the work of the military government teams.[47]

Policy deficiency was a concern of Major General John Hilldring (Ret.), wartime chief of all American CAMG activities. In a letter in 1951 to Dr. Edward H. Litchfield, he wrote that "after six years [of experience] we are in no better shape to handle military government than we were in 1941." [48] He saw as the solution the establishment of firm procedures fixing ultimate responsibility for overall planning. Finally, James L. McCamy, who devoted a section of his study of *The Administration of Foreign Policy* to "The Occupation of Foreign Lands," noted that: "The whole truth is that the United States embarked on the policy of postwar occupation with little notion of what it would be like and with little preparation for the realities of the task. Most serious, we did not recognize that military government was a crucial factor in both the formulation of foreign policy and in the exercise of foreign relations." [49]

These pessimistic conclusions must be weighed against the steps which have been taken to develop a modern and comprehensive civil affairs policy. However, if we limit the discussion only to the military occupation aspect of the new policy, it appears that McCamy's observation could accurately be applied to the current situation. We are still lacking in this field.

As unpleasant as the prospect might be, the possibility, and perhaps the likelihood, that future occupations will be necessary must be given serious consideration. In the autumn of 1962, for example, the probability of an invasion of Cuba was very real indeed. Had it taken place, what occupation policy would have been applied? It is fruitless to judge or speculate too much upon a policy which never came into being. Yet it is worthwhile to enumerate some of the difficulties that would have befallen an American occupation force. Initially, the need for making policy decisions, either by Washington or the field commander, would be most pressing. What were to be the immediate and long-range goals of the occupation, and what guidelines for day-to-day conduct would the invading army adopt?

One possibility was that the reins of government would be turned over to the exiled Cuban leaders as quickly as the line of battle advanced. Then when the American Army had shattered the regular units of Castro's military force, it might withdraw and leave the mopping up of guerrilla bands to the re-established Cuban regime. However, such a hasty American withdrawal would have been unlikely. This country would have invested too much in resources and international prestige to consider departing before a reasonably stable situation existed.

A withdrawal of large American combat units would more likely have been preceded by the deployment of advisory groups and the transfer of individual officers from CA organizations to these advisory groups would have taken place smoothly and with little fanfare. Their presence would be a continuous reminder to the Cubans and others that the United States was prepared to intervene militarily again if necessary.

Framers of military policy for Cuba would be forced to reach agreement with officials in AID and the State Department so that the overall task of initiating economic and political reforms could be coordinated in a single effort, rather than approached in a piecemeal manner by each agency. But while Washington was wrestling with the perennial difficulty of inter-agency cooperation, the military commander on the scene would be forced to undertake many precedent-setting actions. Some of these would be designed to insure the health and safety of his troops, while other directives would fulfill the commander's responsibilities under the war law codes. Decisions he might see as primarily routine in nature could be important enough to merit night-long debates within Washington offices. For instance, the reopening of the Havana casinos, hotels, and amusement centers might be given the green light by the commander. After all, his troops need recreation facilities and the local economy certainly could use the revenue. From his vantage point a connotation that the U. S. was approving the return to influence of the international gambling interests and syndicates could easily be overlooked.

Since the post-World War II occupations the goal of political re-education has continually gained in importance. Consequently, there was a good chance that in 1962 a program would have been conducted to "reorient" the Cuban people and diminish the popularity of the Castro image. The serious implications of any venture of this type are obvious. Yet presumably, if America were willing to go to the extreme of invading and occupying Cuba, it would also be willing and prepared to use its power to purge pro-communist doctrine from textbooks and pro-communist teachers from the schools.

Another perplexing question for the makers of occupation policy would have been the disposition of Castro and his chief lieutenants if they had been captured. Would they have been tried for war crimes? Certainly, pressures from American public opinion for such treatment would have reached major proportions. If they had stood trial, would the proceedings have taken place before a court convened by the U.S. sponsored Cuban regime which replaced the communist government, or would the case have been heard by an international war crimes tribunal of some sort? In either case, to what extent would the Nuremberg Doctrine have been invoked to deal with the Castroites?

A final example of the type of problems the U. S. would have encountered involves the role to be played by other friendly states. Members of the Organization of American States would likely be encouraged to participate in planning and implementing the occupation policy as well as the military phase of the operation. Any form of invasion and occupation would raise sharp reactions throughout the hemisphere, especially in those countries having well-organized left wing movements. A joint U. S.-OAS effort would be condoned with more sympathy than a unilateral American action. But after taking a daring gamble in launching the invasion, Washington might be very reluctant to settle for less than a free hand in establishing once and for all a solidly friendly government. A corollary problem would be created for the United States in the United Nations, where Washington is also sensitive and responsive to criticisms by nations outside the hemisphere which usually side with the U. S. on important world issues.

These are only a few of the major and inescapable policy considerations which would have resulted from a Cuban occupation. Yet in 1962 when invasion appeared a strong possibility, Washington made no attempt to spell out to the American people its goals for Cuba beyond the immediate destruction of the missile bases. We are left to conclude that our leaders were resigned to pursue an occupation policy which would be formulated on a day-to-day basis. This is reminiscent of the manner in which the U. S. has typically developed its policy in the past. In fairness, we must assume that some tentative emergency plans were drawn up in the Pentagon and the State Department and were withheld from the American people because of their security or propaganda implications. It is reasonable to suggest, however, that the problem of occupying Cuba could have proven more difficult and complex than the military campaign.[50]

Though the Cuban dispute was settled without the need for direct armed intervention, the broader policy question which it raised remains unsolved. That is the matter of framing in advance a military occupation policy suitable for small war situations. Also in the case of Vietnam, the dilemma has been that once again little prior thought was given to this problem. While the idea is distasteful, the issues at stake are grave and warrant immediate attention in both governmental and nongovernmental circles. Cuba, followed by the Dominican Republic, was perhaps a prologue to future problems in Latin America. And the next eruption may spark an invasion and occupation.[51] The fixation of the average American citizen with ingenious weapons systems is understandable, but it is shortsighted in the light of the challenges posed by cold war confrontations and wars of national liberation.

This leads to the question whether this country has ever had a clear understanding of the goals it was actually seeking to achieve through military occupation and civil affairs operations. Has policy over the years reflected a pattern, or has it been haphazard and *ad hoc* for each venture? In view of the modern nature of the international struggle, what results would the U. S. wish from an occupation in Latin America, Africa, or Southeast Asia?

When contemplated in perspective, problems such as the selection and training of personnel become secondary in importance to the choice of the policy which should be implemented. The need for officials to become more sensitive to local social conditions, customs, and languages—as well as the broader matters of political education, inherent unpopularity, and choice of civilian and/or military agencies — are all issues of lower magnitude. While intrinsically bound up with the policy question, they properly should be treated as *dependent* rather than independent considerations. There is little hope that they can be resolved satisfactorily if confusion continues about the identity and meaning of the *basic forces* that mold and guide American actions in occupations and newer CA programs. These are the fundamental elements or ingredients at the root of policy which, as they interact among themselves, can be thought to represent policy itself.

Sufficient evidence is available to substantiate the hypothesis that policy can be viewed and analyzed as a consistent pattern of forces which planners consciously or unconsciously relied upon in formulating basic occupation goals. On the surface it might appear that different operations had little in common, yet by probing beneath the variations in immediate problems the outline of a theoretical framework is discernible. Its elements have functioned as both positive motivations and negative restraints in conditioning the approach Washington adopted. On this plane of abstractions and high level generalizations it is possible to analyze the policy question. Drawing insights from a comprehensive cross section of typical situations, the writers are mindful of the primary task of searching for the nature of policy and seek to avoid a simple recitation of what happened.

First, major civil affairs actions have been examined in order to determine the extent to which they were guided by the concept of national interest. This approach made it possible to trace the evolutionary development of policy in relationship to the continually changing interests of the United States. It also provided an opportunity to summarize for the reader who might be unfamiliar with the field the highlights of major operations in their appropriate chronological sequence. Additional but minor occupations were conducted by the Army during the period of Westward expansion, by the

Marines in Central America in the 1920's, and by the Navy on numerous small Pacific islands during the nineteenth and early twentieth centuries. These were omitted from this study because they too were based upon the same factors which can better be understood by focusing attention upon the almost identical forces which came into play during the major occupations. To avoid undue repetition in later sections, Chapter II is confined to an analysis of only those considerations which reflect the role of national interest.

In addition to the influence of national interest, evidence clearly demonstrates that national principles have been important in the formulation and implementation of civil affairs policy. An effort is made to present a theoretical framework by which it can be seen that the political beliefs of the American people have been translated into concrete directives and actions in occupied territories. Principles should be weighed and considered in close relationship with the concept of public mood. This too is an abstract element, but it too is nevertheless incorporated into policy. To a marked degree, principles and mood have reinforced each other or battled each other repeatedly within the policy framework.

The personal role played by the individual official who assumes responsibility for events in the field is another policy ingredient which stands out as being more significant than is usually recognized. He may be a military officer who has been delegated a wide latitude for discretionary action, or he may be a civilian official in Washington who insists that his ideas be enforced with only a minimum of local deviation. Regardless of which he is, his influence is sufficiently critical that it becomes a part of policy itself.

Individual leadership, public mood, national principles, and national interest are the abstract hooks within the policy framework and upon them are suspended the concrete actions which characterize military occupation and civil affairs. Factors such as international law, American and Allied agencies, writings by journalists, actions of political interest groups, and Congress are the media through which the fundamental drives and motivations of policy are transmitted. Since these are of a lower order than the theoretical ingredients they can be analyzed and evaluated more directly. Their true meaning, however, rests not in themselves but rather in the fact that they reveal the existence of an orderly pattern of U.S. military occupation policy.

Chapter II

NATIONAL INTEREST

In dissecting military occupation policy one must accord first consideration to the consistent thread of national interest. Its influence comes from the desire to achieve war aims and sometimes from new international developments which occurred while the occupation was in progress. The following analysis, though limited to particulars and in some respects exceptionally inclusive, deals with three historical periods of substantial duration each indicative of a characteristic approach to policy. The emergence of an overall pattern, particularly applicable to the Army's civil function but also related to other phases of American foreign policy, is discernible in all three eras.

While all the facets of interest were constant factors in policy, specific ones were emphasized in the different periods. Interests are examined here within three historic spans which parallel the growth of American occupation policy: (1) territorial expansion and economic growth, (2) maintenance of the *status quo,* and (3) survival and power. A look at these evolving forces will help explain the policy dilemma in which the U.S. government now finds itself.

Differing Emphases of National Interest

The early formative years of the Republic were dedicated to westward expansion and further consolidation of regions already under the American flag. Though European powers continued to covet the hope of regaining or at least of retaining as much of North America as possible, they were involved in European affairs and lacked the necessary capability and/or will to launch another broad undertaking against the ex-colonies. And the new country, though not dismissing lightly the threats from across the Atlantic, was becoming increasingly confident of its demonstrated ability to defend itself.

President Washington's farewell admonition to avoid foreign entanglements was reinforced by Europe's engrossment with its own problems. Behind its ocean barrier and basking in the enthusiasm of the new political experiment, the United States seemed to have little to fear regarding its security. Economic growth and territorial expansion became the twin goals of its policy.

Initially, the primary effort was to develop the territory already within the recognized jurisdiction of the United States. Soon, however, the need for additional land led to expansion. Where purchase was impossible, war became the instrument of national interest. Of necessity, occupation followed. The number of times military occupation was used is both surprising and revealing. In each case troops were employed to insure the enforcement of national policy, though some debate still persists on the precise legal categorization of these military occupations. For a policy analysis, however, the record is sufficiently clear. *Public Affairs Bulletin* No. 16, issued by the Library of Congress in 1942, presents an authoritative history of U.S. occupations. Benjamin Akzin compiled it in order to give World War II policy planners a better perspective of American experiences. Officially titled *Data on Military Government in Occupied Areas: With Special Reference to the United States and Great Britain,* it provides the basis for the classifications of occupations:

Louisiana (annexed territory) 1803-1812
West Florida (forcible annexation) 1810-1812
East Florida (forcible annexation) 1813-1821
Mexico (belligerent occupation) 1846-1848
New Mexico (belligerent occupation; subsequently annexed) 1846-1850
California (belligerent occupation; subsequently annexed) 1846-1850
Southern States (insurrection; under executive authority) 1862-1866
Southern States (disturbed conditions; under congressional authority)..1866-1877
Alaska (annexed territory) 1867-1884
Cuba (belligerent occupation; subsequently under peace treaty) 1898-1902
Philippines (belligerent occupation; subsequently annexed) 1898-1901
Puerto Rico (belligerent occupation; subsequently annexed) 1898-1900
Tientsin-Pekin area, China (joint intervention;
      subsequently consensual) 1900
Panama Canal Zone (intervention; subsequent consensual) .... 1903 to date
Cuba (consensual) 1906-1909
Nicaragua (consensual; except for a brief period in 1926,
      when intervention) 1926-1933
Mexico (intervention) 1914
Haiti (intervention; subsequently consensual) 1915-1934
Mexico (intervention) 1916-1917
Dominican Republic (intervention) ....1916-1924[1]

For more than a century, the emphasis of national interest continued to center upon the policy of territorial expansion and economic growth. The approach adopted toward the Philippines and the Caribbean and Central American acquisitions represented the culmination of the era. During the War with Spain the American nation matured and achieved a new position of influence in world affairs. Dominance upon the North American Continent was now an accomplished fact. National boundaries were fixed and the level of wealth was beginning to engender worldwide respect. Within the Western Hemisphere, the primacy of U.S. influence was recognized, even if the Monroe Doctrine's confident claims of U.S. capacity to prevent foreign interference in hemispheric affairs were not backed by adequate military power. A point in the history of the American people had been reached where additional acquisitions no longer appeared necessary. Instead, the problem became one of protecting and preserving the American realm.

Simultaneously, the policy of maintenance of the *status quo* was gaining importance because of broader international considerations. These relied basically upon the manner in which the U.S. saw itself as a participating member of the world community. In Washington perhaps the assumption existed that international stability rested, first, upon U.S. hegemony within its established geographic sphere, and second, upon European hegemony throughout the remainder of the world. This approach was consistent with the traditional American drive for growth and expansion, as well as being harmonious with the developing new concept of maintaining the *status quo*. When the U.S. decided to enter World War I the new trend became thoroughly established.

At that time actual military attack posed little threat to national security. However, President Wilson recognized the long-range dangers for America and the world if Germany gained dominance over Europe. His policy of participation in the war centered largely upon the national interest of maintaining the *status quo*.

Military occupations, of necessity, followed. And for the U.S. at least, they were based upon the premise that Europe had been saved intact and could re-emerge in its former structure. Once again the Continental Powers would insure peace and stability throughout the world, except for those regions within which U.S. influence would remain uncontested. Washington's emphasis upon this goal can be seen clearly through the approach adopted toward the Rhineland occupation. Only minimum restraints were imposed upon the daily activities of the German people. For example, unlike most belligerent occupations in modern times, citizens of the defeated state were even permitted to retain and use personal firearms.

The policy was consistent with the President's ideas on collective security and the League of Nations, as well as being in line with his sincere espousal of internationalism. He and his advisors obviously believed that a nonpunitive occupation would speed the rise of a stable and democratic Germany. At a future date, the ex-enemy nation itself would be invited to join the collective organization and resume its full role within the European power complex.

American occupation policies, concentrating upon the *status quo* goal of national interest, were implemented in the following cases:

Luxembourg (belligerent occupation of neutral territory) 1918
Rhineland (belligerent occupation) 1918-1923
North Russia and Siberia (joint intervention) ....1918-1920[2]

Every evidence suggests that the United States held to the idea of perpetuating the existing international order during the interwar period and even through the series of events surrounding participation in World War II. Pearl Harbor forced America to involve itself in world affairs and the outlook within national interest remained one of helping Britain and France again stabilize the international scene. This time, however, the decision was made to rid the world of the German threat. As a result, initial occupation directives were harsh and had little in common with the relaxed occupation policies of World War I.[3]

Events overseas were forcing America to abandon its stress upon the *status quo* interest in favor of an emphasis upon the goal of *security*. The primary international developments which propelled the U.S. toward this decision occurred while the post-World War II occupations were still in progress. First, the realization that England and France were incapable of solving their domestic reconstruction problems without outside aid came as a shocking surprise. Also, it was apparent that their capacity to fulfill their traditional worldwide responsibilities was evaporating. The decline of two of the strongest World Powers, which so recently had played key roles in winning the war, presented a difficult concept for U.S. policy makers to accept. Its true meaning might have been ignored even longer had not the Russians emerged as a worldwide force.

Moscow furnished ample clues regarding its future policy intentions during the course of the initial negotiations on the division of occupied territories. With the U.S.S.R.'s take over of Eastern Europe and the development of the atomic bomb, the certainty of a shift in U.S. national interest was ordained. America began to accept the role of Western leadership and engaged in a struggle with the Soviet Union. At stake were the U.S.'s own self-preservation and security. In the light of the new interest, the rebuilding of Europe became important within a different context. Europe, including Western Germany and Italy, was necessary to the United States as both ally and buffer.

Digressing slightly it is necessary to explain the definition of security, the newly emphasized national interest. Its contemporary meaning was first introduced by the founders of the Realist School of International Relations. Professor Kenneth W. Thompson suggests that foremost among these intellectual innovators were Reinhold Niebuhr, Hans J. Morgenthau, Nicholas J. Spykman, and E. H. Carr.[4] Though coming from diverse personal backgrounds, these four arrived at a new theory of the behavior of nations and created a new philosophical approach which accommodated the traditional poles of isolationism and internationalism. A concept of power politics operating within a constantly changing society was inherent in their theoretical framework.[5] In essence, foreign policy as seen by Morgenthau has one purpose, "the security of the nation."[6]

An exploration of the precise forces involved in security has stimulated a continuing dialogue among the theorists as well as having generated countless tracts by other eminent scholars, writers, and political craftsmen. Among the more widely known and respected of these have been George Kennan, Charles O. Lerche, Jr., Robert E. Osgood, and Walter Lippmann.[7] The single point upon which each of these experts and most other authorities agree totally is the idea that survival takes precedence above all other policy ingredients. It may be labeled with a variety of titles, e.g., self-preservation, self-defense, or self-protection. However, authorities generally find little argument with Osgood's concise statement that, "Basic to all kinds of national self-interest is survival or self-preservation."[8]

Beyond this point, however, the scholarly exposition of security and national interest becomes rather unclear, especially when the problem is approached from the angle of American military occupation policy. A number of vital questions present themselves. Is security really a simple matter of self-protection? Is the concept of power inherent within it? If so, does one consider the balance of power within the world community or the superiority and/or maintenance of a favorable power ratio by America? Does the protection of specific geographic areas fall within the maintenance of security? Is selfishness in the national purpose a part of security, or will such lack of idealism eventually retrogress into domestic dictatorship rather than progress into true security?[9]

The authors have chosen at this point to suggest a definition of security which appears to them workable within the context of military occupation policy. Admittedly, this conceptual approach may not hold true for the entire spectrum of foreign policy, nor will it entirely answer all of the questions posed above. Nevertheless, it is an honest attempt at definition. It is possible to agree with the experts that self-preservation and/or survival must, above all other factors, be included and considered first.

Below this basic premise, all additional policy factors are included in our definition insofar as the United States can afford to carry them economically and ideologically to their necessary ends. Therefore, the most important idea is the need for the U.S. to maintain preeminent power, or as Morgenthau expressed it, "not balance — that is, equality — of power but a superiority of power in [its] own behalf." [10]

Disagreement can be made, however, with the belief that the reason for the elevation in importance of this element is simply power valued in the accepted sense. Rather, the emphasis appears to us important because if power is lost, honor is lost. And to any segment of the military establishment, the idea of honor and prestige occupies the position of a far more significant power in terms of its impact as a realistic force. The Oriental notion of saving face is not wholly unrelated.

On the third level stands the maintenance of the balance of power in favor of those nations which are friendly to the American concept of stability, peace, and order. This is viewed as being on the third rank because should the involvement be only threatened, and not precipitated, then honor can sometimes be ignored.

A further classification is frequently included under the catchall phrase *vital interests*. Though these are not held to be paramount to the survival of the national substance, Osgood suggests that, "Within this category one might place equal commercial opportunity, the protection of citizens and property outside the nation's territorial limits, and the control of immigration." [11]

The following is a list of occupations which have been conducted on the basis of policies which reflected a primary emphasis upon security:

Bases in British, Dutch possessions, etc. (consensual)	World War II
Iceland (consensual)	World War II
Greenland (consensual)	World War II
North Africa (civil affairs; consensual)	1942-1944
Sicily (belligerent occupation)	1943-1947

Italy (belligerent occupation) 1943-1947
Austria (belligerent occupation; zonal control) 1944-1955
Germany (belligerent occupation; zonal control) 1944-1949
Germany (under High Commissioner) 1949-1955
Berlin (belligerent occupation; zonal control) 1945-
Norway (civil affairs) 1944
Belgium (civil affairs) 1944
Netherlands (civil affairs) 1944
Luxembourg (civil affairs) 1944
France (civil affairs) 1944
Japan (belligerent occupation) 1945-1951
Ryukyu Islands (belligerent occupation) 1945-1950
Ryukyu Islands (under High Commissioner) 1950-
South Korea (belligerent occupation) 1945-1949
South Korea (consensual) 1949-
South Vietnam (consensual) ....1964-[12]

The vast array of all the occupations listed in this chapter is rather surprising. During its relatively short history, the U. S. has undertaken at least forty-five ventures of note, not including the additional actions undertaken by the Navy and Marines. The true significance of these operations can be appreciated only when their relationship to national interest is considered and the degree to which military occupations have played a role in the larger area of national security and foreign policy is realized.

CIVIL AFFAIRS OPERATIONS AND THE IMMEDIATE GOALS OF NATIONAL INTEREST

When considered on a theoretical plane, the relationship of occupation policy to long-range national purposes is often minimized or even ignored. At best the connection seems unclear. However, the role of military civil administration as a vehicle for advancing policy in the field has been visible, on occasion dramatically so; more frequently, however, it has been unexciting and little known to the world at large.

The cumulative effect of these small and unnoticed actions can be shown by investigating specific instances of reforms and projects which were undertaken during the post-World War II occupations in Europe and Asia. These efforts admittedly were designed for the primary function of serving U. S. national interests. However, they sometimes benefited markedly the local political and economic system.

The case of the Berlin occupation illustrates difficulties and opportunities open to officials. Russian endeavors to terminate the Western presence in the city continued both before and after the Airlift and the Wall were problems. An embarrassing contrast between conditions in the Eastern and Western zones has been apparent to non-European visitors as well as to the Germans themselves. Refugees fleeing in mass from the East attested to the general favor accorded U. S. policy over that of the Soviets. American policy since the initial postwar era centered upon rebuilding a German economic and political structure compatible with local wishes. And programs sponsored by occupation authorities in Western Berlin were no exception. The repeated attempts by the Russians to starve the Allied sectors of the former capital into submission and the construction of the Wall symbolize both the frustrations of the Kremlin and the successes of Washington. Propaganda values from this situation alone can be seen as working to the advantage of U. S. interests throughout the world.

The specific contributions of military government in this protracted venture must not be overlooked. The physical presence of occupation troops was important. During the Airlift, for example, the existence of a force in being provided unquestioned legal justification for a prompt and decisive American response. On the operational level, the success of Washington's overall policy hinged largely upon the ability of the military's efforts in providing emergency supplies and facilities for the civilian population during the crisis. U. S. forces in Berlin, experienced in the problems of occupation and civil assistance, were capable of rendering a caliber of efficiency which could not have been expected from outside units dispatched to the scene in a hurried and temporary fashion. Aware of the local situation, the small occupying group served as a guiding nucleus for the augmentation units sent into the city.

Within a broader perspective, however, the significance of occupation actions in Berlin rested upon a continual series of lesser struggles and accomplishments. For example, currency problems are endemic to nearly all occupations and civil affairs operations. In any combat or *post-bellum* situation the local money tends to be unstable in value and highly inflated. U. S. servicemen themselves contribute to the difficulties through their traditional affluence. Balancing the American and indigenous finance systems side-by-side is exceedingly complex and poses obvious implications of national prestige as well as problems of sound fiscal management.

Even more burdensome is any attempt on the part of an occupying army to reform the local currency system. Economics Sections, and Money and Banking Sections of civil affairs units are equipped for handling this undertaking by having the technical staff and physical means required to implement the changeover. In postwar Germany, however, the prime difficulty was diplomatic rather than technical. East-West disagreement over the future fate of the ex-enemy nation was evident in the currency dispute.

Soviet efforts to gain a toe-hold in the Western sectors though this avenue began early in the history of the occupation. Being an island within Russian controlled territory, Berlin was particularly vulnerable to Russian pressure. The city's monetary question was not unique in terms of the nature of the trouble. It was unique, however, in the sense that the solution eventually reached for the remainder of Western Germany could not be applied automatically in Berlin. In other zones the U. S. exercised its legal right and unilaterally introduced a new form of currency when negotiations with the Russians reached an impasse. Berlin, however, was under joint administrative control of the Four Powers, and the conversion to a new money had to be on the basis of a multilateral agreement among all the Allies.

The clandestine maneuvering of both sides on this issue in Berlin constitutes a classic occupation story of modern times. Soviet craftiness during the early stages of the German occupation had been responsible for the circulation of vast sums of *phony marks*. These unauthorized bills had actually been manufactured because of the initial gullibility of Western leaders. However, when the June 1948 conversion took place it was evident that U. S. authorities had learned their lesson well and their surreptitious and meticulous advance planning made possible a smooth transition to the new money throughout the Western zones. Berlin, being exempt, continued to use the old Reichsmarks.

In that city Soviet-American negotiations were immediately intensified. Previous discussions concerning the peculiar monetary status of Berlin had labored the same theme endlessly. Soviet authorities insisted that the currency in use in Eastern Germany also be used as the sole form of money in all occupation zones in Berlin. The constant refusal of the American delegates to consider this proposal was based upon a knowledge of the ultimate Soviet motives. These were, first, to undermine American claims to sovereign rights in its zone, and second, to control the total Berlin economy through currency manipulation. If permitted, economic chaos among merchants and manufacturers would generate far reaching political repercussions.

The final showdown came during the late evening of June 24, 1948, four days after the money and banking reform was announced for

West Germany. Delegates met in the Allied Control Council Building in Berlin, the scene of many previous heated exchanges. At approximately ten p.m. a Russian messenger arrived and informed the deadlocked negotiators that Soviet authorities would immediately and unilaterally begin city-wide conversion to East German currency. The conference adjourned at once in an apparent air of Soviet triumph.

But the Russians had underestimated American talents. Quantities of Deutsche Marks had secretly been brought into the city by U. S. agents, and were already distributed in strategic locations awaiting the moment when American authorities would themselves announce a surprise conversion. These bills were identical to those circulated in the other Western zones, with the exception that a large B had been stamped in indelible ink on each note. This designated that the bill was solely a part of the Berlin monetary system.[18] The trusted German officials who were aware of the American plan had been anxiously awaiting the opportunity to circulate the new money and establish a stable money and banking system for the city.

The Russian announcement of unilateral action automatically provided Western authorities with the justification for setting their own plans in motion. American sponsored currency exchange proceeded with clocklike precision while the Russians became bogged in a morass of red tape. Immediately, it was clear that their attempt at a *fait accompli* had backfired, but an even worse difficulty was yet to confront them. Soviet officials had decided to forestall the printing of an entirely new set of bills by the use of an inexpensive expedient. An identifying tab was to be placed on each old bill, denoting that it was usable as new currency. What the Russians might have anticipated soon took place: forgers quickly began reproducing the stickers in large numbers.

The significance of the currency incident in Berlin points up one of the most important applications of occupation policy within the scheme of overall foreign policy. Civil affairs officials have the capacity for furthering interests through a series of relatively small programs and projects. These, in turn, can lay a foundation upon which statesmen are able to press successfully for the higher aims of policy. When programs such as civic action and pacification are added to the list of more traditional occupation programs, the potential offered the nation through the effective use of the Army for civil administration becomes apparent. Military occupation does have its positive side, at least when national interest is the criterion used in judging its worth.

INTERNATIONAL COOPERATION AND ALLIANCES

A vexing and increasingly important problem faced by policy planners has been the achievement of American goals when other countries have participated with the U.S. in joint occupations. Many successes in these situations were by-products of the immediate civil affairs role in supporting the combat effort. Historically, the general idea of *allied* ventures in war and occupation developed simultaneously with the gradual acceptance of the desirability of mutual security policies. World War I marked the beginning of this era for the United States. Since that point Washington has placed ever greater emphasis upon the need to plan and conduct operations under conditions where the overall responsibility and costs would be shared by other states, provided that American interests were not jeopardized in the process.

Sometimes operations which technically were mutual undertakings have been predominantly American. While on the surface other nations appeared to play a major role in the formal administrative machinery, they actually exercised only minor influence in determining and implementing policy. This was the case in post-World War II Japan, where the Far Eastern Commission and the Allied Control Council supposedly possessed the power to govern the occupation. For all practical purposes, however, the American general in charge of SCAP conducted the program strictly in line with the wishes of the United States government.

In other occupations of the Second World War a more equal sharing of responsibility and control was achieved. During the North African, Italian, and Western European operations, American civil affairs officers served in units of the Allied nations and *vice versa*. The Allied Control Commission, which functioned in Sicily and Italy, for example, formulated directives on the basis of consultation among leaders and representatives of several countries. Allied Military Government in Venezia Giulia (Trieste) was a case where orders were received directly from the Combined Chiefs of Staff.

To achieve the active cooperation of the population of the states which had been overrun by the Axis powers, a system of civil affairs agreements was inaugurated. The establishment of sound relations with the government in exile proved to be a distinct aid to the American efforts. The countries involved were Norway, the Netherlands,

Belgium, Luxembourg, and France. Regimes from these friendly nations required an organized plan for assistance if they were to assume responsibility for civil administration as soon after the invasion as possible.

Great Britain took the lead in defining an orderly approach to the problem. Since London was the seat of the exiled governments and closest among the Allied capitals, its leadership could have been expected. In addition, Britain's keen understanding of European political affairs as well as her recognized experience in handling colonial administration helped thrust her leadership into the foreground.

The first agreement was reached with the Norwegians, and it became the prototype for later negotiations and settlements. Procedures for transferring sovereign authority from the military command to local officials, as well as the question of the relative rights of military and civilian agencies after the transfer had been effected, were among the problems discussed. While the arrangement was of considerable assistance to the Norwegian government, the primary motive was the benefit which would accrue to the British Army in the field. It would not be forced to contend with civil difficulties except during the initial invasion. After the expulsion of German troops, governments throughout Europe were found to be in a state of chaos. It was reasoned that these nations' own officials, including those in exile, could best minimize local disturbances which otherwise would necessitate the diversion of tactical units for security duty.

Satisfied with the cooperative spirit of the Norwegian leaders, the British proposed similar agreements with the Netherlands and Belgium. At this point American authorities expressed a strong desire to play a role in determining future pacts. Since the United States was making the most substantial military contributions, the British had no choice but to acquiesce. So, according to the official Allied record, in the early summer of 1944, Norway, Belgium, the Netherlands, and Luxembourg were brought under this form of agreement. During August of that year a pact was finally signed with French authorities. The delay had resulted from differences between Washington and London over the complex question of legitimate French leadership.

Generally, the civil affairs agreement system proved extremely effective. Belgium was the only country where any serious difficulties occurred, and these were resolved through the intervention of the Supreme Allied Commander. In retrospect, the events surrounding the civil affairs question during and after World War II clearly revealed that cooperation among nations in this field was practicable and workable, and definitely to U.S. advantage.[14]

The joint venture in Korea further illustrated the possibilities opened through international alliances. Having been a Japanese possession, Korea was occupied in the wake of the Second World War. It was treated as a friendly rather than a hostile nation which was consistent with the approach adopted toward the countries of Western Europe. Technically, the American Army conducted a civil affairs operation rather than a belligerent occupation. But since economic and political conditions in 1945 were in a state of chaos, U.S. military government units performed major administrative duties during the initial period.[15]

The pattern for the operation had been set much earlier. As a part of the Cairo Declaration of 1943, the wartime Allies had agreed to a joint and short-term Korean occupation. The main concern was the presence of Japanese troops who were sure to be stranded there at the end of the war. It was necessary to have some means of accepting their surrender, insuring their disarmament, and providing for their transportation home. An arbitrary line was drawn across the peninsula at the 38th parallel; and Russian forces were to occupy the northern zone while American and Allied soldiers handled affairs in the southern portion. Originally assumed to be a temporary expedient pending the creation of a single Korean government, the division line soon became a fixed boundary separating communist and non-communist territory. The well known result was a series of disputes which resembled the zonal difficulties occurring in Germany. Upon reaching a final impasse in negotiations over unification, the two major occupiers sponsored separate regimes for their respective areas.

As an experience in international cooperation among the Western Powers, the Korean case stands as a prototype for the utilization of the United Nations machinery. Attempts to resolve the problem through its agencies proved futile since the U.N. had the power only to supervise free elections in the southern sector, which it did in 1948. The resulting South Korean regime was recognized as the legitimate government by practically all non-communist states. To this extent at least, U.S. goals were realized through multilateral agreement. American forces were then withdrawn, except for a small military assistance team. Washington seemingly accepted the situation as a permanent settlement. And by 1950 some question existed as to whether any portion of Korea was within the U.S. defense perimeter. When the conflict erupted, the immediate and primary U.S. problem was military, and the U.N. proved valuable in garnering international support.

During the initial combat operation a form of military government was used by U.N. forces. Not until May 1952 when the battle line had been somewhat stabilized was a comprehensive civil affairs agreement reached between U.S. and Korean officials.[16] Until then American forces dealt on a rather informal basis with the Korean civilian population. The continuous presence of U.S. troops since World War II, though in small numbers during much of the period, helped create a precedent for cooperation when hostilities began.

Though the military campaign was the paramount center of attention, as much as possible was done to assist civilians. Korea was the first instance where Washington policy makers saw the problems of waging modern combat in the midst of an underdeveloped society. Without design, the civil affairs units began to find solutions. For example, as the invaded people fled for their lives, CA officers provided medical care, clothing, housing, and other necessities to the limits permitted by the combat situation. In return, U.S. forces gained the use of Korean public utilities, transport, communication facilities, air fields, quantities of locally produced products and local labor. The latter was mobilized for such vital and hazardous tasks as road building and hand-carrying food and ammunition to troops manning dangerous combat outposts.

Korean national and local officials cooperated actively with the American and UN contingents. However, in fairness to the record, it must be admitted that as the front line was stabilized and the Armistice drew near, the earlier air of informal cooperation became less visible. Minor irritations gradually emerged as both governments started to lay long-range plans for the future. Nevertheless, U.S. interests continued to be served through the mutual unanimity.

One can observe the wartime international understanding which occurred during the Korean Conflict and conclude that it was quite successful for fighting the war and solving the civilian problems. And from these successes, the United States pursued two broad courses regarding international alliances. Through one avenue an attempt was made to establish common civil affairs procedures for joint military operations, most notably through the North Atlantic Treaty Organization (NATO), the Southeast Asia Treaty Organization (SEATO), and through direct trilateral arrangements among the United States, Canada, and the United Kingdom.

The NATO and SEATO treaties were pacts stipulating that the participating states were in basic accord on ultimate policy goals.

But the subject of regularizing procedures was left for future negotiations by lower level officials, with the result that a system for standardizing civil affairs activities took shape. The Standardization Agreements of NATO (STANAGs), as well as those of SEATO (SEATAGs), were patterned after the results of an earlier round of negotiations among the United States, Canada, and the United Kingdom on the same topic. These had been titled Standardization of Operations and Logistics Agreements (SOLOGs), and were gradually expanded in scope during the early 1950's.[17]

Since 1957, the U.S. has achieved concurrence among its NATO and SEATO allies on issues such as the following: (1) principles of CA operations, (2) standardization of documents such as proclamations and ordinances, (3) uniformity of subjects to be taught in civil affairs courses, (4) principles of unit organization, and (5) CA training principles for the general indoctrination of combat forces.[18] Though conceived solely as a device for establishing closer coordination among armies engaged in a joint combat campaign, the SOLOGs, STANAGs, and SEATAGs touch upon broader political and economic questions. As a result, American staff officers assigned to the treaty organizations are forced to exercise caution and insure that implementing agreements do not commit the U.S. to occupation goals not in line with the wishes of Washington.

The second theme involves the United States' continued interest in the use of international organizations for civilian relief and reconstruction. Their presence in battle areas has become an accepted part of international relations since World War II, and several have owed their existence to the policy of the American government. Examples are the United Nations Relief and Rehabilitation Agency (UNRRA) which functioned in Europe during the immediate postwar years, and the United Nations Korean Relief Agency (UNKRA) which operated only within one country. While international in membership, such groups have been under the indirect, and often the direct, domination of the nation providing the chief contributions.

In reviewing the effects of both the civilian relief agencies and the military alliances, it is plain that Washington has usually been able to control the manner in which they functioned. Consequently, through them the U.S. utilized international machinery to further its own national interests.

CHAPTER III

CHANGING PRINCIPLES AND FLUCTUATING MOODS

In the previous chapter the discussion of national interest was confined narrowly to unimpassioned reasons for entering wars and conducting occupations. These included geographic expansion, economic development, and national security. At this point it becomes necessary to consider two areas which are much more difficult to define—national principles and national mood.

Substantial controversy has surrounded the question of the relative importance of national principles or values as an aspect of policy. For example, the Realist School of international relations theorists accords nodding acceptance of their presence, but insists that the national interest is of paramount and overriding significance. Though on the one hand, Professor Osgood can state that the "pursuit of national self-interest without regard for universal ideals is not only immoral but self-defeating."[1] The primary argument of the school is nevertheless that the U.S. would be deluding itself if it imagined that principles had ever been given serious consideration in the guidance of major overseas efforts.

Other authorities, notably those associated with the Idealist School, suggest a different interpretation. They agree with the Realists that interest will and must be the primary element in policy, but they believe that deliberate and careful attention must be given to the set of ideals which are implicitly a part of overseas actions. In their judgment, principles are sufficiently weighty that it is possible and practical to identify them as constituting an element distinct from national interest. While not being totally committed to the idealist approach, Reitzel, Kaplan, and Coblenz articulated that position when they noted that:

"*Principles* is used to mean the enduring modes of behavior or the relatively established guides to action that characterize nations . . . *principles* are deeply imbedded in the general culture and political philosophy of a society and are powerful, if intangible and subjective, guides to action. There are real cultural limits on the extent to which *interests* that are in basic conflict with *principles* can be determined and pursued. Thus although principles cannot be easily identified and are often modified in action, they represent the underlying patterns of value that guide national action and to which determinations of *interests, objectives,* and *policies* tend over the long run to conform."[2]

Such qualities as "enduring modes of behavior" describe many of the most profound ambitions of man, and express the long-range goals of individuals for themselves as well as for humanity in general. In this sense, the merit of the particular value in question is of lesser importance than the concept that people will reject an unprincipled policy but support one which is principled.

America's set of ideals consists of a complex array of broad and specific hopes for the future. Expressions of these have included the altruistic aims of the Four Freedoms: liberty of speech and worship, and freedom from fear and want. A belief in the worth of the individual is a central theme. And man is considered the most important element in society, while social institutions are regarded as little more than convenient means for regularizing relationships. Democratic thought rejects the notion of the existence of a national interest separate from the needs of individual citizens. Consquently, it would be unjustified to sacrifice the welfare of citizens for that of the fatherland. According to the pattern of American values, the state exists solely to promote the well-being of its people and to secure their rights. From this general construction of personal self-determination emerges the belief in national self-determination.

Individual values, which are to be pursued within the context of a free society, are both intangible and numerous. As an illustration, humanitarianism can be cited because of its special significance for the policy question. A serious concern for the general welfare of mankind has been a constant factor in our national character and is probably a reflection of its Judeo-Christian heritage.[3] Values and principles such as these stand as the most unselfish motives which nations can offer the world; seldom are they the reasons for wars. Only infrequently are ideals in evidence during modern struggles, except in slogans such as "making the world safe for democracy."[4]

Theorists and policy planners have found it convenient to ignore the question of principles in the national security policy. Admittedly, ideals are difficult to articulate and often tend to create an oversentimentalized image in the practical mind. Perhaps national principles would be dismissed from this study were it not for one critical fact: they have indeed played a part in occupation policy. When policy is approached from the viewpoint of civil affairs and military government, the consistent role of principles is present.

Since interests have not had the total impact on occupations which they have had on war, the polciy vacuum has typically been filled by a combination of national principles and an additional element. The latter ingredient can be defined as the mood-of-the-day, temper-of-the-times, or climate-of-opinion. The national mood is inclined to fix upon immediate and short range goals and alternatives, and represents the reaction of a mass of individuals to pressing problems. A strong emotional content is presumed. While not necessarily being the least desirable of man's motivations and behavior, it is likely to express his expedient self. For example, in response to the challenge of military occupation, sentiment has somtimes called for benevolence toward the former enemy, but more often it has been characterized by a pressure for revenge and the imposition of harsh restraints.

Within this frame of reference, the balancing of popular sentiment with national principles can be seen as the process by which civil affairs policy is finally evolved. Of course, the assumption still holds that the policy ingredient of national interest is always present to at least some degree. The point is that under some circumstances leaders cease using interest as the primary guidepost, and that the importance of principles and mood is then increased to the extent that they can become a major or even predominent factor in policy.

The role of mood and principles stands out when their impact upon the approach America adopted toward occupied peoples is considered. Any serious attempt to determine their relative role within a complex policy structure requires the application of some form of conceptual framework. From the standpoint of the aims of this study, a logical device involved grouping America's occupations under three headings. The first is titled "opposition" and includes instances where it was possible to conclude that mood and principles exerted conflicting pulls within the established policy. A good example is the Civil War occupation. The military's code of conduct expressed high principles, but Congress and the electorate demonstrated a mood which sometimes prevented their being applied. As a result of mood and principles working at cross purposes, the national interest was not fully served.

A second division of occupations is termed "unintentional support." It includes those cases in which the popular temper and principles were mutually reinforcing and working to support national interest, though without intending to do so. Instances and illustrations can be drawn from the operation undertaken as a result of the Mexican War, from the actions in Cuba and the Philippines stemming from the Spanish-American War, from the American participation in the

Rhineland occupation following World War I, and from the later phases of the World War II occupations.

The final category seems best described by the title "public indifference." Both principles and national interest are visible forces; however, public mood appears not to be a highly solidified factor in policy. These conditions have been most clearly exemplified during minor or limited military engagements. Civil affairs policies for the Siberian Intervention, the Korean conflict, and the Vietnam war reflect this situation.

Opposition

The single most significant policy statement of the Civil War relating to principles was the military code officially titled *Instructions for the Government of the Armies of the United States in the Field.* It appears to have been a natural outgrowth of General Scott's previous experience in Mexico. Francis Lieber, who furnished the Union Army with its war law code, earned his prewar reputation as a professor at the University of South Carolina. While he agreed with the Union cause, it seems obvious that his influence was accepted by Confederate leaders as well as Northern partisans. The document laid much of the groundwork upon which the U.S. formulated the standards of conduct for its military forces in later wars and occupations. The project of establishing a formal code was initiated by President Lincoln at the request of Union generals. Soon after fighting commenced it became apparent to them that they required a manual which would spell out in uncomplicated language the laws of war which they were to observe.

In some quarters the code was criticized as being too severe; certainly it did embody a rather extreme view of the rights of the occupier over the occupied. However, this was consistent with the precedents established in former wars. It was also criticized for being excessively academic in its references to military necessity. In spite of the possible validity of these charges, the overall importance of the code has been recognized generally. It represented the first major effort to establish rules in an area never before subjected to a code.[5] The line of thought reflected in the Lieber code can be seen in the following short excerpt:

"Martial law is simply military authority exercised in accordance with the laws and usages of war . . . Military oppression is not Martial Law: it is the abuse of the power which that law confers . . . As Martial Law is executed by the military force, it is incumbent on those who administer it to be strictly guided by the principles of justice, honor, and humanity—virtues adorning a soldier even more than other men, for the very reason that he possesses the power of his arms against the unarmed."[6]

The Lieber code was written somewhat in isolation from the popular temper. Its author, a legal scholar, felt a strong personal dedication to lay down a set of morally just standards which could govern the conduct of the Army. These would transcend momentary emotional consideration. Of special significance was the implication that the Civil War was being fought to further the status of inherent human rights which could not be ignored or legitimately taken away either by the Southern slaveholder or by the Northern military occupier.

Congress, unfortunately, found it impossible to act with the same detachment from the pressures of the moment. Its responses in framing occupation policy were characterized by highly emotional struggles between the radicals, who wished the South punished severely, and the moderates, who favored a lenient policy. The result was a stalemate in the legislative process which, in turn, contributed to the creation of a partial policy vacuum. The stage was set for an occupation wherein principles and mood clashed.

UNINTENTIONAL SUPPORT

The World War II initial occupation of Germany exhibited the traits of a developing battle between principles and mood. The Atlantic Charter, signed by President Roosevelt and Prime Minister Churchill, set forth a "declaration of principles" for the Allies to follow. Among the Atlantic Charter precepts were such high ideals as the "abandonment of the use of force," "improved labor standards, economic advancement, and social security." It went so far as to pledge help to all nations' economies, "great or small, victor or vanquished."[7]

On the other hand and also felt by the victors was the worldwide cry for revenge. Punishment must be meted out to the German people for their diabolic and savage atrocities against the Jews and other minority groups. Twice within the same generation American youth had been killed and maimed in wars against Germany; this must never happen again. The mood of 1945 was voiced by a loud and near universal American chorus demanding extremely harsh occupation regulations for all Germans, leaders and followers alike.

In the light of the conflict between ideals and revenge, it would be possible to classify the policy applied in postwar Germany as an occupation of opposition like that applied following the Civil War had it not been for one development. In about 1948 the American mood shifted from a hatred of the Germans to a fear of the communists. This factor, coupled with a resurgence of attention now paid to the national interest of security, provided American policy makers with an opportunity to put into practice the high principles of the Atlantic Charter. Thus, this occupation serves as an example of the second classification, unintentional support, wherein the mood and principles developed for different reasons and along different tracks but supported and reinforced each other in an overall accomplishment.

The earlier occupation of Mexico is another example of unintended support. The American people, although understanding the reasons for the Mexican War and the ensuing military occupation, still did not like it. From the birth of the Republic they themselves had been faced with the continuing problem of maintaining the independence of the United States. The idea that America was now initiating the policy of expansion at the expense of another established state made honest citizens feel guilty. The sentiments of many were expressed by Senator Corwin of Ohio, a noted Whig orator. He said that if he were a Mexican, he would say to the Americans: "Have you not room in your own country to bury your dead men? If you come into mine, we will greet you with bloody hands; and welcome you to a hospitable grave."[8]

This sense of public guilt was not lessened when the first American commander in Mexico, General Zachary Taylor, permitted his subordinates to deal with the Mexican civilians as they saw fit. Numerous cases of alleged atrocities were reported, and a national scandal was created by the conduct of Taylor's men.[9] Transfer of command to General Winfield Scott soon brought about a more ambitious campaign strategy and a revamped system of controlling the local population. He decided to strike directly for Mexico City rather than confine hostilities to the border regions. This meant that the American Army would be placed at the mercy of the Mexicans living along the extended supply route. Success of the bold strategy depended upon persuading them either to cooperate with the U.S. troops or at least to refrain from serious interference. And the key was the type of overall occupation policy America would choose to apply.

President Polk and Congress had attempted to establish an approach, but their efforts met with little success. At least two major reasons were responsible for the vacillation within national leadership.

First, inexperience in meeting the problems of belligerent occupation necessitated debate and deliberation before basic decisions could be reached. Closely related but of even greater long-range importance was a second difficulty. This was America's inability to see itself, let alone accept itself, as being a military master over foreign civilians.

The orders which were issued to Scott prior to his assumption of command reflected the dilemma of the Administration and the American people. Congress merely directed that in dealing with the enemy population the Army's actions be governed by the *law of nations*. These were considered to be fundamentally moral restraints upon military authority. On the basis of this vague dictum the new commander developed his famous General Order Number 20.[10] More credit must go to Scott than to any other official in the American government for initiating the policy implemented during the Mexican occupation.

Through General Order 20 and related directives Scott attempted to resolve two basic military occupation questions. First, what rules should govern the conduct of individual members of the occupying force toward the civilian population? And second, what general attitude should the occupier adopt toward the civilians-at-large in contrast to the enemy government and its officials? In answering the latter question, Scott's policy emphasized that his force had an obligation to distinguish between civilians who were merely citizens of the enemy state and those who were officials of the enemy government. He proclaimed to the Mexican people that the Americans had entered their homeland solely because of the tyrannical actions of their own government. The occupation troops were actually the friends of the Mexican people. To demonstrate that this was the case, Scott ordered his forces not to disturb civilians in their peaceful customs, traditions, and institutions. He took particular pains to avoid interfering with the local churches unless they were used as military strongholds. He attended Catholic Mass even though he was a Protestant and he instructed his men to salute both priests and magistrates. Such orders were especially striking because at this time anti-Catholic agitation was at a peak within the United States.[11]

The second major policy question Scott dealt with concerned the rules which should govern the relationship between American troops and Mexican civilians. For this purpose he established a well defined set of regulations which were unusually strict for their day. If occupation forces were to be respected and accepted as liberators rather than exploiters, logic dictated that their deportment must be just and chivalrous. Scott's orders bound both his own troops and the local inhabitants under identical legal and moral sanctions. Murder, rape, theft, and other crimes were not to be tolerated, whether committed by Mexicans or Americans. Here again the impact of principles upon policy guidelines can be seen in sharp perspective. The American concept of just and proper standards of behavior constituted the actual source for the regulations. And the penalties for breaching the code were to be no less humane than punishments for like crimes committed within the United States.

Scott had defined the law of nations to be a set of occupation goals and codes which could operate in such a manner as to reinforce his military efforts. His sensitivity to the political and moral pressures of the time were at the root of his ability to forge a model policy. In the search for concrete guidelines, Scott was forced to take it upon himself to develop, interpret, and implement a policy based mainly upon a combination of principles and generally recognized popular sentiments. These were, of course, coupled with the factor of military expediency.

Operations in Cuba and the Philippines furnish another set of examples of unintentional support. This was an era of national adolescence. The popular feeling of self-satisfaction bordered upon national smugness, smugness for the record of American successes which disproved foreign criticism that the system could not work, smugness in the sense of a cocksureness that the answer for the ideal political order had at last been found.

There is little wonder that the yellow journalists were able to exert considerable influence upon the American people at the turn of the century. Citizens wished to be moved and swayed, and probably wanted to believe the William Randolph Hearsts. He and his numerous imitators prospered, to a great extent because they met a need or supposed need of the moment. A sensational press stressed continually the superiority of American political and social values, and was inclined to see the world as an arena open and waiting for the embracement of these ideals. The notion of a national cause which should be pursued with messianic zeal was implicit.

More than altruism, however, was behind the press's agitation. A "Congressional Commission" established under the auspices of Mr. Hearst was sent to Cuba in 1896. Composed of three Senators and three members of the House, it reported that the "Future of Cuba is American" and the "Americanization" of the island could be completed in twenty years through the "exploration of Cuba by American capital."[12] Clearly, the yellow press had an ulterior motive in stirring up the populace. Yet, it is true that the struggle of the Cuban people for their independence from Spain did arouse the sincere sympathy of America which had itself gained its freedom by revolting against a European master. The sense of comradeship was strengthened by an uneasiness over the armed conflict being fought ninety miles away.

When the Madrid government sent General Valeriano Weyler to the island in 1896 to put down the uprising the problem came to a climax. His policy of severe repression resulted in a general break-down of the economy and widespread sickness and starvation. Not only the American press but also the man on the street reacted by making Weyler the symbol of Spanish autocracy and misrule. The situation was further agitated by José Martí's Cuban Revolutionary Party which maintained headquarters in New York. This exile group flooded the desks of newspaper editors with exaggerated accounts of rebel heroism and Spanish atrocities. Since such stories were good copy, they were often printed as though they represented objective reports rather than deliberate propaganda. Several newspaper ex-tracts reveal the type of stories which bombarded the American public on the eve of the sinking of the *Maine*.

Hearst's *New York Journal*, for example, reported: "It is not only Weyler the soldier . . . but Weyler the brute, the devastator of haci-endas, the destroyer of families, and the outrager of women . . . Piti-less, cold, and exterminator of men . . . There is nothing to prevent this carnal, animal brain from running riot with itself in inventing tortures and infamies of bloody debauchery."[13]

Even the more responsible *New York World*, under the publisher Joseph Pulitzer, considered it proper and necessary to indulge in similar expressions. Also dealing with the Cuban question, the *World* found: "Blood on the roadsides, blood in the fields, blood on the doorsteps, blood, blood, blood! The old, the young, the weak, the crippled—all are butchered without mercy . . . is there no nation wise enough, brave enough, and strong enough to restore peace in this bloodsmitten land?"[14]

As the United States became emotionally involved with the Cuban question, it increasingly sought more straightforward ways through which to share the "blessings of liberty" with the island's inhabitants. Every session of Congress between 1895 and 1898 witnessed the in-troduction of measures to come to their direct aid.[15] The popular mood was ripe for a widespread discussion of the possible purchase or annexation of the Spanish colonies, especially Cuba. The addition of Cuba to the Union as a State had earlier been urged in the 1850's by Southern leaders who saw in it an opportunity to alter the failing balance between slave and free states. Others saw Cuba, so close to Florida and the Keys, as a logical extension of the American Union. In the decades following the Civil War the rapid expansion of trade with Cuba also contributed to keeping the matter of annexation a live issue.

But typically, the American people did not face up to the need for any major policy decisions until after the war was well under way. The question of annexing the former Spanish territories had now to be weighed in terms which were both immediate and irrevocable. In the fall of 1898 President McKinley sent Robert P. Porter, a trusted personal friend, to Cuba to gather information which could help guide the Administration in the formation of a long-range policy toward the island. Following his return from Havana, Porter wrote a book, *Industrial Cuba,* and an article in the *North American Review,* in which he expressed strong support for total annexation. When he wrote that Cuba's future should be sought through "complete union with the greater Republic,"[16] he was probably voicing the sentiments of Administration leaders as well as his own. If not an outright statement of McKinley's private opinions, Porter's writings at least functioned as a semi-official sounding board through which Washington could better gauge the reaction of the American people to the idea of annexation.

Among Congressional leaders, Senator Henry M. Teller's statement of 1894 that "I am in favor of annexation of Cuba" revealed this prewar popular thought.[17] Interestingly enough, this is the same senator who four years later authored the noted Teller Amendment designed to "leave the government and control of the island to its people."[18]

Had the politicians been able to deal with the annexation question in isolation from other forces, the fate of Cuba and the Philippines might have been far different. However, their future was directly affected by the changing attitudes of the American citizen, especially the new viewpoint which emerged during the six month period following the sinking of the *Maine.* Until then the prevailing sentiment had operated to reinforce the principles of humanitarianism and freedom which were implicit in the foreign policy of that day. The belief existed that it was necessary and appropriate to forge a policy which used the Army for the purpose of translating popular domestic values into a reality overseas. In addition, the ventures were assumed to be economically profitable steps.

Once the new territories were actually occupied, the popular mood favoring annexation or self-government began to change. A feeling of disillusionment perhaps best describes the reaction of both the Army and civilian officials upon their first contact with the local people. In Cuba, for example, the yellow press's "dashing rebel bands" were soon being described as "dagoes." The American troops, especially those from the Southern states, were shocked and infuriated upon discovering that large numbers of islanders were "inferior" Negroes.

To the disciplined military men, the guerrillas were slovenly in the formalities of soldierly conduct. This might have been excused had not the local bands engaged in open exploitation of their benefactors. Refusals to take orders were coupled with rampant thievery of Army equipment and personal property. Such acts were regarded as doubly unconscionable because Cuban leaders often abetted the crimes of their subordinates. With the breakdown of a sense of comradeship, American commanders turned increasingly to using the local forces as labor troops. Obviously, digging trenches and cleaning stables were demeaning and thus inspired little desire on the part of the Cubans to reform. The attitude of U.S. troops was revealed by Stephen Crane, the *New York World's* correspondent, when he reported that "both officers and privates have the most lively contempt for the Cubans. They despise them."[19]

The extent to which the Army had reached definite conclusions on the island's future was further stated in an interesting interview given by General William R. Shafter, who headed the expeditionary Army. He was questioned in December 1899 about the possibility of the Cubans developing self-government. In emotional and colorful language he said they were absolutely unready and unfit to govern themselves.[20]

Pursuing the same theme, an increasing number of dispatches from a variety of sources reached the American public. The *Detroit Tribune* editorialized that the Cubans were incapable of erecting a stable government and the best course might be "the military subjugation of the people we went to war to save."[21] The *Hartford Post* praised McKinley for his strong stand and wrote that "had it not been for our chief magistrate, these good for nothing allies of ours would have been established as an independent nation."[22] The respected liberal leader Carl Schurz noted that "There are multitudes of Americans who say now that had they known what a sorry lot the Cubans are, we would never have gone to war on their behalf." But since this has now happened, "the same Americans should at least not permit those same Cubans to take part in governing us," which they eventually would do if they were granted statehood and representation in Congress.[23]

Problems of a similar nature were developing in the Philippines. The friendly attitude of the American journalists toward the islanders was replaced by hostility as it became known that the two peoples exhibited different ethnic and social traits. To use a term which came into vogue a half-century later, the cultural shock took Americans by surprise. Admiral Dewey found it necessary to ask Washington to send "a small commission composed of men skilled in diplomacy and statesmanship . . . [who could] adjust the differences."[24] A succession of Military Governors between 1898 and 1902—Generals Merrit, Otis, MacArthur (Douglas MacArthur's father), and Chaffee—sent back a constant stream of pessimistic reports. They questioned the wisdom of permitting the Filipinos any substantial control over the government and economy of the islands.

Another major force contributed to the rapidly changing attitude toward the Philippines and Cuba. This was a growing belief among Americans that Washington officials were taking undue advantage of the occupied peoples and acting in an undemocratic manner. For example, the Cuban postal scandals of 1900 started a widespread demand for a reappraisal of foreign policy goals. David F. Healy reported that "The American public . . . was shocked and disillusioned by the suggestion of robbery and corruption in Cuba, supposedly the show place of American rule."[25] The resulting debate in Congress soon progressed to the broader issue of whether this country had any right to be governing on the island at all.

America had talked itself into believing that it was taking liberty to the ex-Spanish colonies; and now it found itself faced with bitterness, hostility, and even open insurrection by the very people it had befriended. The Cuban armed forces were retreating into the hills with the apparent aim of launching raids upon their benefactors. In fact, the situation was so ripe for bloodshed that General Brooke issued orders that no Cuban insurgent troops would be allowed in Havana to attend the ceremony terminating Spanish sovereignty. They were not permitted to celebrate their own Fourth of July.

The American public was also unwilling to accept gracefully what was happening in the Philippines. José Rizal, the George Washington of the Philippines, had gained worldwide fame for his struggle for national independence against the Spaniards. Before the war began he had looked continuously toward the United States for leadership and sympathy. In 1897 he and other rebel leaders had established a Revolutionary Government and had written a Provisional Constitution which was clearly influenced by its U.S. counterpart.[26] However, shortly after the defeat of the Spanish, Rizal felt compelled to turn his energies against the nation he had formerly idealized. The American people were asking themselves why, and the answer took the form of self-blame. The fact that force had to be used to subdue the "little brown brothers" was widely interpreted to mean that something was basically wrong with the policy being applied. "Civilizin' 'em with a Krag" seemed somehow an inappropriate and contradictory device for spreading democracy.

During 1899 the First Philippine Commission tried to discover a long-range solution to the difficulties, but it was caught in the same dilemma that faced the general public. On the one hand, the delegates told the Filipinos that the U.S. would enforce its supremacy throughout the islands. Simultaneously, they proclaimed that the local inhabitants would be guaranteed their individual civil rights and granted a degree of self-government. Their first line of reasoning seemed consistent with the imperialist notions of Senator Beveridge, while their second proclamation mirrored the idealistic sentiments of Senator McEnery.[27]

Confusion about the policy goals was further compounded when the Commission took its next step and added its own judgment about the manner in which the occupation fitted into the historic development of the American nation. It opined that the administration of the Philippines should follow the precedents laid down by Madison and Jefferson at the time of the Louisiana Purchase. Though perhaps unintended, the implication was that eventual statehood was an accepted goal of the occupation policy, and new doubts and suspicions were raised. The net effect was a Philippine, as well as Cuban, policy born more of confusion and indecision than design.

A third and closely allied force was also operating to bring about a change in attitude. The perennial weariness for the problems of occupation set in. Increasingly, the call for substantial expenditures to suppress uprisings and bolster bankrupt foreign holdings encountered voter resistance. This conflicted sharply with the earlier belief that the ventures would be profitable. In addition, the human costs were being scrutinized in a more dispassionate light. Atrocities against troops in the Philippines, in particular, raised further doubts. When

Theodore Roosevelt described the Filipinos as "Malay bandits" and "Chinese halfbreeds,"[28] and Leonard Wood referred to Latins as "a race steadily going down for a hundred years,"[29] they were expressing a new-found scorn and disdain shared by a large segment of the public.

Such opinions were factors in the crystallization of sentiment regarding the future of the new possessions. Concern for the moral and political welfare of the occupied peoples was replaced by contempt. Church leaders continued to refer to the new opportunities for missionary work which had been opened. But many religious leaders and laymen were reacting with disfavor to the suggestion that the Catholic Church in both Cuba and the Philippines was being treated with deference by occupation officials. Anti-Catholic prejudice, voiced through organizations such as the American Protective Association, became an issue whenever the status of church lands and schools was debated.

Gathering pressures both at home and overseas could not be ignored indefinitely. A responsibility had been assumed. While many Americans would have welcomed an immediate withdrawal from the occupied areas, such a move would have invited Spaniards to return and reimpose their same colonial misrule. The solution for Washington lay in finding a justification for a uniquely "American" colonial policy which emphasized current national principles, accepted moral and democratic ideals, and supported the momentary flurries and backlashes of public opinion.

Elihu Root, who was successively Secretary of War and Secretary of State during this period, provided guidance. More than any other single official, he had the practical insight to see the problem in perspective. Writing many years later in a letter to Philip C. Jessup, the aged statesman reflected upon the manner in which he had weighed the relationship between colonial administration and "the American dream." In the hope of finding inspiration for an enduring policy, Root had searched through his collection of documents relating to British and Dutch actions:

"I read them until I came to the conclusion that . . . [we had] to take the lessons we could get from the colonial policy of other countries, especially Great Britain, and apply it to the peculiar situation arising from the fundamental principles of our own government . . . [which are] based upon certain definite principles and fundamental rights of man . . . I came to the conclusion that there are certain things the United States Government couldn't do [in the colonies] because the people of the United States had declared that no government could do them—the Bill of Rights. There is a moral law which prevents the Government doing certain things to any man whatsoever. We haven't always stuck to it."[30]

Though America had wished to become a colonial power rivaling Britain and France, it could not bring itself to take the final and necessary steps in that direction because they would have been too much in opposition to national principles. Three broad policy alternatives were opened through the defeat of the Spanish and the resulting establishment of military governments in her former domain: (1) annexation and eventual statehood, (2) self-government and eventual independence, or (3) full-fledged colonial exploitation for an indefinite but certainly prolonged period. Yet, because the popular mood and national principles operated in unintentional support of one another the ultimate choice was almost assured.

The decision was made to renounce imperialism and remove the country as quickly and gracefully as possible from the international race for empire. Self-rule was soon granted to Cuba and a sincere attempt was made to fashion a new government there following the pattern which had proven so successful for the free people of the United States.[31] While it was obvious that the Cubans would have to face many difficulties as they labored to change from foreign rule to democratic government, supporters of U.S. policy could argue that America itself had arisen out of the turmoil of oppression and revolution. Cuba would be given the same opportunity.

While events followed a different course in the Philippines, the same overall policy of presuming their eventual independence was applied. Though military and civilian administrators remained on the Pacific islands for many years, this was recognized as a temporary and transitional arrangement which would yield to full self-government and sovereignty. Puerto Rico was also to be accorded an increasing measure of self-rule. However, because of its small size and population, it never symbolized the issue of empire and imperialism as did the larger and more important Cuba and Philippines. The maturation of policy during the Spanish-American War era can be viewed as a prelude to the military administration of the Rhineland following World War I. In this occupation also, principles and mood functioned together as policy ingredients and provided unintentional support.

Under General John J. Pershing, the U.S. commander in Europe, the American Third Army took charge of a tactical occupation of Luxembourg which extended from November 10, 1918, to June 1,

1919. During this period the military government in the Rhineland was under the command of Brigadier General H. A. Smith, who held the post of Officer in Charge of Civil Affairs in Occupied Territory. In this transitional period the Army exercised the type of occupation functions associated with combat operations, including wide executive, legislative, and judicial powers over the German civilians. The Tactical Phase in the Rhineland occupation ended on June 1, 1919, when the Advance General Headquarters was dissolved and the Commander of the American Third Army, General Smith, became formally the Military Governor for Occupied Germany.

In this early phase the General Headquarters of the Third Army developed a plan for the conduct of the postwar occupation. The Army envisaged a direct type operation under which military government officers would continue to exercise authority over German officials. The French military high command also supported this idea, which would have retained long-term control by the generals. Under the U.S. Army's proposal, the next administrative stage would be the establishment of a separate military government command under Army control and civil affairs officers already operating would be reassigned from their tactical units to the new organization.

In the spring of 1919, President Wilson sent Pierrepont B. Noyes, a civilian, to act as his personal representative in negotiations relating to a final occupation settlement. Officially, Noyes had the title of American Delegate to the Inter-Allied Rhineland Commission. In this capacity he played a decisive role in shaping the future of Germany. Noyes opposed any approach which stressed revenge or allowed non-Germans to dictate the final outcome of the Rhineland question. His opinion was that "in the Rhineland a hostile military occupation is seen at its best; and at its best, I can say from personal observation [the occupation] is brutal; it is provocative; it is continuing war."[32] Reflecting what he knew to be Wilson's sentiments, Noyes opposed those who insisted that a prolonged occupation should be enforced through a system of martial law.

At the May 7, 1919, session of the Versailles Peace Conference the civilian representatives of the French Government, as well as the French and American generals, were adamant on the necessity for conducting a harsh occupation. The military attitude was championed by French Marshal Ferdinand Foch; and of course, Noyes did not approve. As a result of the sharp exchanges which took place, it was decided to turn the entire matter over to the Supreme War Council, which was instructed to draft a suitable occupation statute.[33] Since the Council was composed of Army leaders, it was not surprising that they adopted a version of the military's earlier plan, a severe policy which was to be implemented by the generals. They suggested that the authority of military governors should include a veto over issues such as German legislation, industrial questions and the functioning of local civilian officials.

Noyes reacted to this development by sending a passionate personal appeal to Wilson. In his now famous letter of May 27, 1919, the envoy expressed the belief that "force and more force must inevitably be the history of such occupation long continued."[34] He told the President that the only practical solution for the long-range problem rested in the acceptance of what he termed a *skeleton plan* for administration.

Noyes's proposal called for the establishment of a civil commission empowered to exercise final authority over both policy and administration. However, its prerogative would be limited to framing only those minimum regulations necessary to insure German compliance with the Armistice provisions. The military would be deprived of its policy making role and would be restricted to the sole duty of stationing in designated compounds a few troops which the commission could call upon in an emergency. Without surprise, Noyes's formula for civilian control was bitterly criticized by Marshal Foch, though it was espoused with total enthusiasm by Wilson. Since the dispute over the policy had to be resolved without further delay, a decision was made to transfer the issue to the Loucheur Commission with instructions to reach a final and satisfactory compromise. This body, appointed by the delegations at the Peace Conference, accepted the two central ideas of Noyes and thereby created the civilian controlled policy that remained in effect throughout the Rhineland occupation.

The ultimate irony was that the United States did not ratify the Versailles Peace Treaty because of the unrelated provisions dealing with the setting up of the League of Nations. Not being a signatory to the peace treaty, America could never officially recognize the sovereign authority of the Rhineland High Commission. Yet Washington had been responsible for the establishment of a civilian rather than a military occupation.

The pressure for Wilsonian idealism was unintentionally reinforced by the popular mood for isolationism. The American policy of encouraging a limited and temporary postwar occupation constituted a logical extension of the decision at the turn of the century to forego colonialism. Earlier overtures in that direction, both in Cuba and the Philippines, had ignited quarrels and dissension within the

United States which few wished to see repeated after World War I. The popular desire for noninvolvement was strengthened by the clamor to return quickly all American troops to their homes. Most citizens adopted the attitude that the soldiers had completed their full task in Europe, and that it was senseless to ask them for further sacrifices in the name of a Rhineland military "dictatorship."

Another opinion held was that Germany, being an advanced Western nation unlike Cuba or the Philippines, was capable of establishing self-government and understanding democratic institutions. It was believed that given the opportunity the former enemy state and its people would develop a workable political order which was consistent with the values of Western liberalism. Following this line of reasoning, the victors should provide encouragement through a magnanimous occupation policy permitting the Germans to work out their own problems.

PUBLIC INDIFFERENCE

Military occupations have occurred under a variety of circumstances. Historically, they fell within two general operational classifications. Under one system programs were implemented while combat was in progress, while in the other they were conducted following hostilities. Confusion can arise in assessing the impact of the civil affairs issue upon wars because of these traditional habits of definition.

The most familiar form of belligerent occupation is that which has followed major conflicts. Within this type of operation, national interest is the motivating policy goal and the ensuing occupation is undertaken only because the war has been won. Unfortunately, there is no automatic assurance that the particular interests which served as the basis for the conflict will also furnish an adequate foundation for the occupation policy. An additional problem is that the relative strengths of particular interests sometimes changed during the course of the total operation.

In small war situations, however, the policy picture has been different. Formal belligerent occupation after the war had been won was not envisaged as a final stage. Rather, concurrent pursuance of war and peace aims was to be followed by simultaneous termination of both the conflict and the occupation. Consequently, the more general aims of these conflicts can be seen in terms of the policy which was adopted toward the civilian population and its institutions. Such an approach necessitates an analysis of pertinent factors discernible on the theoretical level of policy. Related conceptual policy characteristics include (1) a prominence of national interest, (2) an espousal of national principles, and (3) the absence of a solidified public mood among the American people. The term public indifference has been applied here to describe this type of occupation.

Since the public mood has proven to be a major policy element it can be used on the level with principles and interests. At the same time, this label, public indifference, is broad enough to encompass both civil affairs and direct military combat. Further, the prevailing mood is always subject to change even in traditional situations. In small wars the possibility of its emergence and consequent impact makes policy even more vulnerable to change.

Numerous studies have approached the question of limited war from the standpoint of deterrence and other strategic problems of weapons systems and combat techniques. This book attacks the policy problem from a different perspective: namely, through the miltary occupation and civil affairs aspect of foreign interventions. This phase has been characterized by Robert W. Komer as "The Other War."[85] A variety of terms such as pacification, civil affairs, revolutionary development, civic action, or simply the American military's role in the civilian life of the country in question have been used.

Regardless of the descriptive phrase attached, the essential idea is that a form of occupation and war are occurring simultaneously. A presumption exists that a systematic policy approach is being followed in these armed involvements which are less than total in terms of military means utilized and political gains demanded. The Siberian Intervention of World War I, the Korean Conflict, and the Vietnamese War have evidenced these policy characteristics and can be considered examples of modern small wars. An evaluation of the effect of principles and mood upon policy planning is possible through a brief recounting of American experiences.

MOOD AND PRINCIPLES IN THE DOMESTIC POLICY PROCESS

Few presidents have been more aware of the need to accommodate ideals within policy than was Woodrow Wilson during the Siberian Intervention. He stated in 1913 that "It is a very perilous thing to determine the policy of a nation in the terms of material interest."[86] From his overall approach to international relations it was apparent that he believed that ideals should stand in their own right as a valid element of policy. Yet as president, Wilson had to face the necessity of ordering troops into North Russia and Siberia in 1918 in an action which might have been interpreted by the world as a betrayal of America's idealistic motives. The justification for the U.S. interfering in the internal affairs of a friendly though weak Russia required explanation from the White House. In the course of answering American and world opinion Wilson laid down the theoretical guidelines for policy in occupations of public indifference which have been followed to the present day.

The President sought to accommodate both national principles and national interest. Richard D. Snyder and Edgar S. Furniss have summarized the Wilsonian approach as follows: "Political instability in weak countries creates situations dangerous to American security. Such instability is caused by the immaturity of governmental institutions." The United States must serve as the example for these nations because its level of maturity in terms of popular sovereignty is the most advanced. "Strategic and ideological interests thus coincide; in fact the latter is a steppingstone on the way to the protection of the former."[37]

Wilson's contribution rested upon his insight that in cases where a discernible public mood was absent, idealism provided a logical justification for intervention. The propriety of the Siberian affair was justified to the public through White House emphasis upon the notion that principles were guiding American actions, even though the chief consideration within the policy was obviously national interest. Political instability had to be curtailed in vital areas of Russia or the U.S. military position on the Western Front would be made more difficult. It is clear that, had the intervention been undertaken openly in the name of interest, the credibility of the American role as the leader of a moral crusade against German aggression would have been undetermined.

The President chose to avoid personal and national embarrassment over the motives behind the Siberian Intervention through the written policy statement, the *Aide Memoire*. This document was framed in sufficiently ambiguous phraseology that even his most idealistic supporters could point to passages which seemed to express the spirit of self-determination for all peoples. On the other hand, the policy was vague enough that an extremely practical minded Army commander could interpret it as a blueprint of logical material goals. The following excerpt from the *Aide Memoire* illustrates the Wilsonian technique:

"It is the clear and fixed judgment of the Government of the

United States, arrived at after repeated and very searching reconsideration of the whole situation in Russia, that military intervention there would add to the present sad confusion in Russia rather than cure it, injure her rather than help her, and that it would be of no advantage to the prosecution of our main design, to win the war against Germany. It cannot, therefore, take part in such intervention or sanction it in principle. Military intervention would, in its judgment, even supposing it to be efficacious in its immediate avowed object of delivering an attack upon Germany from the east, be merely a method of making use of Russia, not a method of serving her. Her people could not profit by it, if they profited by it at all, in time to save them from their present distresses, and their substance would be used to maintain foreign armies, not to reconstitute their own. Military action is admissible in Russia, as the Government of the United States sees the circumstances, only to help the Czecho-Slovaks consolidate their forces and get into successful cooperation with their Slavik kinsmen and to steady any efforts at self-government or self-defense in which the Russians themselves may be willing to accept assistance."[38]

In summing up the precedent setting Siberian Intervention, it becomes clear that the official espousal of idealistic goals was undertaken in close alliance with the absence of an influential national mood. Attention was focused upon the war in Western Europe and the need for returning to peace. The only people concerned enough to take a vocal stand were the immigrants from Russian and Eastern Europe who had recently arrived in the United States. But their worry over the Bolshevik issue did not bring substantial pressure upon Washington, partly because many of them still lacked citizenship and the right to vote.

At a much later date, the approach adopted by the White House toward the Korean Conflict reflected a similar situation. National interest again constituted the most important policy ingredient. Popular sentiment lacked crystallization, resulting in a void in mood that could provide little guidance for President Truman. As a rational and acceptable explanation for the actions of the Administration he too seized upon idealism. He said to Congress, "I think it is important that the nature of our military action in Korea be understood. It should be made perfectly clear that the action was undertaken as a matter of basic moral principle." America "was going to the aid of a nation established and supported by the United Nations and unjustly attacked by an aggressor force."[39] The Chief Executive stressed that the policy was proper because of its consistency with national principles.

The creation of the United Nations furnished Washington leadership with a strikingly effective and idealistically arguable justification for involvement in the type of war and occupation that ensued in Korea. Policy planners could formulate both military and civil affairs programs in the absence of a clear expression of popular sentiment and have fewer misgivings about violating long-range American aspirations. Washington had, in effect, discovered a new basis for military action under executive authority which gave relative safety and insulation from momentary fluctuations of mood. Candidates for national office, whether Democrat or Republican, could more easily gloss over or ignore the most basic of all issues; precisely what was the United States attempting to accomplish over the long haul through its foreign policy.

Again during the Korean War the fighting seemed to concern or arouse few people outside the government agencies directly involved. Certainly, the families of the soldiers who were drafted for the conflict did not share the general mood of apathy, but they were the exception. As an illustration, the dismissal of General of the Army Douglas MacArthur, who ranks among the foremost national heroes of the twentieth century, generated an outpouring of homage and respect for the man, but it failed to spark an overnight intensification or garnering of sentiment regarding the larger issue of the war itself. While some leaders and laymen, including the venerable Senator Robert Taft, were stirred, most refused to take a definite stand.

The gradually expanding casualty lists, threats of inflation, and the campaigning of presidential candidate Eisenhower aroused some popular concern. In fact, an argument can be advanced that Eisenhower's appeals to end the fighting aided his campaign and excited a distinct national mood. However, in retrospect, it seems that both parties were committed to the limited military action launched by the Truman Administration.

"Bring the boys home" once again appeared as a slogan reflecting as much a popular disinterest as a disgust with the manner in which the war was progressing. Had the candidates in 1952 chosen to adopt sharply differing foreign policy platforms, the public might have listened. As it was, the sentiment appeared to move steadily and without design toward a demand for honorable disengagement in lieu of a conventional military victory.

Involvements as recent as that in Vietnam have also followed a rather similar path. President Johnson's speech delivered on February 23, 1966, at Freedom House leaned heavily upon American idealism as a rational basis for intervention in Vietnam, and presumably in other states threatened by communist takeover. Referring specifically to the Vietnamese situation the President affirmed that: "Washington will not impose upon the people of South Viet-Nam a government not of their choice. Hanoi shall not impose upon the people of South Viet-Nam a government not of their choice. So we will insist for ourselves on what we require from Hanoi: respect for the principle of government by the consent of the governed. We stand for self-determination for free elections—and we will honor their results."[40]

Once again the same pattern emerged in Vietnam. Initial effects were that neither protest marches nor savings bond drives mustered the enthusiasm of the total citizenry. The similarities of Siberia, Korea, and Vietnam suggest a policy insight which is significant for small wars. The formula is that so long as national leaders are able to conduct a military operation without calling upon the people for a mass army and severe sacrifices, the ordinary individual remains basically unmoved. However, a prolonged conflict inevitably requires an increased expenditure of resources, and the policy will move toward disengagement or withdrawal with honor. At least, this repetitious theme is consistent with the historical trend.

When public indifference operates as a significant influence within policy an interesting and important paradox develops. In traditional belligerent occupations, Washington has continually encountered the problem of framing policy in an atmosphere charged with deep emotions, often of hate and revenge. Many officials probably believed that if only the citizenry would remain silent and permit the experts to handle matters, the results would be better for all.

Yet when the mood is absent, as typically has occurred during small wars, Washington finds itself facing an equally serious problem. The fear of accidentally violating a potential public outcry poses a major threat to both the policy and the policy maker. A safe course is to place a high priority upon caution. Weakness in mood consequently functions to paralyze the policy machinery just as effectively as does the unreasonable demands of the vocal and shortsighted during major wars. When the popular sentiment remains an undefined quantity, a distorted rather than a balanced approach to solving both military and civil affairs questions is present. Political leaders are unwilling or unable to bring the full capability of the nation to bear upon the small conflict for fear that the public and the policy are not attuned to one another. Conversely, total withdrawal from the military action poses the same problem.

THE IMPORTANCE OF MOOD WITHIN THE OCCUPIED COUNTRY

In occupations of opposition as well as in those of unintentional support, the mood of the civilians within the occupied area is initially important only in so far as it affects the Army's capacity to exercise control. Providing that hostile activities such as sniping and looting can be curbed, the attitude of the enemy civilians is considered as being sufficiently receptive to adopt, with proper guidance, the principles and institutions associated with the democratic way of life.

However, during occupations when the domestic American mood is quiescent, the significance of public opinion in the combat zone assumes greater proportions. This is true, not only because of the void at home, but also because modern small wars are fought on the territory of friendly foreign states. The civilians, therefore, are considered allies rather than enemies. For example, in the Philippines, where the population had been friendly to the West, communist inspired insurgency has created a difficult situation. Continuing opposition to the authority of the central government suggests that the ultimate solution there depends upon more than temporary and intermittent civic action and pacification measures. A military program spanning decades may be the only alternative for the modernization of the new nations along democratic lines.

Unlike traditional belligerent occupation, the conclusion of combat operations in a modern small war need not be sealed through the negotiation of an international peace treaty or similar instrument. Again citing the Philippine case, during the initial postwar years the Hukbalahaps (HUKS) made striking gains in establishing control on the village level. Through military civic action and the successful use of the army as a police agency, government hegemony was reasserted and consolidated. Once the insurgent power had been broken, the matter was left there without the need or desire for a treaty.

Civil affairs requirements have not always been identical in small wars, even though the need for a policy of some sort has always existed. In instances where the local population was solidly behind the actions of the indigenous government, U.S. policy could be confined largely to providing and distributing supplies for civilian relief and rehabilitation. This occurred during the latter stages of the Korean Conflict. Earlier in that war, however, the civilian problem for the American forces had included a major security duty. North Korean sympathizers and infiltrators operating south of the battle zone had to be intercepted, identified, and prevented from jeopardizing the security of the United Nations contingents. During the first stages of combat the South Korean agencies were ill equipped to deal with the problem.

American Military Police issued and checked identification passes and enforced curfew regulations until the Republic of Korea (ROK) units could be trained to perform such tasks. While the primary civil affairs effort was in this direction, as much as possible was being done to provide critically needed services to the local population; U. S. Army Medical Officers, for example, were furnishing care and treatment for villagers to the limit of their facilities.

The rate at which the civil affairs functions could be transferred depended upon the proficiency of the Americans in training the Koreans. Indigenous civilian officials and ROK Army officers had to be taught to recognize that the successes of the war effort hinged upon the relations established between the Korean forces and the villagers. It was vital to create the popular psychology that the conflict was a patriotic war, and that the Seoul government and the foreign UN troops deserved trust and support. The Korean Military Advisory Group (KMAG), which was a U. S. Army training organization, played a key role. The speed with which the Koreans took over responsibility for the civilian problem was largely the result of KMAG's effectiveness, but the process of training officials, as well as gaining local cooperation, proved to be a slow and difficult chore. Only gradually did the Koreans first take charge of the security function, and later assume a major role in the welfare function of civil affairs.

Correctly evaluating U. S. military goals within the overall national security policy may be the prime factor which determines the success or failure of the foreign effort. Wars of national liberation can be classified as civil affairs wars, and as such, the satisfaction of civilian wants is imperative. This is true even if local demands take the form of economic and social reforms. While Army officers may be unfamiliar with these problems, policy makers can devise methods by which armed forces can help achieve these changes.

The situation in Vietnam initially paralleled that in Korea in many respects. Training of local leaders again became critical, and the winning of the war centered upon the question of civil military relations. But in Vietnam, the U. S. encountered much greater difficulty in shifting its civil affairs emphasis from securing internal stability to furnishing civilian services to the villagers. Promises by President Johnson of a massive aid effort for the region stalled indefinitely pending the solution of the security dilemma.

Civil affairs projects and programs such as the construction of strategic hamlets, pacification, and revolutionary development, all shared the common goal of establishing order in the countryside and solidifying the authority of the Saigon government. These were planned and conducted jointly by American and Vietnamese military and civilian agencies. Regardless of which government assumed responsibility, no action was undertaken as a countermeasure to thwart a communist civil affairs policy which had proved successful.

The United States Agency for International Development remained the most prominent civilian organization on the scene. It is reasonable to categorize and define broadly many of its activities, such as those mentioned above, as constituting a form of civil affairs policy. AID functioned in Vietnam within a social and political climate characterized by a breakdown of domestic law, and the substitution of military necessity for civilian rule. Organized hostilities converted the area into actual or potential battlefields, despite the fact that the enemy consisted of insurgents and guerrillas rather than conventional military units. Success or failure for the defending army's strategy was predicated upon the effectiveness of the means chosen to handle the civilian population.

Experience gained in developing civil affairs programs for Korea has been applied as communist challenges emerged in Southeast Asia. Unfortunately, many of the earlier successful approaches proved not as transferable as Washington originally hoped. The new arenas for wars of national liberation have long histories of colonial exploitation and anti-Western leanings. Some of the suspicion and hostility exhibited against Caucasian personnel appeared to be manifestations of racial and religious antagonisms which give way very slowly. For example, in Vietnam the cleavage between Catholics and Buddhists had more than internal consequences. Americans were unavoidably drawn into the dispute because of Catholicism's identification with the West.

Throughout much of Asia, generations of villagers have fought the authority of whatever national leaders happened to be in power at any given moment. They learned the techniques of insurgency well. In Vietnam local resistance reached proportions which necessitated a major break from the earlier Korean approach. The decision to confine the primary efforts of the Vietnamese troops to pacification and rely upon American units for combat duty was evidence of the extent of difficulty encountered in the provinces.

Vietnamese army and para-military forces, aided by American advisors, have engaged in a prolonged series of civil affairs projects. These sometimes took the following form: a pacification team (1) entered a village which was known to be under the control or influence of the Viet Cong, (2) encircled it with barbed wire and other fortifications designed to keep out the Viet Cong, (3) interrogated local inhabitants, (4) recruited a few soldiers for the Saigon Army, (5) distributed a basic supply of food and drugs, (6) gave guns to a cadre which promised to use them against the marauders, and (7) conducted a political propaganda campaign. When the hamlet appeared calm and under governmental control, the pacification team moved on to pacify another village.

Unfortunately, the story often did not end here. The team's exit was frequently the signal for the Viet Cong to return, tear down the barbed wire, execute a few inhabitants who had cooperated with the pacification team, confiscate the weapons from the protective cadre, recruit soldiers and spies, and reimpose its domination over the life of the people. Perhaps later another pacification group would be sent to rebuild the barbed wire barricades, conduct more propaganda talks, and generally repeat the whole process. But for Washington, the problem remained unsolved; after the same village had been pacified for the fourth time, had anything been accomplished?

Such happenings suggest a critical policy breakdown. It *may* be impossible to win an insurgent war if both a favorable foreign mood and a positive domestic mood within the United States are lacking. Failure of the Vietnamese to give the kind of backing which had characterized the Korean and Philippine counter-insurgency operations was not taken into adequate account. Neutralism and indifference of a type exhibited by Southeast Asian peoples is of special importance in the light of the absence of a crystallized popular sentiment among the American people. For Washington planners, the void in mood at home and the overseas predispositions have to be interpreted in conjunction with each other.

Irrespective of the geographic location of the military involvement, whether Southeast Asia or elsewhere, the local attitudes should be examined prior to the commitment of U. S. forces. Pessimistically assuming that small wars will have to be fought in the future, the type of military policy which is best suited to the situation can be developed through a knowledge of whether local sentiment is moving gradually or rapidly in favor of, or against, U. S. intervention.

In deciding whether or not to play an active part, Washington needs to recognize that the first priority in countering wars of national liberation involves the capability of estimating foreign popular moods. Many agencies are already available for providing this advance insight. Organizations such as the Peace Corps, the Agency for International Development, and the U. S. Information Service could be employed. Since they operate on a worldwide scale, their capability extends to the regions where future wars of national liberation are likely to arise.

Peace Corps Volunteers are particularly well trained in sensing the currents of local thought. Their experience can be tapped as a source of information about the state of mind in the world's underdeveloped provincial regions. Daily the Volunteers encounter incidents which reveal the feelings of villagers regarding their ultimate political aspirations, as well as the general cultural direction in which the countryside is moving.

U. S. Information Service branches conduct numerous surveys which are designed to elicit similar data. AID teams furnish technical assistance to local groups seeking to raise agricultural production. The members of these teams also gain a perspective on what is taking place in the smaller communities. Foreign assistance specialists, as well as the organizations which they represent, can provide a composite picture of whether the indigenous population would support or resist an intervention by the U. S. Army, and if so, under what circumstances.

Another vehicle through which the popular sentiment might be ascertained is the U.S. Army's own civic action teams. These groups of military professionals operate within a host country and help its army devise projects which can raise local economic standards. Though the Army has played the primary role here, the contributions of Air Force and Marine Corps teams should not be slighted. The Pentagon has made some halting steps in the direction of expanding their use, particularly in Central and South America. But the more traditive minded in both the military and the State Department have attempted to keep alive the hope that national security policy could be preserved in reasonable separation from the rest of foreign policy. They also saw as their first priority the requirement to prepare for a possible World War III with the Soviet Union, a war which again would see Europe become the focal point of strategic concern. Army as well as State Department thinking, therefore, continued to employ the standard concepts of organized warfare waged to a conclusion which would take the form of either a conventional military victory or defeat. The result has been a general lack of attention being paid to fostering and exploiting the civic action concept. This is regrettable.

When officials neglect to employ the full potential of the civic action device they rob themselves of an invaluable listening post. These teams, if their reports are seriously sought and evaluated, can gauge local conditions before a revolution starts. And they will see the situation from the background of trained military observers. Foreign policy leadership would then have the advantage of a sensitivity for the civilian problem, which is the essence of small insurgent wars. With this knowledge transmitted to the White House from the Executive agencies, America might avoid entering a future war like that waged in Vietnam, or at least, the President would be better informed as to the possible consequences of such an involvement.

State Department leaders, as well as the Joint Chiefs, could then consider the foreign mood in balance with the likelihood that the American people will fail to understand or support with great sacrifices a military commitment which draws too heavily upon domestic resources. Before another war/occupation dilemma faces the United States some concrete steps can be taken. The advisability of assessing anti-Western hostility or pro-Western cooperation within the probable battle zone seems uncontestable. Each and every available means, including the total gamut of federal agencies, should be exploited. Mistakes of the past are difficult to counteract. However, planning for future crises must be more systematic.

ADDITIONAL ELEMENTS OF THE ROLE OF
JOURNALISTS AND POLITICAL INTEREST GROUPS

On occasions, American newsmen and editorial writers have had the capacity to influence the formulation of foreign policy, including its military occupation aspect. Within the limited context of this study, their roles are examined in terms of their direct impact upon the electorate and governmental officials.[41] Instances involving the activities of reporters have been cited under earlier headings in order to demonstrate manifestations of national mood. However, their contributions merit further consideration.

The title "journalist" is used in the present context to describe reporters, newscasters, and others employed within the broad field of gathering, editing, and disseminating information through the mass media. Authors of books which have a topical rather than scholarly orientation can also be included within the category.

A variety of reasons are responsible for the degree of political power in the hands of this group as well as for the fact that its influence far surpasses that of other occupational groups of a similar size. Reporters and editorial spokesmen for major news organizations are taken seriously by political leaders because the journalists wield considerable influence on public opinion. In addition, the opinions expressed by journalists are respected because the American press enjoys a reputation for accuracy and fairness. Certainly one of the most important bases of journalistic prestige is their monopoly over a vital service. For those who must be well informed about the daily events around the world, there is no practical substitute for the private news media.[42]

The specific means by which journalists have helped shape occupation policy can be summarized under two main headings. First, as Bernard C. Cohen has suggested "the press provides policy makers with the ingredient that has long been assumed to be its chief contribution: a measure of public opinion."[43] He describes the situation in these terms: "The newspaper is a source of a daily *feel* as to what is going on, and the public reaction to it."[44] Naturally, both the State Department and the Pentagon are concerned with the interpretation given by the press to policies which are subject to frequent change, such as military occupation programs.

The capability of the journalists to engage in conscious agitation affords a second avenue of influence. They have unique access to immediate happenings as well as to confidential sources of information; and their opinions tend to have special weight in cases where the bulk of dispatches and editorials expound a uniform condemnation of a particular policy.[45] When a definite viewpoint is constantly repeated by newsmen, the public is likely to pay attention or even become aroused, resulting in an intensification of political pressure through interest groups and other private power centers. This has occurred in several civil affairs incidents, some more dramatic than others.

During the Spanish-American War era the press made serious charges against the occupation policy. Reporters were almost unanimous in their criticism of alleged cases of misconduct and faulty judgment by military government authorities. Partial credit for abandonment of imperialism after the turn of the century can be given to the journalists. Another illustration of the power of press agitation concerns the German fraternization issue following World War II. Many believe today that the exceedingly harsh anti-fraternization measures adopted during the initial postwar period were partly the result of exaggerated dispatches sent to American newspapers. The stories often created the image that the occupation forces were too soft on the German civilians.⁴⁶ Families of soldiers killed by Hitler's troops were disgusted and enraged to see front page photographs of GI's and Germans laughing and joking together. Letters to the editor columns during this period, as well as petitions by patriotic groups, reflected the impact of the reports from overseas.

The Army itself was largely at fault for creating in Germany a situation which fostered the flood of stories on matters such as fraternization and the shortcomings of a few occupation officers. Because of inadequate advance planning, occupation agencies initially paid little attention to the need for public information programs. In the confusion which followed the end of the war, reporters experienced great difficulty in locating accurate and worthwhile material for stories. To meet the demands of their editors and publishers at home, a few succumbed to the temptation to overstate or even fabricate accounts of sensational happenings. Of course, many of the dispatches dealing with sordid events were doubtless accurate. Accordingly the Army gradually improved its informational practices.

Journalists were able to influence the treatment of ex-enemy civilians in post-World War II years partly because Americans were eager for news from overseas. Recognizing this, publishers pressured Washington to permit their correspondents wide freedom in the occupied zones, often over the objections of Army authorities. In some theaters, field commanders were able to curtail dispatches which were critical of the civil affairs policies being implemented. Yet such news items did reach the American public and served to inflame the mood of the electorate. And finally in this rather circular process, the greater the volume of news items appearing, the greater was the pressure placed upon officials in Washington to open additional areas to newsmen.

The future of Germany as well as the future plans for the U.S. troops still stationed there were live issues. Consequently, publishers helped their reporters gain access to news sources whenever possible. In the case of major newspapers and news services, editors did not hesitate approaching field commanders directly if Washington officials refused assistance. And partly as a result, correspondents in occupied

Germany were permitted to move about with reasonable freedom and with little to fear from arbitrary censorship regulations.

While postwar Europe was relatively open to the journalists, the situation in Japan was quite different. After judiciously watching the course of the German occupation, American citizens became rather indifferent toward the Far Eastern operation. Lack of interest created a climate which permitted MacArthur to regulate news coverage strictly, if not actually to manage the press. His controls served to restrict the flow of dispatches, especially those which were critical and might have aroused a public reaction against SCAP (Supreme Commander Allied Powers, MacArthur's headquarters establishment) activities.

Under MacArthur's rules correspondents were forbidden, or discouraged, from leaving the Tokyo area on fact-finding trips. SCAP's public information agencies were prone to release only a minimum of data for publication. On some occasions occupation authorities were not above employing a system of rewards and punishments to prevent critical stories from being sent home. One technique which proved effective was to notify hostile reporters that if they once left the Theater for any reason they would not be permitted to return. Another device involved the allocation of scarce housing for journalists. Those who wrote dispatches unfriendly to SCAP might find upon returning from a brief trip outside the Tokyo area that their quarters had been reassigned." Such petty harassment plagued the Tokyo press corps throughout the MacArthur era.

In a particularly revealing incident, MacArthur attempted to block a fact finding mission from the U.S. composed of writers, editors, and publishers who were well known and respected on the domestic scene. After a series of exchanges between Tokyo and Washington, the War Department overruled his objections to their visit. Thereupon, the Supreme Commander was alleged to have sent the following cable to the War Department on December 1, 1948:

"While continuing my doubts as to the advisability of the contemplated trip of U.S. newspapermen to Japan for a first hand inspection, in view of the insistence of the War Department, I will withdraw my objection. I would like to have an opportunity to pass upon those contemplated for selection before their invitation is accomplished. I believe that the list should not include actual writers but should be limited to publishers and editors and should not include those connected with papers of known hostility to the Occupation. Such papers as the *Christian Science Monitor, Herald Tribune, Chi-*

cago Sun, San Francisco Chronicle, PM, Daily Worker, and others of this stamp whose articles and editorials have not only been slanted, but have approached downright quackery and dishonesty."[48]

While some leading American editors were finally able to bring pressure upon Washington to improve the situation, this incident pointed up the larger issue. Had the news media in general, instead of just the publications mentioned, launched a full scale campaign against SCAP's press policy, perhaps even the Supreme Commander could not have resisted. But since the average newspaper reader showed little concern about Japan anyway, the publishers possibly concluded that a major press effort against MacArthur and his policy was not worthwhile. The widespread public respect and confidence in the Pacific hero, coupled with the General's formidable support from powerful conservative elements of both political parties, served further to reduce the likelihood of a press campaign against SCAP.

Since the journalists in Tokyo could not send meaningful daily dispatches to their home editors, many spent their time gathering materials for books. These personal memoirs were later published after the reporters had returned to the States and were beyond the reach of reprisals. Books such as Robert B. Textor's *Failure in Japan,* Harry E. Wildes' *Typhoon in Tokyo,*[49] were delayed action dispatches which did little good for the image of MacArthur, SCAP, or the total occupation. The point is that the commander who believes that he can effectively silence the American journalists should have second thoughts on the matter. He might ask himself when he would prefer the criticism, now or later, in the newspapers or in the history books?

Interest groups representing large segments of the electorate have also played roles in the policy picture. There is a general awareness that industry, labor, farmers, professional societies, patriotic organizations, religious and ethnic groups, reform forces, and associations of organized women have long influenced many domestic and foreign programs. The persistent individual acting alone can also have a surprisingly important effect; the press itself, particularly certain columnists, has been listed within the pressure group classification by some authorities.[50] Others have emphasized the activities of private nationalist and internationalist groups and pointed out that in 1955 alone there were at least 434 nongovernmental organizations taking part in foreign affairs debates.[51] The political action campaigns of these groups has shown a marked increase, and their number has grown substantially since 1955.[52]

While those mentioned above constitute quite an impressive list, there is no reason to believe that they encompass the entire spectrum of political interest groups. Richard W. Gable noted that extensive lobbying also exists within the governmental establishment itself.[53] It would be naive to assume that agencies within the administration would refrain from engaging in some form of pressure politics when proposed legislation directly affects their functioning. This of course includes the military. In a recent instance, Pentagon spokesmen testified before congressional committees on an issue which grew out of the occupation of the Ryukyus. Some Okinawans have yet to be compensated for property taken over by the Army Administration during early stages of the occupation. Congressional presentations on such matters constitute lobbying. Besides agencies of the American government, foreign nations also employ lobbyists in Washington. Their activities are especially noticeable when a country is seeking foreign aid from the United States.

Political parties, while cited by some as participants in pressure group activities, are discounted by others who have studied the question. The parties endeavor to influence by helping to elect or defeat candidates, writing party platforms and generally exerting leverage over those whom they have helped to elect.[54] It has been argued that they do not accomplish these goals. Their weakness creates a void which must be filled by interest groups.[55]

The tools used by these organizations are not of particular value to this study. Most Americans are aware of examples of their most blatant overt acts, epitomized by gifts to important officials and mass letter writing campaigns directed at Congressmen. It must be admitted that the techniques they employ are varied, imaginative, and inventive, and need be mentioned here only as they relate to the specific illustrations cited. The government officials and organs approached, the type of results sought, and the effectiveness of the contact are of much greater concern.

Lobbying groups have frequently pressed for the establishment or rejection of specific programs for governing occupied territories. Education associations have had definite ideas regarding the revision of textbooks. Farm and business groups have been concerned about agricultural and industrial expansion which might create future competition for American products. Union leaders have watched closely the attitude adopted toward building strong labor organizations. Spokesmen for the legal and medical professions have been concerned about the future status of their colleagues overseas. Even *ad hoc* groups have been sometimes formed to pressure policy makers for very narrow and specific projects.

There are several avenues through which private associations can operate, some more direct than others. They may openly approach top civilian and military agencies in Washington and plead for a particular program because the facts themselves allegedly prove that its adoption would contribute to the effectiveness of the total policy. One such instance involved a World War II *ad hoc* group which called itself the American Commission for the Protection and Salvage of Artistic Monuments in War Areas. Through this body a number of prominent citizens were able to shape this particular aspect of occupation policy. A 1946 *Report* on the Commission's wartime activities by its Chairman, Owen J. Roberts, provides a revealing account of pressure politics being applied to civil affairs questions.[56]

The idea of forming the Commission was proposed in the fall of 1942. A suggestion was made jointly by the President of the Archaeological Institute of America, the President of the College Art Association, the Directors of the Metropolitan Museum of Art in New York and representatives of the National Gallery of Art in Washington. They approached Chief Justice Harlan F. Stone, whose personal interest in the fine arts was well known. In turn, the Chief Justice used his influence to lay the foundation for a governmental body to deal with the problem. Its task was to undertake the protection of irreplaceable art treasures and libraries which might be destroyed unintentionally by American combat troops.

The Commission also contacted the Chief of the Civil Affairs Division of the War Department and the Army Intelligence Service, seeking their support and cooperation. Once official recognition of the private body was secured, its leaders became increasingly active and were instrumental in the development of the War Department's Program for Protecting Monuments, Fine Arts, and Archives. Implemented under the direction of the Civil Affairs Division, the program extended into every overseas theater. The Commission also played a vital role in the selection of personnel to administer the project. It compiled a list of professional archivists and related experts who were already serving in the Army. Through the direct intervention of Washington, these specialists were reassigned to civil affairs units operating in the field. In the case of the Commission, the success of an interest group was not only rewarding to its individual members, but also contributed a valuable service to mankind.

On some occasions, private groups have sent their own agents directly into the occupied area as either full-time workers or observers. For example, in the wake of the Korean Conflict numerous philanthropic, educational, religious, and cultural groups maintained offices in Seoul. Their number became so large that the Army was forced to establish a special agency to coordinate their activities and minimize their interference with military programs. According to the available reports, in 1955 a total of fifty-five different nongovernmental bodies claiming to be engaged in some form of civil assistance work were registered with American authorities.[57] This figure did not include the representatives of other private associations who periodically conducted brief reconnoiters.

While very possibly accomplishing altruistic deeds, interest group leaders have posed problems for field commanders. If he does not furnish adequate housing or Post Exchange privileges, he runs the risk of being accused of harboring an arbitrary and militaristic attitude toward civilians. On the other hand, if he does extend total hospitality the charge of waste and extravagance can ensue. The impact of interest group politics sometimes extends even below the level of the headquarters of major commands. Scarce officers become tour guides and the routine of important business is often disrupted by the visitors who wish to observe grass-roots operations.

Activities of interest groups often perform a positive service because the civilian leaders are immune from reprisal by military authorities. Consequently, they are in a position to relay to the highest levels appeals for help from local officials whose efforts are being frustrated by excessive Army bureaucracy. Typically, civilian leaders who were allowed to enter occupied areas secured such permission because they were privy to the highest political and military councils in Washington. Upon returning from overseas, they had the opportunity to report their findings directly to top leadership in the Administration and in Congress.

In fact, Congress has often been the arena in which pressure groups have worked to exert influence. This is undoubtedly their most publicized though not necessarily their most effective vehicle. An illustration of this type of lobbying activity which affected military government occurred during consideration of the Displaced Persons Act of 1948. The aim of this measure was to loosen immigration and naturalization restrictions in the aftermath of World War II. The Germans during the war, and the Russians later, had moved a large number of people from their homes. Some were placed in temporary camps while others were allowed to exist somehow by living off the countryside. Over a million people were reportedly in this condition, but European states could accommodate only a few of them.

Military occupation personnel recognized the problem since they encountered it daily, particularly in Germany. President Truman tried first in 1947 to have Congress pass proposed legislation permitting an increase in the flow of these displaced persons (DP's) into this country. In January 1948 when he repeated his plea, Congress acted. However, the legislation which was finally passed in June was not, according to Truman, satisfactory.[58]

The pertinent concern here is the lobbying which took place during 1947 and 1948 over this issue. One of the best financed and largest of the group efforts was billed under the heading of the Citizens' Committee for Displaced Persons. At one point, it maintained a staff of thirty to forty workers in its New York office alone. In addition, several lobbyists represented the group in Washington.

Stephen K. Bailey and Howard Samuel cite one case where a field representative recalled his reception in a small Wisconsin town. He began with a single telephone call to the local secretary of the YMCA which eventually culminated in a mass meeting. Those attending the conclave included public officials as well as civic minded citizens prominent in the community. As a result, many of the participants took immediate action in support of the DP legislation by writing and telephoning their Congressmen. The Wisconsin experience was probably not unique. In twenty-nine states Displaced Persons Commissions were established, and while their overt purpose was to take care of newly arrived DP's within the states, they worked actively in mustering pressure for additional laws.[59]

Evidence also suggests that ethnic groups which were already in existence took part in the campaign, at least indirectly. Senator Homer Ferguson, who had been less than excited about the original Truman proposal, eventually became a strong supporter and even pushed passage of the law. It is reasonable to believe that influential Polish societies among his Michigan constituents helped change his mind.

When the Judicial Branch becomes a target for interest group activity, the total spectrum of government could be open and available to their influence. The record of the courts, however, appears almost untainted in comparison with the other two branches. Yet political pressure can be exerted before judges are selected or even nominated. Spokesmen for labor, business, and other organizations can register publicly or privately their support or opposition for particular candidates.

The practice of allowing interested parties who are not directly involved in the case to testify has sometimes furnished groups with an opportunity to participate within the judicial process. *Amicus curiae* have discovered many ways of having their briefs read by the court. In other instances, test cases lead to decisions which fill the void of legislative inaction.[60] Clement E. Vose suggests that special interests have been drawn into important cases for two reasons. First, judicial review has become a major aspect of the American governmental system. And second, the vital nature of the issues of public law at stake before the courts demand that they take some action.[61]

After both World Wars lengthy legal disputes arose over the ultimate disposal of German cartel holdings the U. S. government had earlier confiscated. American interests owning stock in the cartels sought restitution while some business associations and labor unions opposed any change in the existing situation out of fear of heightened competition. In other cases alleged violation of civil liberties by occupation courts, as well as citizenship and nationality claims, were presented by organized groups.

While emphasizing the executive, legislative, and judicial avenues available and used by pressure groups, many authorities deal with one additional approach. This is the infrequently used device of direct legislation. We have not considered it extensively here since there is little evidence to confirm the success of this method in shaping military policy. The fact that the initiative and referendum have been employed successfully on the state level by special groups suggests that the possibility cannot totally be ignored.[62] Through an extension of this approach, constitutional conventions could theoretically be called by the states if they decided that national leaders should be curbed in their handling of policy for a military occupation.

INTERNATIONAL LAW

International law has not prevented any major war and has often seemed powerless even to mitigate the cruelty associated with warfare. Some believe that it has accomplished much because it has been a constant source of inspiration and higher aspirations toward which government and men could strive. Its champions hold that a legal approach is the best means of settling occupation questions. We have not found international law to be the basis for occupation policy, though it is an ingredient of policy and cannot be overlooked. In the first chapter an attempt was made to define the status of international law within the policy framework. Here we explore some of the broader implications involved, for example, the evolution of the various war and occupation codes which bind the military governor to definite standards of humane behavior.

However, since the book seeks to delve into the essence of the policy process, it is necessary to omit lengthy discussions of the aspects of the legal quandary which relate primarily to the implementation of policy rather than its formation. In assessing the role of law as it fits into occupation efforts, the question of its connection with principles and mood must be considered.[63]

Doris A. Graber pointed out in her study *The Development of the Law of Belligerent Occupation* that there "are general principles intended to be as representative as possible of international public opinion."[64] The provisions of the various war and occupation codes which developed were expressions of a world conscience striving for some means of injecting order into a traditional arena of world chaos.[65]

The law of belligerent or military occupation evolved slowly, but the growth was consistently in the direction of greater emphasis upon the principles of justice and humanitarianism. From the beginning of civilization until as late as the last century, the military occupant had the right to work his will upon the occupied people without having to answer to any specific international code of conduct. This was true because none existed. Traditionally, the invader in war became the absolute ruler over all of the territories and inhabitants brought under his control, and for legal purposes the defeated population was subjected to the domestic law of the victorious state. The sole statutory restraints upon the manner in which the conqueror treated the vanquished were whatever regulations the government of the occupying army chose to enforce upon its own troops. Within this setting of war devoid of law, the ideas of scorched-earth and to-the-victor-belong-the-spoils often guided the actions of armies.

While the nineteenth century witnessed the pioneer movement to establish detailed codes for regulating occupation, much theoretical groundwork had been laid earlier. Long before the concept of just behavior in occupations was considered, the broader dilemma of the role of justice in warfare itself received attention by theorists. Hugo de Groot, or Grotius, (1583-1645) made a fundamental contribution through his *Law of War and Peace,* written in 1625. Grotius wrote the treatise because, as he stated: "I saw prevailing throughout the Christian world a license in making war of which even barbarous nations should be ashamed; men resorting to arms for trivial or for no reasons at all, and when arms were once taken up no reverence left for divine or human law, exactly as if a single edict had released a madness driving men to all kinds of crime."[66]

Grotius went on to speculate as to whether justice or utility constitutes the more important basis for actions in war. He concluded that justice is the more important and in fact is "more than utility, because it is part of the true social nature of man, and that is its real title to observance by him."[67]

The next milestone was the work of Emerich de Vattel (1714-1769). In his study, *The Law of Nations* (1758), he stressed the belief that *nature* conferred upon the state certain rights, among them being its right to continued existence. From this it followed that when one state occupied the territory of another in consequence of war, the presence of the invading army constituted only a provisional situation. Legal possession or transfer of territory could result only from a peace treaty acceptable to the participants in the conflict.[68] The general adoption of this precept stands as a first tangible and significant step in tempering the conduct of invading armies.

Since the occupant would eventually be re-establishing peaceful relations with the defeated nation, extreme cruelty on the part of the victorious force could result in needless difficulty at the peace conference. Within a broader context, the idea that occupation was inherently temporary can be cited as a factor of much importance. Gradually, a worldwide opinion took shape that the occupier must act under some form of *international* obligation that transcended momentary political considerations. Governments increasingly came to recognize and accept the premise that justifications of a higher order than simply national self-interest were necessary in order to invest occupation policies with the mantle of legitimacy.

During the next century legal theorists enhanced and amplified the concepts attributed to Grotius and Vattel. Statesmen moved slowly, however, in translating these ideas into formal occupation codes. As a result, it fell to the United States, a new arrival among the military powers of the day, to play a pioneering role. Necessity rather than choice was responsible. Difficulties in developing a policy for handling Mexican citizens during the 1840's forced American leaders to take the initiative. Expediency and the absence of a workable alternative can be credited with the Administration's official acceptance of the idea that a *law of nations* based upon moral principles should guide the actions of military commanders in dealing with foreign populations.

Less than two decades later the Civil War erupted. The new conflict was immeasurably larger in scope and complexity, but again combat strategy dictated the need for a systematic and consistent approach to occupation. Francis Lieber's code was the outgrowth of this requirement. The still fresh memories of Scott's and Taylor's experiences provided a practical foundation upon which to build. To these were added, first, the historic insights of legal scholarship; second, provisions of existing treaties and international agreements having pertinence to the war law issue, and finally, the unique set of articulated principles upon which the American nation was founded. Together, these considerations formed a framework for a comprehensive legal statute which was applicable in both combat and post-combat situations.

Fully recognizing that the object of war is victory, Lieber contended, however, that such a laudatory goal does not absolve the military commander of certain fundamental responsibilities and restrictions. Extreme ferocity on the part of the enemy cannot in itself be used as an excuse for acts which violate the law of humanity or the basic guarantees of individual rights expressed in the Consitution.

The American theorist's instructions to the Union Generals reflected an awareness that conditions and institutions affecting the mode of warfare were changing rapidly. In both American and Europe new ideas about economic and political organizations were forcing a re-evaluation of long accepted assumptions and values; and an increase in the zeal of armies was noticeable. Simultaneously, military technology was taking advantage of new means of transportation, communication, and weaponry. The ability of the civilian defender to flee or hide from the invading battalions was evaporating. Lieber saw that the need for applying systematic restrictions upon military behavior transcended the immediate requirements of the American insurrection. The worldwide attention which soon focused upon his work testified to the fundamental significance of the U.S. contribution.

It remained for the European States of the nineteenth century, however, to take the next step in developing a more widely applicable set of international statutes covering occupation. European powers became interested because the idea of a war law code fitted logically into the balance of power system under which they operated. During the last half of the century the Concert of Europe idea was under attack from within. New states were arising and challenging the old order, sometimes resorting to vicious military adventures to demonstate their claim to sovereign rights. A war law code could serve as a constant reminder to the new powers that their long range aims would be defeated by excessive cruelty. Against this background, the Brussels code of 1874 was formulated; both its form and substance followed closely the pattern laid down by Lieber. The code was more considerate of the humane rights of civilians because it limited the areas in which military commanders could act arbitrarily. Though the United States did not participate officially in the Brussels negotiations, and while the resulting code was never officially ratified by the major powers, it still carried great weight since it was the first modern war law code developed at an international assembly. And its provisions formed the basis for the war law sections in the military manuals of the leading nations.[69]

A quarter of a century elapsed before the next major efforts were made to restrict further the conduct of armies during wars and occupations.[70] Much has been written about the importance of the two International Peace Conferences* held at the Hague in 1899 and 1907, and the war law codes that resulted from them. United States delegates attended both meetings. The 1899 conference included representatives from twenty-six nations, primarily European. However, the 1907 conference was attended by delegates from forty-four states; among them were several from Latin American republics which were gaining their first experience in this type of international conclave.

Both conferences were called primarily for the purpose of devising means whereby disputes among nations could be settled peacefully. While there was general agreement that this distinctly commendable aim should be pursued, little success was achieved. One result was the creation of the unsuccessful Hague System of international arbitration. While not able to prevent World War I, the approach developed at the Hague did become the basis for the later League of Nations and United Nations Systems.[71]

Since the conferees at both meetings were unable to cope with the root problems involved in preventing war, they turned their attention to the lesser matter of adopting conventions designed at least to humanize war and military occupation. The 1899 conventions contained provisions for occupation which closely resembled those

---

*In both the Hague Conferences and the Geneva Conference a number of separate agreements were reached on particular matters. These agreements are variously referred to as *conventions, statutes,* and *regulations.*

of the earlier Brussels and Lieber codes. One innovation was that the contracting states now bound themselves to issue concrete orders to their armies to obey the conventions. But no penalty was provided for countries whose armies failed to live up to the mandates of the new law. Perhaps the underlying significance of the 1899 Conference and war law code was that world leaders felt compelled to reach any agreement on the question at all. The notion that a sovereign state should seriously consider respecting any law other than its own in the critical area of war-making represented another marked step in the direction of states accepting international responsibility for their actions.

While the Second Hague Conference of 1907 produced few changes that would prevent or eliminate war, it did adopt several statutes related to the occupation question. An important innovation was the decision that governments violating the rules of the law of land warfare would have to compensate individuals who suffered because of illegal acts. This basic idea was incorporated into the statutes which dealt specifically with military occupation. At present, the United States is a party to five of these which are spelled out (in various field manuals of the armed forces)[72] for the guidance of military commanders and civil affairs officers.

In summing up the development of the early codes from 1863 to 1907, two points stand out. First, the right of the occupied to enjoy life and property received continuing attention; and second, the codes reflected a shift in emphasis regarding the role the occupant could play in the territory controlled by its forces. The Lieber code stressed the occupiers *rights* which were to be exercised with stipulated limitations, unless military necessity dictated otherwise. In contrast, the Hague Regulations emphasized the occupant's *duty* to preserve, as far as practical, the *status quo* in the area. The broad occupation powers granted under international law were not to be used to change or drastically to alter the conditions and institutions of everyday life.[73]

But world politics was entering a period of rapid and fundamental change. The balance of power system, with its emphasis upon moderation, was replaced during the first half of the twentieth century by a set of new ideas. World War I ushered in an era in which the ambitions of nations pitted against one another in major wars could seemingly not be satisfied short of the wholesale destruction and defeat of the enemy. Yet the Hague rules for military occupation, with their implementing amendments, continued to serve as the basis for the war law manuals used by the major governments of the world.[74]

In terms of ferocity, perhaps World War II was no more cruel than World War I for the fighting man. However, the advent of strategic bombing during the Second World War brought the physical tortures of the conflict to a greater proportion of the civilian population than ever before. The occupying force often found itself in possession of a once proud city that was now only rubble and starving civilians.

Paralleling the introduction of weapons designed to ravage areas behind the fighting lines came the general acceptance of the political and military idea that every citizen of the state was part of the war effort and thus all enemy citizens could be considered proper targets for combat action. The more genteel Victorian traditions and manners which had protected women and children were increasingly submerged in national psychologies of hate.

Yet, the ideals embodied in the Hague Conventions were not entirely dead. Governments of the major powers continued to preach and practice those international principles, at least to the extent they did not impair the war effort. Nevertheless, when the fighting finally ended in 1945, it was recognized that changes in the traditional relations between victorious and vanquished nations would take place.

On May 8, 1945, Admiral Doenitz formally surrendered in the name of the German government, whereupon he and his staff were immediately placed under arrest by the Allies. In the Declaration of Berlin, issued less than a month later, the victorious nations assumed "supreme authority with respect to Germany, including all the powers possessed by the German Government, the High Command, and any state, municipal or local government or authority."[75] In August, the Potsdam Agreement affirmed that the occupying powers intended to abolish certain laws, reorganize the German economy, and make fundamental changes in German educational, legal, and political institutions.[76]

Litchfield noted in his work, *Governing Postwar Germany*, that the Allied policy decisions to make sweeping changes in Germany made a conventional legal occupation inconceivable. "There may have been limits imposed upon the conduct of occupation affairs, but they were the product of the culture from which the occupants came and not of international convention or articulated international law."[77] The postwar occupation proceeded on the basis of assumptions and premises which might be termed extra-legal. Litchfield further suggested that the following constituted the most important of these underlying assumptions and *modus operandi*. First, military victory would be used for the purpose of acquiring what was termed "supreme sovereignty," which represented in fact the powers of legal sovereignty. Second, the occupying governments intended to abandon, at least temporarily, the traditional doctrine of internal self-determination even though this principle had been repeated and affirmed as recently as the Atlantic Charter. Third, during the period of the occupation "political or popular sovereignty [would] not and could not be taken from the German people. . . ." And fourth, "legal sovereignty itself was [to be] held in trust until such time as the trustees might decide that the possessors of popular sovereignty were prepared to undertake its responsibilities" in accordance with political and social values and institutions deemed proper by the victors.[78]

Litchfield's conclusion was that the guiding force behind the occupation of Germany was primarily political rather than legal. His points can be overstressed since America had not abandoned its concern for the part that moral principles should play in military occupation. During the immediate postwar years this continuing concern was reflected through two legal steps. First, through the Geneva Conventions of 1949 a strong effort was made to insure that *states* conducting wars and occupations would henceforth be bound by a more detailed code of conduct. Second and perhaps of greater significance, the U.S. sought through the Nuremberg doctrine and the United Nations to bring *individuals* acting as agents of states directly under the authority of the provisions of international law.

The Geneva Conventions of 1949 were the result of meetings which had been urged by the International Red Cross to deal with the total range of war law problems. These meetings afforded an opportunity for the Western Powers, especially the United States, to formulate a revised set of regulations. Regarding the occupation aspect of war law, a need existed to update the statutory provisions so that once again they would be consistent with the realities of contemporary international politics and military strategy.

In addition, both the meetings and resulting conventions were especially important to the U.S. because they provided a respectable vehicle through which it could again affirm that its policies were in line with traditional national principles and the higher ideals of mankind.

The new ideas which emerged from the 1949 sessions provided an even stronger shield for protecting the citizens of the occupied territory from unjust outside domination.[79] They were more inclusive and detailed on the formal rights of both the occupant and the occupied in the following areas: (1) treatment of civilians, (2) deportations, (3) destruction of private property, (4) collective responsibility, and (5) procedures to be followed in occupation courts. The conventions also contained far-reaching humanitarian obligations in the fields of health, welfare, and relief.[80] Under the revised law the victor would be acting in the name of an international conscience whenever the question of choosing a new or modified form of government for the defeated nation arose. The conqueror would be called upon and expected to submerge its own particular national interests to the higher goal of internationally recognized principles.

Acting under UN authority, the International Military Tribunal sat in judgment of German and other fascist military and civilian leaders who had been accused of committing atrocities. These cruelties against the Jews, other racial and religious minority groups, prisoners of war, and non-German civilians who had lived under German military rule were alleged to be crimes against humanity itself. Few modern legal precedents for trying individual military and political officials for war crimes existed.

The United Nations Charter included provisions which seemed clearly to outlaw war atrocities. A legal problem arose, however, because the Charter was written after the alleged crimes took place. Objections centered upon the contention that holding trials would violate the principle of *ex post facto* immunity. Yet, world opinion and world conscience demanded the trials, and the trials were held. In its deliberations and judgments the Tribunal did not presume openly that it was laying down permanent legal doctrine which should and would henceforth be part of international law. Nevertheless, that was tantamount to what happened because of the work of another body, the International Law Commission.

In November 1947 the UN with American support established this Commission as an organ of the General Assembly. It was to include members representing the various mainstreams of civilization and the major legal systems of the world. The UN Statute under which it was to function stipulated that its activities should be directed toward two general goals, each bearing upon the law of war and military occupation. First, the Law Commission was to develop new formulations and principles of international law for those matters not adequately dealt with in the existing statutes. Second, it was to codify the already recognized principles stemming from international agreements, conventions, treaties, court precedents, customs and usages, and other sources of international law. Thereby it would further the general understanding of Law and eliminate confusion about which provisions currently were enforceable. Later in the session the Commission was charged with a third task. It was to formulate the principles of international law growing out of the Nuremberg trials, and further to prepare a *Draft Code of Offenses Against the Peace and Security of Mankind.*

In 1950 the Commission transmitted to the Assembly its first report. It was a formulation of seven principles of international law which were derived from the decisions of the International Tribunal (decisions heretofore called informally the Nuremberg doctrine). For military occupation, the more pertinent of the Law Commission's Nuremberg Principles stipulated that the perpetrators of crimes would be held personally responsible and accountable for their actions. Provided a moral choice is open to them, individual officials are not relieved of their obligations either because the act is not punishable under the law of any particular country, or because they act as Heads of State or responsible governmental officials, or because they act under superior orders. When charged with a crime against humanity under the provisions of international law, the individual must be granted the right to a fair trial in the state where the offense occurred, or granted a trial before an international tribunal. The principles also enumerated and defined in a general way crimes against peace, war crimes, and crimes against humanity. As a final relevent principle the Commission ruled that complicity in any one of these acts also constituted a crime under international law.

The International Law Commission's draft code of offenses against the peace and security of mankind was prepared and transmitted to the Assembly in 1951. It was confined to offenses of a political nature such as those which endangered or disturbed international peace, fomented civil strife, or violated treaty obligations concerning armament limitations. Provisions of the code also provided that an individual acting as a Head of State or as a responsible governmental official could not claim that his position as agent of the state provided immunity from his responsibilities. Because the Assembly decided to link the draft code to the broader question of defining aggression in international affairs, final action on the code was postponed and has yet to be taken.

But the meaning of the Law Commission's Nuremberg Principles and the Military Tribunal's earlier Nuremberg doctrine are clear for the individual civil affairs officer. Military commanders as well as political leaders will operate in violation of the enumerated principles of international law if they order their subordinates to engage in actions which are in contradiction to the law of humanity. And all who order or engage in such acts, official and subordinate alike, are personally liable for criminal prosecution and punishment. Under these legal tenets, for example, U.S. bomber pilots downed over North Vietnam could conceivably be tried for committing war crimes against unarmed civilians.

Since no agreement is in force which spells out the acceptable standard of ideological values and goals, Guenter Lewy has expressed the grim view that "most of the international law of war lies in shambles and the 'dictates of the public conscience' have seemingly surrendered to military expedience." [61]

The postwar efforts in this direction have major significance for the future of American civil affairs policy. The recent events, as well as the long trends of history, suggest that definite gains have been made in making the military occupier adhere more strictly to humane principles. But advances have been measured in centuries, rather than decades.

General MacArthur perhaps made the truest assessment when he observed that: "Convention after convention has been entered into designed to humanize war. Yet each war becomes increasingly savage as the means for mass killing are further developed. You cannot control war; you can only abolish it. Those who shrug this off as idealistic are the real enemies of peace—the real war-mongers." [62]

THE IMPACT OF THE UNIVERSAL DECLARATION OF HUMAN RIGHTS UPON MILITARY OCCUPATION

While the individual civil affairs officer's significant place among the prime ingredients of occupation policy will be discussed in the next chapter, the relevance of the Universal Declaration of Human Rights to the leadership question can nevertheless be seen at this point. Approved by the United Nations in December 1948, the Declaration was the outcome of an attempt to establish an internationally sanctioned code of legal standards for the relations between governments and citizens. Within this study of the occupation policy process, the background and development of the Declaration furnishes still another illustration of the way in which American national principles and American national mood play their roles as primary policy elements.

Efforts to create a code regulating the conduct of officials can be interpreted as a move to establish a force which could counterbalance the Nuremberg doctrine. Prior to the precedent setting decisions of the Tribunal, the military officer always had legal right on his side so long as he followed exactly the orders of his superiors. Nuremberg deprived the officer of this; no longer did he have automatic justification for his actions. A disquieting and dangerous void had inadvertently been created because the new principles were of little help since they were limited to stipulating that the criterion for just and legal acts by the official was the official's own conscience. In the ensuing search for a more precise and uniform code of authority, the Universal Declaration of Human Rights took on an important meaning for national security planners.

The hope that the world was at last ready for the framing of an international bill of rights reached a high pitch of enthusiasm during the immediate postwar years. And its aim was to define what constituted just conduct by all governments in their dealings with private citizens, which theoretically included both military occupation situations and constitutional governments' operations.

The idea of developing an international code or set of statutes to protect the citizens of all countries against the caprices of unjust governments was not totally new in 1945. In fact, the first serious attempt took place in 1929 when the Institute of International Law, a private organization which maintained close ties with the League of Nations, drafted an international bill of rights. It consisted of six articles closely patterned after the American basic documents guaranteeing political rights and freedoms.

Official statements during World War II encouraged the belief that once the conflict ended the United States would accept leadership in this area. President Roosevelt's famous Four Freedoms speech to Congress, as well as pronouncements at the 1944 Dumbarton Oaks Conference, seemed to demonstrate the Administration's sincerity. The first steps were taken in 1945 at the San Francisco Conference which was convened to create the machinery for the United Nations. Through the insistence of the U.S. delegation the Charter adopted went further in the area of human rights than had been anticipated at Dumbarton Oaks, and the UN became the chief promoter of "human rights and fundamental freedoms." This development resulted as much from the lobbying of the forty-two private interest groups present at the Conference as from the wishes of the State Department. Throughout earlier official talks and meetings, the British and the Russians had been reluctant to grant the new agency power to deal with these questions. They had preferred that its role be confined strictly to the maintenance of international peace and security.[83] But world opinion appeared to be on the side of those who saw a broader role for the UN.

Once the Charter with its mandate on human rights had been signed, Washington seemed to gain enthusiasm over its prospects. Secretary of State Edward R. Stettinius reported to the President that the new organization "will have the opportunity to work out an international bill of rights . . . just as there is a Bill of Rights in the American Constitution," and that "the United States, as a nation which takes pride in its free institutions, is particularly interested in the promotion, through international means, of human rights throughout the world." [84]

The popular mood favoring this role for the United Nations was surprisingly strong and seemed to infect political leadership. Respected officials and private citizens were seriously suggesting that the UN Charter *itself* represented a world declaration of principles and that it might even be the World Constitution for the new era of peace and harmony which had been ushered in by the defeat of the fascists.

Through sessions of its special Commission on Human Rights, the UN began the project in 1947. The core of the problem was that the contemplated law of humanity involved more than the traditional relations *across* national frontiers. At stake was the delicate issue of setting standards for governmental conduct *within* sovereign states which automatically brought under scrutiny the very foundations of different political systems. Potentially, the results would bring the international approval of some systems and the outlawing of others. As appreciations of these implications spread, the venture received more thoughtful attention in the foreign offices of the world. Even the cynics could no longer dismiss it as merely an idealistic sop for the do-gooders.

Complexities of the undertaking soon forced the Commission to divide the project into three distinct phases: (1) writing a Declaration, (2) writing a Covenant, and finally (3) establishing measures for implementation. The Declaration of Human Rights was to be a statement of principles embodying the highest political and social aspirations of mankind upon which international agreement could be reached. Attention was to be focused upon the civil and political freedoms which all states were morally and legally bound to grant their citizens. The next stage of the project, the Covenant, would cast the principles enumerated in the declaration into the form of legally binding statutes. Lastly, the Commission intended to deal with the establishment of administrative machinery for hearing complaints against alleged violations of the covenant. New organs or *courts* would be created and granted authority to encourage, if not directly to enforce, compliance with the covenant.

Early deliberations on the declaration were marked by the diligent cooperation of governments and private groups. Organizations such as the American Law Institute and the American Society of International Law provided advice, and in some cases, submitted detailed proposals.

Two opposing points of view developed over the type of provisions to be included in the Declaration of Human Rights, reflecting the ideological differences which separated the democratic and communist states. American delegates argued that individualism and a system of private enterprise were the most basic of all guarantees, and that any statement which was universally to be applicable must be narrowly drawn to insure that governments did not deprive their citizens of these rights. From the U.S. standpoint, the new code should be confined strictly to protecting the political and civil liberties of the individual from arbitrary actions by any and all officials who happened to be in power. In line with traditional Western liberalism, the tone of the enumerated principles should be essentially negative. The basic concept was that man has the best chance to build the perfect society if he is protected from capricious exploitation by government.

Representatives from the communist states said that they too wished to see the Declaration provide a basis whereby the level of human welfare could be raised. However, they held that the provisions must center upon the economic and social rights of man. Governments must be placed under a positive obligation to provide the individual with services such as education, employment, and social security. Unless these exist, the idea of political rights is meaningless. They felt that the state alone was in a position to guarantee these services which the individual could not provide for himself. Government must be more than passive; it should play an active part in furthering economic and social advances.[85]

Though this view was originally expressed by the communists as an affirmation of their own philosophy, the representatives of under-developed, noncommunist nations came increasingly to favor this general approach. These former colonial areas which had recently gained political independence had vast economic and social problems. They were beginning to realize that the acquisition of political freedom did not, in itself, meet their most immediate needs. Lacking accumulated capital, developed natural resources, and an educated citizenry, the emerging nations were attracted to the communist position.

The debate between American and Russian diplomats over these issues merits thoughtful attention. Few occasions have provided a comparably complete public record of the ideological discord which separates democracy and communism. In contrast to the more commonplace East-West confrontations over political ambitions, the human rights dispute reached the foundation of the two philosophies.

American critics of the Russian approach termed it socialism. U.S. representatives argued that legalizing the state's power to so supervise the life of the citizen could lead to the loss of personal freedoms and the establishment of tyrannical governments, tyrannies which would be worse than any in the past because they could now legally excuse individual persecution on the grounds of the need for general or collective improvements.

The Amercian view prevailed, partly because the U.S. Constitution's set of principles had long been the ideal beside which the citizens of other countries measured the actions of their governments. On December 10, 1948, the draft of the Universal Declaration of Human Rights was adopted by the General Assembly by a vote of forty-eight to zero. The Soviet bloc plus two other states abstained. Of the thirty articles included in the Declaration, only eight dealing with social and economic rights had crept in over American objections. For example, the right to free compulsory elementary education was recognized. But the U.S. delegation had succeeded in phrasing the language of these articles to keep them consistent with their country's national principles.

As the Carnegie Endowment's respected study of American policy in the UN concluded: "The United States had blazed the trail for internationalizing human rights through the United Nations, had led in the work of drafting, had seen many of its basic rights and freedoms embodied in the Universal Declaration, had for the most part fended off attacks successfully, had made clear the nature of its reservations on necessary points, and had watched the rest of the world

flock to this common standard in such unity that even the archantag-
onist had found it the better part of valor merely to abstain rather
than vote against this proclamation containing much that was
anathema to his system and would destroy it. Such at the end of
1948 was the success of the United States in furthering through the
United Nations its objective of carrying traditional American rights
and freedoms to the rest of the world, in the interest of peace." [86]

The initial goals of the Commission had been accomplished when
the Universal Declaration of Human Rights was adopted by the
General Assembly. Unfortunately, the second and third aims, en-
acting a human rights Covenant, and establishing implementing or-
diances, did not fare as well. Partial blame can be placed upon a
shift in mood within the United States away from internationalism.
Responsible for this change in attitude was the aggressive intent of
world communism, evidenced by the takeover in Eastern Europe,
the Berlin blockade, and the invasion of South Korea. Americans developed a pessimistic attitude regarding many international efforts
for peaceful cooperation and McCarthyism became a manifestation
of these new suspicions.

In particular the State Department was accused of actively working
through the UN to undermine the American system. Its effort to
promote human rights within a world organization was pointed to
as proof of this and responsible officials were scarcely heard when
they tried to explain that this effort had been as much a response to
apparent popular convictions. Southern spokesmen charged that
Washington's flirtation with the human rights code had been a "red
and pink" plot to force racial integration upon their region. On
broader issues, influential Senators such as John Bricker and Tom
Connally introduced proposals to limit the foreign policy powers
of the President. And the Senate became increasingly adamant in
its refusal to ratify the UN Convention on Genocide, which U.S.
representatives in the Assembly had endorsed in 1946 and 1948.

These pressures in themselves might have been sufficient to halt
further action on a convenant, but international opposition was also
solidifying. The underdeveloped states in the UN appeared more
disillusioned and uncertain about the desirability of democratic
ideals. This was especially evident as the Commission on Human
Rights met in session after session in attempts to refine the articles
of the Universal Declaration into concrete statutes which should be
included in the Covenant. The debate which had characterized
earlier meetings continued. Now, however, the emerging states were

intractable; they insisted that it was necessary to emphasize the duty of governments to act in the areas of social and economic affairs.

Pressures from at home, abroad, and within the UN were compelling Washington to drop negotiations concerning this international endeavor. However, Mrs. Eleanor Roosevelt, who had been one of the chief architects of the Universal Declaration, argued that a U.S. abandonment of efforts for a Covenant would be a serious mistake. To withdraw from the project would eventually cost America its ideological and political leadership among the new nations. She was also concerned as to whether the communists might take over the writing of the document in the absence of U.S. representation on the Commission.

A variety of views about the situation emanated from Washington. One State Department group reportedly felt that writing a satisfactory covenant was now impossible. They advocated a total withdrawal from the project. Another group attempted to seek a middle ground, and suggested that the proposed Covenant be split into two sections, one dealing with civil and political rights and the other dealing with economic and social rights. Through this approach the U.S. could still play a major role in formulating the overall covenant, though it was recognized that the Senate would never ratify the section dealing with economic and social issues.[87] In 1953 the incoming Eisenhower Administration decided to withdraw completely and the official attitude expressed by Secretary of State Dulles was that if the UN adopted a covenant, the White House would not present it to the Senate for consideration.[88]

To avoid the charge that the underdeveloped states were being abandoned, Eisenhower pressed for UN sponsored technical assistance programs. But the decision on the covenant meant that at least temporarily Washington would forsake the notion that it should exercise world leadership in working further for an international law of humanity, even though that law might be based upon American national principles. However, one irrevocable step had been taken with the adoption of the Declaration of Human Rights.

CHAPTER IV

LEADERSHIP, IMPLEMENTATION, AND ADMINISTRATION

It is necessary to look within the military establishment itself to find several of the problems which have plagued the United States in past occupations. The Army's well-known hierarchy, bureaucracy, and rigid discipline tend to create, especially in the minds of those unfamiliar with its actual workings, the picture of a machine composed of inflexible human gears. Presumably, the policy established by leaders in Washington is implemented in the field with speed and precision. This image of efficiency is more illusion than fact, at least so far as occupations are concerned. As Professor Zink has pointed out, "military organizations are made up of men just as political organizations, and the result is that theory or no theory, they operate very much as do other human groups."[1]

An agency created to administer any type of policy, whether military or civilian, is a blend of three distinct factors or influences. There is first, the nature of the goals sought; second, the type of administrative structure utilized; and third, the personal traits of the individual leaders who occupy the key posts within the agency. These three factors must be balanced harmoniously if the organization is to function effectively. Through long experience and study the Army has developed combat and administrative units, which do achieve an extremely successful equilibrium of these components. In combat situations these units have demonstrated a high degree of administrative stability and rationality. But this internal balance is all too often destroyed when occupation rather than battle becomes the major activity. Difficulties arise because a set of political objectives is suddenly substituted for the previous military goals. Political problems do not lend themselves to the same approaches as do more conventional Army tasks, and the organization which has been so successful in bringing about military victory now tends to flounder when it is confronted with administering a military occupation.

Instead of accepting the need for reshaping its administrative machinery, the Army has consistently resorted to a simple, but not always successful, expedient. Field commanders have been permitted an unusually broad gamut of decision making powers in dealing with civilian problems. While the basic directives spelling out occupation policy always originated in Washington, the manner in which the policy was applied has been determined largely by top ranking officers overseas. The history of America's civil affairs ventures from the Mexican War through the present is filled with such instances, and several illustrations are included in this chapter.

Many of the accomplishments and failures in past programs can be traced directly to theater commanders assuming policy-making roles. On the surface the continued existence of this problem could imply sinister motives on the part of the generals, who consciously wish to usurp political authority from civilian leadership in Washington. While this is a possibility, the facts do not support any sweeping allegation of conspiracy. With the exception of a few isolated cases involving political generals, administrative and technical considerations rather than power struggles have been responsible for the field generals' powerful position.

The development of the telegraph and later the radio made it possible for national leaders to participate directly in making vital decisions in the field. Yet the new innovations have been somewhat offset by the increasing scope and complexity of modern conflicts. And as might be expected, individual generals have seen their role *vis-a-vis* Washington in different terms. Some officers have operated on the apparent assumption that they possessed substantial discretionary authority, but in turn, that this power need not be shared with subordinate generals within their theater.

Others have had less confidence in their own supreme authority. In these instances, Washington leaders could deal more directly with subordinate generals who were then in a favorable position to plan and implement their own policies. Consequently, the pattern of military leadership and organization utilized has played a direct role in influencing and even in determining the extent to which Washington's goals were pursued. Thus leadership itself became a major element of policy.

One must assess the situation in a framework which is broadly applicable. Subjective and intangible pressures, such as mutual trust or distrust between particular generals, as well as personality traits, should be supposed present and taken into account. Recognizing these and other difficulties, a meaningful examination can be made. America's major occupations are first divided into two general groupings. Each of these is marked by a distinct leadership pattern or approach; one category reflects *centralized control*, while the second is characterized by *decentralized control*.

In centralized operations the theater commander laid down the policy that all important matters be handled exclusively by him or his headquarters staff. In decentralized situations the theater chief permitted his subordinate field generals to develop their own methods of dealing with problems and also allowed them to make relatively important decisions. These two approaches, of course, represent differences in tendencies and do not stand as hard and fast absolutes. Even in the most centralized theaters, subordinate levels were expected to solve purely local problems and handle minor emergencies. By the same token, theater chiefs in even the most decentralized organizational structures never allowed lower commanders to disobey explicit and detailed orders.

In fact, one of the critical distinctions between the two approaches hinges on the nature of the instructions and directives issued by theater headquaters. When these were specific and detailed, subordinates interpreted this to be a signal that the theater commander desired that they play only a minor role in framing policy. But when directives were vague and ambiguous, lower level units tended to assume that the directives were flexible guides. Consequently, officials in the field felt justified in formulating their own set of implementing instructions. As a result, subordinates became deeply involved in the policy process without being fully aware of the import of their actions.

DECENTRALIZED CONTROL

Campaigns in North Africa and the Mediterranean were America's first major encounters with civil affairs during World War II. Much of the confusion which surrounded the establishment of a policy for controlling civilians in these areas resulted from haphazard planning, complicated by a multiplicity of civil affairs agencies and combat command headquarters sharing overlapping functions. Besides having different types of organization, these groups often sought diverse policy goals.

As the American Army moved into North Africa, the plan was to limit military occupation activities on enemy territory to securing the supply lines to the rear of the fighting. This quickly proved unworkable and the result was a policy gap at the field unit level. In Sicily once again, planning was faulty. To illustrate, military government officers landing with the invasion troops immediately posted proclamations outlawing fascism. Yet more than a year elapsed before comprehensive directives were issued on a theater-wide basis which spelled out precisely how this goal was to be accomplished.[2] Further reflecting the problem, handbooks containing the location of Sicilian public buildings such as police and fire stations were unavailable until after the occupation was underway.

Once Sicily had been secured, American forces turned toward the invasion of the Italian mainland. Rome became the headquarters of U. S. military government, and it was here that an even wider range of difficulties emerged. Regional occupation officers going to Rome in search of advice and instructions seldom found headquarters very helpful. Often when solutions to pressing local problems were suggested by Rome, these would be of little value and sometimes were even detrimental to other aspects of the overall program. Thomas R. Fisher was highly critical when he reported that if the regional or city CA chief insisted upon receiving concrete decisions on policy matters he might be told, "You are doing all right, just deal with the problems as they come up."[3] Such abdication of responsibility by the central agency resulted in widespread confusion. And with unfortunate regularity, adjoining sectors and cities were applying dissimilar policies to identical problems.

The lack of adequate centralized direction during the Italian and Sicilian actions has been corroborated in numerous authoritative accounts.[4] In an exhaustive and well documented study, John A. Hearst reports that "A review of the history of actual operations leads to the almost inescapable conclusion that, in almost all instances, low-ranking officers in the theater of operations were the chief architects of American and British policy."[5] He identified the two who played the most influential roles as Lieutenant Colonel Charles M. Spofford and Lieutenant Colonel Charles Poletti.[6] During the initial post-combat period in Sicily and Italy, Poletti became probably the most controversial American occupation official in the theater.

It is significant that even his known critics have found that an accurate description of the occupations is impossible without citing several of Poletti's personal accomplishments, though his name is frequently omitted. Poletti never reached the rank of general, and his most important assignments were with field units where he dealt directly with civilians, namely in Palermo, Naples, Rome, and Milan. Several decisions he made, as well as procedures he developed, became standard elements of American occupation policy and were enforced throughout the Italian and later the German theaters.

Poletti entered the picture as a formulator of policy during the

Sicilian campaign. Soon after the July 10, 1943, invasion by Allied troops, the structure of the Sicilian government collapsed. Key local officials fled or went into hiding for fear they would be purged and punished as fascists. Absence of local leadership, coupled with the unanticipated severity and scope of war damage, necessitated that military government officers personally take charge of the rehabilitation of public services such as medical care and the distribution of food and water. Indirect rule through agencies of the former enemy regime, which had been a basic assumption of the occupation plan, was out of the question.

Sicily became a testing ground in which a policy was sought whereby a small number of civil affairs officers could govern successfully large enemy populations. If the Sicilians who held deep antipathy for the Rome government could not be persuaded to cooperate, some serious shortcomings in the basic policy had to be corrected immediately. Out of the process of facing and solving the immediate problems which arose in Sicily, a more flexible approach to implementing policy gradually took shape. This included a fuller recognition that the imagination and resourcefulness of the military government officer in the field should not be stifled unduly by policy provisions which were obviously unworkable and unenforceable.

In an unfamiliar and hostile environment where the combat troops would soon move on and leave the civil administrator largely on his own, only limited progress in achieving some goals could be expected without jeopardizing local cooperation. Aims which called for sweeping and immediate changes in community life were self-defeating. Poletti, as well as numerous other American officers scattered across Sicily, appreciated the critical need for establishing an image of mutual respect and confidence with the occupied civilians.

In return, the defeated people would be more willing to cooperate with any reasonable request which did not appear to be in direct conflict with their long-range interests. For example, the policy which dictated the arbitrary dismissal and purging of local leaders who, though associated with the previous fascist government, were regarded with honor by local inhabitants was actually undermining the possibility of achieving American desires.*

---

* Probably the most publicized military government officer of World War II was the fictional Major Joppollo in John Hersey's novel *A Bell For Adano*. While in occupied Sicily gathering materials for a book, Hersey heard about the strong-willed and resourceful American Major who was the Allied military governor of the small seacoast town of Licata. The 1944 novel was an outgrowth of a week which Hersey

Upon assignment as the Regional Commissioner in Sicily with headquarters in Palermo, Poletti first directed his energy toward the problem of recruiting capable Italian leaders who would be willing to accept posts in the new government. Being sensitive to the traditional Sicilian resentment toward the *alien* regime in Rome, he played upon the chord that henceforth Sicily would enjoy a greater degree of administrative autonomy and self-rule under the Allied occupiers. Initially he appointed the Italian Prefect of Palermo to the newly created post of High Commissioner of Sicily. Recognized as an able respected lawyer, he was a Socialist but had never joined the Fascist Party.

With assurances that a new independence had arrived for the island, the Prefect and Poletti were successful in recruiting a group of competent new administrators. Largely because of the personal trust that the civilians had for Poletti, potential leaders came forward who otherwise probably would have avoided any involvement in public office. From this point onward, the Sicilians themselves began to carry the burden of local government. As they wrestled with the problems of relief and rehabilitation, they gradually assumed responsibility for ensuring that a reasonably uniform set of rules and regulations was enforced. This was an accomplishment which the occupiers were ill-equipped to bring about exclusively under their own power. Poletti demonstrated that military goverment could rebuild political institutions in a systematic fashion and proved that it was possible to reestablish efficient indigenous administration when the local political situation was dealt with correctly.

While in Palermo, Poletti was also responsible for developing the first practical system for swiftly screening and weeding out dangerous fascists from the ranks of public employees.[7] The original plan for implementing epuration (de-fascistization) had relied heavily upon the ability of the Army's Counter Intelligence Corps to provide military government with lists of both those employees who should be

---

spent with Major Frank E. Toscani. Toscani was wrestling with many problems in his efforts to restore order, including replacing the town bell which had figured prominently in the prewar life of the village. Licata's ancient bell had been seized by the Mussolini government to be melted down for munitions. In recognition of his wartime contribution, a street was named Via Toscani. And in 1962, he and Mrs. Toscani were invited by the people of Licata to return for a celebration in his honor. Among the remembrances given to the Major was a centuries-old bronze bell inscribed as follows: "Presented to Colonel Frank Toscani by the People of Licata on his 'Return to Adano' October 28, 1962, Licata, Sicily." See "Salute to Colonel Frank E. Toscani, USAR," *The Army Reservist*, 9:5, December, 1963.

retained and those discharged. Unfortunately, the task of conducting background investigations on all civil servants, from mayor to janitor, soon swamped the CIC's limited facilities.

In an attempt to break the bottleneck, Poletti, through his small Political Intelligence Section, developed a questionnaire designed to measure the extent of the employee's involvement with fascist activities. Under severe penalty for falsification, the officials and workers placed a mark beside the names of the various fascist organizations to which they had belonged. The counterintelligence people could then on a selective or random basis compare the Sicilians' answers against lists of known members of fascist clubs, societies, and similar groups.

Initially, the plans for epuration stipulated that all fascists had to be purged. Poletti's *Sicily Scheda Personale,* or questionnaire, set forth the concept that dismissals for political reasons would be on a selective rather than an absolute basis. The genius of the idea lay not only in the questionnaire, but also in the development of a workable system of purging by categorization. Public servants who were classified as Original Fascists, Veterans of the March on Rome, and Party Leaders were barred indefinitely from holding office. However, those who played only a passive role in minor groups were permitted to retain their posts, since many in this category were essentially apathetic toward politics and had joined merely as a condition of employment.

Colonel Poletti's pragmatic approach to the epuration problem met misgivings and resistance from those combat commanders who saw the war as a crusade against fascist ideology. This was an understandable reaction, but since his scheme constituted the only workable and systematic proposal to be advanced, it gained theater-wide acceptance. In December 1943 it was published in the form of a directive by the Allied Commission and on July 29, 1944, the reorganized Italian government issued its epuration decree which contained essentially the same classifications as those developed in Palermo prior to November 1943.[8] The Italian *Scheda Personale* became the model for the even more significant *Fragebogen* denazification questionnaire used in Germany.

Poletti's handling of the Sicilian administration quickly established his reputation for aggressive and imaginative leadership. When the American forces moved from Sicily to the Italian mainland, occupation problems became even more complex. In February 1944 when Poletti was named Regional Commissioner of Naples he again put his political talent to work. The city administration was chaotic as a result of conflicts and petty bickering among local leaders and factions. Prior to Poletti's arrival, other civil affairs officers had found it impossible to secure for local posts a sufficient number of candidates who were both competent and able to command the general support of the citizenry, but the problem was somewhat different from Sicily.

In Naples, as well as throughout Italy, Committees of National Liberation had been formed by local leaders in anticipation of the ouster of Mussolini. The Committees were amalgamations of various anti-fascist bodies which welcomed the coming of the Americans primarily because of their dislike of the former regime. But since they often included leftist elements, a cloud of suspicion surrounded their actions. Were they working to establish a democratic Italy or a communist Italy? U.S. military government officials faced difficult decisions whenever they dealt with these groups, because in many cases, including Naples, the Committee stood as the sole source of able candidates for offices in the new government.

In that particular city the Committee was composed of six parties and was led by the highly respected attorney and Socialist, Enrico de Nicola who was later elected the first postwar President of the Republic of Italy. By coincidence, the Committee chairman, was married to a former American and this perhaps aided Poletti in planning his course of action. De Nicola volunteered a list of potential candidates who would be acceptable to all local factions; this saved the military government much time during an exceedingly critical period.

The Naples Committee then assumed the task of drafting, subject to the approval of occupation authorities, a law which would be suitable for dealing with the epuration problem on a national basis. Through its efforts, the Allied Commission issued a theater-wide directive on the subject in November 1944 which was little more than an official affirmation of the proposals advanced by this Committee.[9] And subsequently the re-established Italian government followed suit with an almost identical decree.

The chief significance of the policy process lay in Poletti's decision regarding the best method of handling the committees. Once again he saw the value of establishing close relations with local leaders and placing the prime burden for epuration upon the shoulders of the Italians themselves. Allied authorities could then remain in the background and consult the local committees in each city on the question of reconstructing governmental machinery.

Following his assignment in Naples, Poletti was successively Regional Commissioner in Rome and Milan, Italy's political and economic capitals. In this last major assignment he aggravated some of the American professional officers greatly. This can be seen by understanding the story in sequence. Milan had been captured by the Partisans prior to the arrival of the Allies. The U.S. Army commander in the area laid elaborate plans to lead personally a column of his victorious troops down the main boulevard to the city hall where his authority would formally be invested. Everything proceeded according to schedule, except that when the commander entered the city confident of a hero's welcome, he was told that Colonel Poletti had already arrived in Milan, established his office, and was hard at work laying plans for the future of the city. Then and there the general evicted Poletti from the city and for a few weeks denied him access. This act of petty jealousy proved fruitless because the commander soon found himself unable to deal with the Italian Partisan government which had established actual control over Milan. Higher authority intervened and returned Poletti to his post, where he quickly reasserted Allied control.

Considerable conjecture still surrounds not only some of Poletti's actions but also the reasons behind his repeated assignments to critical areas. One view is that he was chosen directly by Washington to head the administration of major Italian cities as they came under American and Allied control. This suggests a U.S. plan to counter the British choice of the experienced diplomat, Lord Rennell of Rodd, who had been Senior Civil Affairs Officer for British military government in North Africa.

The decision to send the already controversial Poletti to govern the vitally important administration of Milan was presumably made during November or December 1944 while Roosevelt was still alive. Ultimately, a choice of this magnitude had to be made in Washington and London. Churchill had a habit of conceding to FDR's wishes on such matters, even though this particular appointment raised sharp protests among British representatives in Italy. Milan, being the economic seat of the country, was a prize which they had hoped to control and exploit to the commercial benefit of the Commonwealth. As for the American generals, governing Milan meant glory. They recalled that in this city Napoleon had once situated his main headquarters. Both the American and British military hierarchies were still piqued over their earlier loss of absolute authority in Naples and Rome to Poletti, and they saw themselves being outmaneuvered again in Milan. Yet his record of success could not be ignored. So, in balance, a fair appraisal would be that he was both condemned and praised by both U.S. and British leaders for his unorthodox methods.[10]

Another factor behind Poletti's ability to step into the policy vacuum and make decisions came from his personal political connections. As a former New York State judge and Democratic Party leader he had risen steadily through a succession of appointive and elective offices until finally reaching the governor's mansion. From 1939 to 1943 he served as Lieutenant Governor, and in 1942 he filled the Governor's chair for a short time. The following year Poletti was appointed a Special Assistant to the Secretary of War, the position he left to join the Army.

As two former New York Governors, both FDR and Poletti had derived political support from many of the same groups. The extent to which Poletti received the direct or indirect backing of the White House during his service overseas is a matter of conjecture but it appears that he came to play a prominent part in the Italian occupation through an unanticipated set of circumstances. Mayor Fiorello La Guardia of New York City was the natural choice to become the President's unofficial representative to the Italian people. However, the Mayor's declining health made his selection impossible, even if he had otherwise been willing to relinquish his New York City post. Speculation suggests that the Poletti designation may have been an outgrowth of both FDR's and La Guardia's negotiations on the problem. The inevitable question arises as to what might have been Poletti's eventual political fortunes had the President and the Mayor lived longer.

His strong political ties within the U.S. were not limited to the White House alone because his Italian-American background furnished a link with powerful local voting factions. Speaking fluent Italian, Poletti was a politician who knew intimately the mind of the large Italian populations in cities such as New York and Buffalo. As an occupation officer he merely practiced the same pragmatic and rule-of-thumb techniques which were commonplace and successful in urban politics. Dealing in Italy with factional groups and machines which fought for control of city hall held little mystery and few surprises for the experienced American politician.

Though many of the Army combat commanders who had charge of the Italian campaign thoroughly disliked Poletti, they dared not treat him too harshly. As an unofficial spokesman for the Italian-Americans, many of whom had close relatives in occupied Italy, the colonel had an unusual opportunity to exercise individual initiative in breaking critical civil affairs bottlenecks. In a reference which, if it did not apply explicity to Poletti, certainly was intended to describe officers having similar civilian backgrounds, Fisher wrote that "to discipline an ex-governor, lieutenant governor, or Congressman, who let it be generally known that he was close to 'the throne' was something that even a general would hesitate to do." And in one case when a "general disciplined a high political figure he was heard to say, 'When you give an order to an ACC officer it becomes a matter for negotiation!' "[11] Obviously, scores of other officers labored in lower level agencies without the benefit of Poletti's freedom of action and insulation from interference by Army brass. Yet his career in Sicily and Italy would not have been a significant chapter in the occupations unless the man himself had possessed unusual talents. Few Italian politicians or Americans who were involved with the occupation will likely forget the Poletti legend.

The structural framework for civil affairs organizations, as well as the pattern of ideas which evolved into accepted practices during the Mediterranean campaigns, became the harbinger of basic policy approaches adopted for the later operations in Western Europe. Several logical reasons accounted for this. When General Eisenhower was transferred to England to lay plans for opening the Western Front, many of his staff advisors and combat leaders accompanied him. After D-Day additional officers who had gained experience in North Africa and Italy were assigned directly to military government units in France and Germany. They augmented the newly arrived officers who had been trained specifically for occupation duty in Germany.

Eisenhower permitted his subordinate combat commanders exceptionally wide latitude in dealing with civil affairs problems. Postwar evaluations of the relative wisdom of the Supreme Commander's approach have been numerous. Among the more outspoken critics, Professor Zink charged that decentralization was inherently defective because it allowed a degree of local independence to officers who were not uniformly equipped or skilled for the responsibility.[12] An inconsistent occupation policy was the result.

For example, at one point at least three different denazification policies were being administered by military government units because differing directives had been issued below the theater level. Yet Eisenhower continued to believe that his approach was sound and at the Potsdam Conference he presented persuasive arguments. He urged "that civilian authority take over military government . . . at the

earliest possible date." And "while the Army would obviously have
to stay in control until order was assured, the government of individuals in their normal daily lives was not a part of military responsibility." But "no matter how efficiently and devotedly the Army
might apply itself to this task, misunderstandings would certainly
arise." In the long run, "American concepts and traditions would be
best served by the State Department's assuming over-all responsibility
. . . using the American Army there merely as an adjunct and supporter
for civilian authority and policy."[18]

A more laudable commitment to democratic principles expressed
by a career general would be difficult to find. However, the price was
a very weak and disjointed administration of the occupation. Whether
Eisenhower was aware of the fact or not, his view that agencies other
than the Army should play the major role was impractical. No civilian
body, not even the State Department, was at that time prepared to
handle the array of complex problems entailed in a major occupation.
Perhaps a degree of rationalization must be read into the Supreme
Commander's desire that a civilian agency quickly take over prime
responsibility. The conduct of the occupation was the Army's job
and it was Eisenhower's job. As an interesting aside, perhaps a study
of the General's decentralized approach to occupation should be
viewed in context with his system of organizing the federal administration when he later became president. His consistency is striking.

While Eisenhower was in command in Europe, he permitted several
of his generals to make important decisions relating to civilians.
Among the commanders of regions were Lieutenant General A. M.
Patch, who directed the U.S. Seventh Army, and Lieutenant General
George Patton, who was the Commanding General of the U.S. Third
Army. While both were extremely competent military officers, they
differed markedly in their record of success in solving occupation
problems. Patch believed that the especially trained civil affairs officers should be used to deal with civil military problems. Consequently,
he welcomed the experts into his zone, whether they arrived as individuals or as members of newly assigned civil affairs units. His
sincerity was reflected through the direct orders issued to subordinate
commanders insisting that in their relations with the military government professionals full cooperation was to be extended and giving
notice that acts of interference would not be tolerated.

In contrast, General Patton never fathomed the modern function
of civil affairs and military government. He appeared to consider it a
useless innovation that merely cluttered up the battle scene. While

he did recognize that the duties assigned them had to be performed by someone, he held little respect for the Army's occupation specialists. Instead of utilizing the trained officers who were assigned to his area, he preferred to use available combat officers. Zink reported that "during one period military government detachments awaiting General Patton's orders sat idly by while military government functions were being performed by surplus tactical officers."[14]

The performance of the latter proved to be wholly unsatisfactory. Pressure was exerted by higher headquarters, and Patton was forced to permit the professional detachments to enter his area and take their assigned posts. However, following the lead of their general, commanders of local tactical units provided little support, and in fact, after the fighting ended they spent much of their time interfering with the operation of military government units. For example, directives issued by smaller civil affairs units were countermanded, and German officials appointed by occupation authorities were sometimes removed and replaced on the order of tactical officers. The situation became so unmanageable and confused that the professional occupation officers often gave up in despair. Extensive surveys were conducted to evaluate occupation activities in the areas controlled by Patch and Patton. These rated General Patch's Seventh Army area far in the lead.[15]

Other examples reflecting the decentralized approach to military government were scattered throughout the entire European experience. But in order to determine if this has been a significant and consistent element of civil affairs policy, the record of earlier American occupations should also be examined. The search reveals many illustrations, the earliest instance cited here being the strikingly independent role played by individual field commanders during and after the Civil War. Since no uniform occupation policy or central authority existed, wartime and postwar military government operated largely on the basis of the whim of the particular general whose troops controlled the local area. Some wartime leaders, notably Andrew Johnson in Tennessee, pursued a moderate course in dealing with civilians and imposed only those restrictions which were absolutely necessary. Other commanders, such as General Butler, adopted a harsh and punitive policy which caused an even wider rift between the North and the South and cast doubt upon the validity of a decentralized approach.

"Old Butler," as General Ben Butler was called when he first entered New Orleans at the head of a Union column, was a political general. He had earned a reputation before the war through his flamboyant manner and outspoken statements. While a staunch abolitionist, he had also expressed some admiration for Jefferson Davis's stand against the economic exploitation of the South by business interests in the North. In political consciousness, he associated himself with the lower classes and tended to look upon aristocrats and well-to-do business-men as enemies of the people. He professed to be a strong believer in welfare and aid for the poor, and obviously enjoyed every opportunity of demonstrating his power over the bumptious established leadership.

He possessed self-confidence bordering on arrogance and was prone to surround himself with officers of dubious reputations. For example, Colonel Andrew Butler, the general's brother, purchased in Texas a quantity of relief supplies intended for the destitute of New Orleans and sold them for a personal profit.[16] Also acting for themselves, others on Butler's staff allegedly intimidated Louisiana planters into selling them cotton for a fraction of its actual worth. As time passed, it seemed that while the general's associates found means for cheating the poor, Butler himself managed to insult the wealthy.

Looking back upon the New Orleans occupation, the fact and fic-tion of his exploits have become so mixed that it is difficult to relate an accurate and objective account of what did happen. It is known that when he entered the city he encountered opposition from local merchants. For example, when he ordered the newspaper *True Delta* to print proclamation notices the editor refused. Whereupon, Butler seized the paper, printed the notices, and resumed publciation of the newspaper himself.

When the male members of the New Orleans aristocracy had been coerced gradually into submission, the resistance movement was taken up by their daughters and wives. Probably their studied insults di-rected against Butler's troops did result from a well-thought through plot rather than spontaneous acts. Whatever the cause, the effect was to enrage the commander. When his soldiers boarded streetcars, all the women arose with a huffy air and got off. In a famous incident, "One Southern girl draped in a Confederate flag, walked up to a soldier standing guard, stared at him, turned toward the street, and ostentatiously lifting her petticoats, spat in the gutter."[17] This war of nerves did not continue for long before Butler acted. He issued his historic General Order 28, which stated that women who engaged in insults against Union forces would be dealt with and treated as prosti-tutes. He now became "beast Butler." Protests were heard from throughout the South and even from Victorian England. The Con-federate Government put a price on his head—dead or alive. The order precipitated an open argument with the New Orleans city officials which ended with Butler's sending the mayor, police chief, a Judge Kennedy, and another minor official to jail.

If this were not enough to create his reputation, the handling of the Mrs. Philip Phillips affair was. She was the fiery wife of a former congressman from Alabama who believed whole-heartedly in the Confederate cause. Previously, she had been thrust into the limelight when apprehended for espionage in Washington. Continuing as a social leader in New Orleans, Mrs. Phillips was able to avoid a direct encounter with Butler until one fateful day when a funeral procession for a Union officer passed her home. She was heard to utter an outburst of laughter from behind her draped window. When taken into custody for violating Butler's order she insisted that she had not laughed at the dead officer. Instead, she claimed, the gaiety was intended for a childrens party being held inside the house. Apparently her excuse was thought questionable, because she was brought personally before the general. When she refused to apologize for an offense which she insisted had never been committed, Butler became livid with anger and called her not "a vulgar woman of the town, but an uncommonly vulgar one."[18] He sentenced her to jail on Ship Island and refused to permit her to communicate with anyone except himself and her maid.

Whether Butler's actions were calculated or imprudent, he certainly was unsuccessful in dealing effectively with local officials. He seemed instead to provoke hatred and create chaos. While his avowed love for the poor was admirable, his disdain for the city's leaders, as well as his terrible temper, prevented the building of an effective administration in New Orleans.

After the war Butler was elected to the U.S. House of Representatives, where again his talent and temper made him the center of some of the most disorderly scenes ever witnessed on the floor. Later he was to become Governor of Massachusetts, but his major place in history books will continue to rest upon his actions as the administrator of the New Orleans military government.

Unfortunately for the future of the South and the entire nation, the wartime New Orleans scandal did not result in the rooting out of the basic causes of the problem. After Appomattox the former Confederacy was divided for occupation purposes into five separate military districts, each headed by a Major General. In all, nineteen different Union officers headed the districts before the system was finally scrapped in 1870.

During the immediate postwar period, the extremely confused political climate in the North blocked the possibility of establishing a
clear and consistent occupation program. On occasions an open question existed as to whether any actual limits curbed the generals'
authority in dealing with civilians in their districts. However, there
was no doubt about the fact that the commanders received little if
any concrete policy guidance from their superiors in Washington,
except, of course, from congressional leaders who acted as their personal patrons. Some of the satraps, as the Northern officers were
sarcastically dubbed by Southerners, adopted moderate policies stress-
ing rehabilitation. Hancock, Schofield, and Meade followed this course.
However, others such as Sheridan, Pope, and Sykes enforced a harsh
and punitive program within their areas.[19]

As might be expected, problems created or aggravated because of
the lack of centralization were not restricted to the five district commanders alone. Because of the decentralized approach subordinate
headquarters within the districts often capitalized upon the situation
and developed their own unique policies. For example, the notorious
Brigadier General Milton Littlefield began his career as the Prince
of Bummers while heading the occupation of Charleston.[20] Subsequently, he led a group known as the Ring. This collection of financial
conspirators engaged in transactions in stocks and bonds in several
Southern states, causing their near bankruptcy. The Wall Street
Panic of 1869, or Black Friday, was also blamed upon his manipula-
tions. The "Rule of the Major Generals,"[21] as Walter L. Fleming described the era, was a direct outgrowth of the case with which individual field commanders could make policy decisions which should have
been made in Washington.

CENTRALIZED CONTROL

America's record of occupation has also included several instances
of centralized control. In these operations the theater commander
insisted that his headquarters alone possessed power to interpret all
directives and orders for the entire command. Of course, exceptions
were always made in the case of minor details of a purely local character. The most recent and significant illustration of this type of
policy occurred during the post-World War II occupation of Japan.
General MacArthur's dominance of that scene is well known. He managed civil affairs with a firm hand and allowed no subordinates in
field units to make decisions which were at variance with the overall

pattern laid down by his headquarters staff (SCAP).

Even his critics acknowledge that the general was a remarkable leader whose actions reflected intelligence and astuteness in both military and political matters. Japan furnished an arena in which he could exercise the full breadth of his talents. Walter Millis has described MacArthur as a "political soldier."[22] While this label is by no means unique in American history, few generals have shown such a long and deep involvement in partisan politics.

Douglas MacArthur was an exceedingly complex individual, which may explain the seeming inconsistency of many of his actions and statements. To the average American, he came to stand as a symbol of far-right conservatism, a badge he seemed willingly to accept. Throughout the decade following the war the general's name was mentioned frequently as a possible Republican presidential nominee. Instead, the more moderate General Eisenhower was chosen. Party leaders appeared to feel that MacArthur's views were too conservative to attract the middle-of-the-road support necessary for election. Many Americans recalled vividly and disapprovingly that as Chief of Staff MacArthur had ordered the Army to break up the Veterans March on Washington during the depression. This incident laid the foundation for a domestic image of authoritarianism and military elitism which he was never fully able to live down, and which he perhaps deserved. He appeared to lack understanding and sensitivity for the forces which were moving the country from the Representative Republic envisaged by the Founding Fathers to a newer form of popular democracy which had inexorably been emerging during the past half century. In a sense, he was politically old-fashioned.

Overseas, however, MacArthur gained for himself quite a different reputation. He had not changed; it was the setting that was different. To the peoples of the Philippines and Japan his brand of democracy appeared both progressive and practical. Throughout the occupation he labored arduously to substitute the institutions of Western liberalism for the authoritarian social and governmental structures upon which prewar Japan had been built.

Extension of the franchise, women's rights, land reform, a Constitution, and the ideas of popular sovereignty and civil rights were among his ambitions. On the one hand, he respected the ancient institutions which were cherished and understood by the people, for example the figure of the Japanese Emperor. Simultaneously, he argued that democratic ideals and practices were better suited to the needs of the modern world and should be incorporated into the future law of the land. The result was, in our judgment, one of the more successful military occupations conducted by the United States.

His talent and drive alone did not account of the image which he projected. Fortune was on his side in the sense that he operated within the context of an administrative muddle which tended to reduce the effectiveness of his opponents. While not responsible himself for creating the confusion, it strengthened his hand in dealing with both Japanese and Washington officials. Since the occupation was conceived as a joint Allied venture rather than strictly American, formal authority to establish policy was delegated to several Allied and United States agencies.

From the beginning MacArthur apparently intended to operate in a highly centralized manner. Since circumstances reinforced his plans, his ability to undertake major projects in the name of the U.S. government increased as the occupation progressed. The Supreme Commander's independence seems to have evolved in a very natural manner during the first two years of his tenure in Tokyo. During the initial phase, the realization that the joint Allied agencies were incapable of establishing a workable policy created the need for an alternate source of direction. Soviet obstruction and bickering at the meetings of the Allied bodies suggested also that the difficulties would not soon be remedied.

SCAP headquarters in Tokyo, which was designed originally to be merely the operational arm of higher Allied authorities, began to take on a new and greater significance. Increasingly MacArthur asserted an independence from their deliberations and decisions. And his ability to do this certainly involved at least the tacit approval of Washington. Both the State Department and the Pentagon were undecided as to the best means for countering Soviet expansionism in the Far East and elsewhere without precipitating a direct showdown with Moscow. Being aware of the impact of this problem on the policymaking process, MacArthur simply seized the initiative.

As time passed, he seemed to turn inward for answers to critical problems and once remarked to Russell Brines that, "My major advisors now, have boiled down to two men—George Washington and Abraham Lincoln. One founded the United States, the other saved it. If you go back into their lives, you can find almost all the answers." [23] MacArthur's admiration for Napoleon is also revealing. He believed Napoleon to have been the greatest general who ever lived when he was on the battlefield. But in political affairs Napoleon lost his faith in his own ideas and listened to those around him.

Perhaps these interpretations of history help explain why the Supreme Commander placed high value in always giving the impression of having complete confidence in himself and in his own opinions. In fact, however, he was not always successful, and his judgment was far more fallible than he assumed.

He demanded that the staff members around him be of unquestioned loyalty. In return for this service he was willing to accept advisors who perhaps had little else to offer. Since he was irritated by criticism, he received little from subordinates. This particular style of leadership has advantages, but it also presents the serious drawback of his not receiving accurate information about existing conditions.

Perhaps the most striking example of MacArthur's unfortunate choice of advisors was Major General Charles A. Willoughby, who as SCAP Intelligence Chief was frequently regarded as the second most powerful American official in occupied Japan. Willoughby was a career officer who had immigrated to the United States from Germany as a boy. In 1910 he enlisted in the Army and earned an early and respected reputation for his military skill as well as for his soldierly manner and bearing. In an immaculate and perfectly tailored uniform, sometimes topped with a monocle, he likely appeared to senior officers as the ideal prototype of any general's aide. Reportedly, MacArthur first met Willoughby at Fort Leavenworth in the mid 1930's and was greatly impressed.

Willoughby's political leanings became widely known through a book he authored in 1939. In an account which was generally sympathetic to fascist regimes, he wrote that, "Historical judgment, freed from the emotional haze of the moment, will credit Mussolini with wiping out the memory of defeat by re-establishing the traditional military supremacy of the white race, for generations to come."[24]

In 1940 MacArthur, who was then the Field Marshal of the Philippines, sent for Willoughby. From this point until the beginning of the occupation of Japan in 1945, Willoughby carried on a close association with the Franco-oriented landholding clique on the Islands, even during their exit to Australia after 1942. The special favoritism shown one member of this locally unpopular circle, Sorianos Elizaldes, resulted in protests from both Congress and Secretary of the Interior Harold Ickes. MacArthur's staff was instrumental in Sorianos' gaining American citizenship as well as a high post in the Philippine government, even though he had reportedly given financial help to Franco and had earlier been denied naturalization by a local Philippine court because of his rightist political activities.[25]

During the American occupation of Japan, Willoughby gained greater stature and importance. As Intelligence Chief, he became the key figure in what seemed to be the SCAP policy of subtle, and sometimes overt, persecution of news correspondents who were in any way critical of the Supreme Commander's conduct. Willoughby was blamed for incidents such as the use of innuendo to imply that the highly respected CBS reporter Frank Costello had communist affiliations. This occurred when Costello attempted to dig into various occupation projects without the assistance of SCAP public relations officers.[26]

Willoughby's high regard and respect for the dictator Franco and his methods continued. John Gunther reported that at a dinner party Willoughby once proposed a toast to: "The second greatest military commander in the world, Francisco Franco."[27] (Of course, MacArthur was assumed to be the greatest.) Following his retirement from the Army, Willoughby visited Spain on a semi-official mission for the American government and described that country in a public lecture as a "cradle of supermen."[28] In Madrid he was toasted by Fernandez Cuesta, Secretary General of the Falangist Party, in these terms: "I am happy to know a fellow Falangist and reactionary."[29]

Later one finds MacArthur's man Willoughby testifying before a Congressional committee on the subject of proposed foreign aid legislation. Speaking on behalf of an organization calling itself the "American Coalition of Patriotic Societies," he expressed disgust for what he alleged to be the "anti-American, anti-West, [and] anti-white" policy pursued by the Indian government's chief delegate to the UN.[30] With continuing admiration for his Spanish hero he said that, "apparently Europe lacks the will to fight. Spain has shown what can be done on a shoestring. She defeated Russia on the battlefields of the Spanish Civil War, 1936-1939, at a fraction of the mutual security grants that cascaded into France and England." Spain "maintains 11 divisions behind the Pyrenees which may yet become the last refuge of the shattered and retreating battlefield."[31] When questioned as to whether he favored stopping military assistance to the United Kingdom, he replied that since Britain furnishes only three to four divisions and Spain provides eleven; that should be the yardstick used to govern the distribution of foreign aid.[32]

But Willoughby's pet project, as expressed before the committee, was the establishment of a Congressional "watchdog committee" over the nation's intelligence services. "There should be a Congressional committee with the assistance, of course, of bright boys like myself who have no ax to grind, at the moment. We work for nothing." He continued, "I am a consultant to Francis Walter's committee [The House Committee on Un-American Activities] as a work of love, because I know he is on the right track and is harassed, abused, and persecuted."[33]

It is part of the enigma of MacArthur that he accepted and permitted an officer of Willoughby's leanings to fill a critical post on his staff. The trust placed in his chief advisor is doubly curious in the light of MacArthur's obviously sincere effort to persuade the Japanese people to abandon national extremism. An explanation for this inconsistency perhaps rests in the general's personality, and this helps explain the management of the occupation.

As an illustration of centralized control, much can be learned from the manner in which MacArthur organized his command. Throughout the operation the United States found it necessary to implement what were termed Urgent Unilateral Interim Directives. These permitted the American government, through the Supreme Commander, to deal with civil affairs problems as it saw fit. The directives covered the major issues upon which the Allied Powers disagreed; and regrettably, these were numerous. MacArthur used these disputes to enhance his own power.

An illustration of this was the Case of the Vanishing War History, a bizarre affair beginning in the most innocent manner. During 1943, when the war was at its height, MacArthur's G-3 Staff for Operations began collecting materials for a history of the war in the Pacific. Being a routine record-keeping activity, it generated little interest. Then on September 8, 1945, the Adjutant General of the Army, C. G. Engle, formally brought up the matter with MacArthur. Engle desired that the War Department receive a full historical account of everything that occurred in the course of the the the just-beginning occupation.

A complete record of civil affairs policy could be useful for practical as well as historical reasons. It would serve as a guide for future occupations, and MacArthur was urged to make the maximum use of Japanese and American sources. He was further informed that the project would be under the technical supervision of the Historical Branch of the War Department's General Staff in Washington. That group was to be kept aware of all history-writing activities undertaken by MacArthur, and it would have final authority over editing.[34] SCAP, it was assumed, would limit itself to writing about the occupation phase of the U. S. operations in the Pacific. And at this point there was apparent agreement between MacArthur and Engle concerning who had ultimate control over the project.

Exactly what ensued after this meeting is unclear; however, it is known that MacArthur began to take a strong personal interest in producing some form of a history. He did continue to send progress reports to Washington until the fall of 1949. They then ceased.[35]

Instead of concentrating upon the occupation, the Supreme Commander's staff set to work on a comprehensive historical work which was to encompass both the wartime and postwar activities of the U. S. forces in the Pacific, including of course the occupation. The manuscript initially bore the title *MacArthur in the Pacific*,[36] the implication being that it would center around all phases of MacArthur's personal involvement. In November 1946, a 695 page manuscript was completed and submitted to the general. For reasons which have never been brought to light, MacArthur rejected it on the spot.

Willoughby was then ordered to take charge of the project. According to reports, he thereupon "threw away more than half of it, rewrote 298 pages and added 187 new pages of his own."[37] Not to show favoritism, MacArthur immediately rejected the Willoughby draft as well. As a sidelight, it might be mentioned that neither the first draft nor the Willoughby draft were ever published or even transmitted to Washington. These were the first of several manuscripts to "vanish" mysteriously.

In the next episode we find Willoughby hastily gathering a larger writing and research staff. The new group included some fifteen Japanese Generals and Admirals, as well as an assortment of American and Japanese writers and artists. In fact, it became such an extensive project that an entire floor of the Nippon Yusen Kaisha Building was taken over to house the staff.[38]

A decision was now made to recast the emphasis of the entire project; who actually made this move, or why, is not known. This time the occupation history was to be omitted in favor of a three volume account of the wartime operations. Speculation exists that a fourth volume, perhaps to deal with the occupation, was intended in 1946 but never received any serious attention. New titles were adopted and instead of the single title, *MacArthur in the Pacific*, the three following volumes were designated: I. *Campaigns of MacArthur in the Pacific;* II. *Japanese Operations Against MacArthur;* and III. *MacArthur in Japan: Military Phases*.[39] When criticisms later appeared in the press over the seeming lack of modesty on the part of the Supreme Commander, the first volume was renamed *Allied Operations in the Southwest Pacific.*[40]

Once the project was launched it took on the air of a super-secret military venture. Reports sent to Washington provided only the most sketchy clues as to what MacArthur was up to with his War History; in no way does this imply that he failed to reply with due courtesy or that he deliberately ignored official queries. Yet as incredible as it may seem, Willoughby went so far as to deny the very existence of the project.[41] "All possible devices were employed to conceal even from visiting official war historians—such as the Navy's distinguished Professor Samuel E. Morrison who already knew of the history—the very fact that the volumes were still in perparation."[42] Those engaged in the research were forced to destroy all notes they made and sign out for all materials. Their work had to be cleared through a special security arrangement, presumably under the personal supervision of Willoughby. MacArthur himself even brushed aside the whole matter by saying that the "only historical work his G-2 Staff had undertaken in Tokyo was the preparation of twelve or more volumes of routine monographs on various aspects of the Pacific war, all of which had been sent to Washington and were in current use."[43]

After roughly six years of work and costs which must have expanded into millions of dollars, the massive study finally reached prepublication stages in the fall of 1950. From the few reports available, most of the work was a thorough and accurate treatment of the military phases of the Pacific war. Supposedly, it contained 350 multicolor maps and about a million words of text.[44] The completed three volumes were, so the story goes, delivered to MacArthur in December, 1950, in the form of some twelve hundred double-column 8x12 inch pages of beautifully printed page proofs.[45] Another version is that the three volumes consisted of a total of approximately 3,000 pages, and that four sets of the completed manuscripts were in existence in December.[46]

The history was set for publication by MacArthur in Japan about the time President Truman relieved him of his duties during the Korean affair. With this act the President was not only scuttling the venerable general, but he was also writing the temporary—or perhaps permanent—obituary to the War History. One can only guess what happened on that morning after the news of Truman's action reached Tokyo, but a playwright might conjure up an exchange such as the following between Willoughby and his chief:

Willoughby: "General, what about the War History?"

MacArthur: "Willoughby, burn it!"

And the history did disappear. Reportedly, the printing plates which had already been made were destroyed. Work copies and other similar evidence vanished and all that remained were the four completed manuscript copies. When the Pentagon was questioned in 1952 about the matter, the Office of Military History replied that, "What has happened to the four sets is known presumably only to General MacArthur and perhaps to General Willoughby."[47]

MacArthur's attitude of independence on the war history and other matters doubtless proved as frustrating to Washington as to the Far Eastern Commission, the Allied body charged with overall supervision over the occupation. Nevertheless, the Supreme Commander's wide discretionary powers served as a convenient device for the United States and enabled it to exercise near complete hegemony over the policy being applied in Japan. While MacArthur had a tendency to act on his own, he was in the final analysis an American General who could be replaced by Washington should he stray too far from the long-range goals of the President and Congress. Kazuo Kawai, a Japanese scholar who experienced the U. S. venture himself, summed up the situation as seen by those most directly involved— the Japanese. To them, the occupation appeared to be "primarily a MacArthur operation, secondarily an American operation, and remotely an Allied operation."[48]

Because of the dominant position of the Supreme Commander and the centralized nature of his role, MacArthur's name has become synonymous with the initial post-war period of Japanese history. In both scholarly studies and popular conversation it has become "MacArthur's occupation of Japan." In an earlier episode in American history another general had his name similarly associated with the operation he headed. "Graves' occupation of Siberia" is clearly understood to mean the activities surrounding the World War I intervention by the United States in that part of Russia. Like MacArthur, General William S. Graves so thoroughly determined policy himself that the influence of other American officials has been relegated to obscurity. Also like MacArthur, he was accorded by Washington wide discretionary power to make important decisions on his own authority.

Unlike MacArthur, however, Graves was not the obvious choice, and his selection came as a surprise to many. Wilson could have appointed an officer whose background reflected a higher sensitivity to the political and moral implications of the intervention. Instead, the President found a man whose earlier assignments had exemplified "a rigid obedience to orders and a willingness, in the case of a confused situation, to act only upon that portion of the orders which were most clear and applicable."[49] With a military chief possessing this cast of mind, the President could reasonably predict the manner in which Graves would set about applying American policy in Siberia. He could safely be trusted with a relatively free hand, enabling Washington to concentrate its attention upon the larger problem of the European war.

Strong pressures were brought to bear upon the American commander in Siberia, especially by Britain and Japan. The overall situation was extremely confused and it was a tribute to his talents that he was able to perceive any specific policy. Once he had discovered what the American policy actually was, he proceeded to implement it with unswerving dedication, regardless of the criticism of United States or foreign officials.

To Graves, the assurance of non-interference was the only part of Wilson's policy that was sufficiently tangible to merit serious consideration.[50] Repeatedly the question of subtle or overt American involvement with one political faction or another posed major policy problems. The situation seemed to demand that Graves take a personal hand in local affairs, but this he refused to do. Whether his actions stemmed from determined dedication or a simple lack of political astuteness is an open question. However, there is no doubt regarding the fact that the military occupation policy put into practice was Graves's handiwork.

THE AGENCY CONFUSION

It is recognized generally that agencies constitute one aspect of the civil affairs policy question. Their functions and locations have been varied, ranging from coordinating groups on the highest levels in Washington to organs in the field having direct control over civilians. A cursory examination of American occupations reveals an extensive dissatisfaction with the manner in which agencies performed their assigned tasks. Because little advanced planning was given to civil affairs, numerous difficulties occurred which have often been blamed erroneously upon the administrative machinery itself. Admittedly, internal management was frequently haphazard and did not follow the proven principles of public administration. Fiscal, structural, and personnel bottlenecks were constantly brushed aside and excused on the basis of their being inherent in all emergency and temporary organizations. As a result, these administrative rationalizations complicated the already difficult operational problems.

However, the chief consideration here is the relationship of the role of agencies to the overall framework within which civil affairs policy is formulated and implemented. An analysis of several major American occupations led to discounting the suggestion that agencies, in themselves, stand in the forefront of policy making forces. Instead, historically they have acted as a subordinate element within a much larger picture and operated as a secondary policy factor within the primary ingredient of individual leadership. Since they can be considered as extended elements of the individual, agencies are discussed here, first, in a decentralized context, and second, as a part of centralized control.

An official faced with a concrete problem cannot wait for an agency in Washington to debate the desirability of various alternatives. The problem is understandable, though not always excusable. A policy review can be, and usually is, a complicated and trying process. Official authorizations and directives must be based upon extensive consultation and study. A suggestion from the field can bring about a policy change only after the request has been read, passed upon, and changed probably by upwards of a dozen different department or bureau chiefs, each preparing recommendations in quadruplicate form. The collective brain can degenerate and become immersed in its own bureaucratic morass. Resultant delays, coupled with the agency's lack of fortune telling ability, can relegate the solution of the problem to those who operate in the field.

From the vantage point of the officer working directly with local civilians, Washington agencies and their problems are apt to seem remote and vague, and his immediate thought will be that the important organs on the theater level can be relied upon for assistance and guidance. The overall efficiency of these groups, and especially the speed with which they respond to local needs, is a major factor in shaping the attitude adopted by the field officers toward the theater agencies. Unfortunately, local commanders have been lucky if they obtained a policy decision or interpretation from the theater level before the situation was entirely out of hand. Consequently, a requirement for immediacy becomes a strong tool in placing policy matters on the shoulders of individual leaders rather than upon the higher organs which theoretically had the responsibility. Army officers have tended either to overestimate or to underestimate the capability of such bodies. They would prefer to take one side or the other, either to see them as superhuman collective brains that should be two steps ahead of every crisis, or to dismiss them as remote and esoteric and ignore their advice.

Despite inherent weaknesses which slow their functioning, the agencies ought to be expected to assume definite responsibilities. They should be held accountable for keeping abreast of the precise nature of the military involvement, understanding subtle changes which may be taking place during the course of the operation, and insuring a broad perspective of the overall situation. In order to achieve these goals, a thorough command of historical data on previous occupations and civil affairs actions is imperative. By proceeding from this basis, officials hopefully will realize that in each venture a consistency in policy direction must be sought.

Concordance is possible only if the agency is aware of how it fits into a comprehensive pattern. Merely possessing the official designation as a policy making body should not lead its officials to develop an inflated estimation of their role and capabilities, though they may well possess the power to issue directives and statements designed to amplify the decisions of the White House, Congress, and the State Department. Leaders in official positions must be cognizant that they themselves are seldom aware of the full impact of their directives until *after* an attempt has been made to implement them. The task of administrative machinery is to be sensitive to this fact by according due attention to reports received from the field as well as dealing with instructions handed down from higher levels.

On the basis of experience it should be apparent which requests emanating from lower headquarters merit serious evaluation and which ought to be discounted. Long delays can also be avoided, or at least minimized, if personnel know whether it is necessary to consult other agencies about a specific problem. However, to ask any administrative organ to make this decision presents difficulties since any modern military operation depends upon the support of a multiplicity of interrelated organizations. But the assumption of responsibilities, ideally, should replace the bickering and buck passing between and among agencies. Otherwise, the military sacrifices will be squandered.

Unfortunately, the record of agencies concerned with civil affairs is quite sad. As a rule, whenever more than one group had a chance to formulate policy, feuding, jealously, and inefficiency resulted. The examples are so numerous and tragicomic that some of them deserve recounting here to show the aggregate perspective.

Washington was the scene of a bitter dispute between military and civilian authorities during the Korean Conflict. Both the Army and the Mutual Security Administration (MSA) claimed primacy in the area of economic assistance for the Korean people. The military's position was that until fighting ceased no civilian agencies of consequence could be permitted to function within the combat zone unless they were under the strict guidance and discipline of Army units. MSA officials came into the picture by contending that they should have the authority to negotiate economic aid agreements with the Rhee Government. These civilian negotiators saw the situation in terms of possible political repercussions and of their own statutory authority to guide America's foreign aid programs. Bickering between the two groups continued until Congress finally intervened, but its ultimate decision did more to encourage the feud than to halt it. While supporting the Army's general position, Congress compromised the economic assistance appropriation by dividing it between the Pentagon and the civilian relief agency. The result was that no single body had unquestioned responsibility for planning a long-range solution.[51]

Modern bureaucratic organs are undoubtedly more prone to problems of duplication and overlapping of functions than were earlier and less complex organizational structures. Yet it would be a mistake to assume that a drastic reduction in the number of offices and the reversion to a simpler structure would magically eliminate the difficulty. The record of the management of earlier occupations belies this easy answer. For example, between 1862 and 1864 the Treasury Department issued, through officials in occupied Memphis, permits to trade in cotton. As a result, twenty to thirty million dollars worth of supplies were furnished to the Confederate Armies of the West by courtesy of the Union Treasury Department. General Sherman, while Military Governor of Memphis, attempted to halt the traffic, but he was soon moved out of the area to another field command, and the illegal movement began again. This allegedly occurred because of the laxity of the new Military Governor.[52]

During the Cuban occupation at the turn of the century, the Post Office Department and the Army had their difficulties. Cuban postal authorities were under the control of their Washington counterparts. This allowed the Military Governor on the island, General Leonard

Wood, only limited power over these local employees. When irregularities appeared in the Cuban Postal Service, Secretary of War Elihu Root directed Wood to correct these difficulties and take appropriate actions to insure that no future corruption occurred. The ensuing clash between Army occupation officials and civilian postal authorities over who held the power and was responsibile for the problem was horrendous. One direct consequence was that a high post office official was discharged; and further, even though Wood did not have charge of the mail service, he came close to dismissal simply by his association with the scandal.[53]

Probing another set of occupations, it is clear that the agency tangle during World War II was especially complicated because of President Roosevelt's personal influence and executive style. He recognized the perennial danger that confronts every Chief Executive, that of becoming a captive of his intimate advisors or, perhaps even worse, of becoming a devotee of the bureaucratic machine itself. In attempting to avoid these pitfalls the President used a divide-and-rule approach. Sometimes he reached directly into the operating agencies and solicited opinions from subordinate officials. This practice infuriated bureau chiefs, seriously disrupted the status system, and undermined working relationships within many administrative organs. FDR was also prone to give similar or nearly identical assignments to different existing agencies, or to create new groups that duplicated the work done by already functioning bodies.[54]

Showing favoritism toward a particular official or agency was another disconcerting habit developed by the Chief Executive. Since his personal support could be quite fickle, top-level administrators frequently had painfully short tenures. It might be assumed that this propensity would generate keen competition and strong efforts to please the Chief through the creating of brilliant policies. Unfortunately, the effect was quite different and it resulted in speculation and gossip regarding every agency's momentary standing with the White House. While these tactics employed by the Commander-in-Chief were enterprising and must in some senses be admired, they did not serve to make the groups responsible for occupation policy more harmonious or effective.

Despite the problem, civil affairs units in the field had at their disposal some basic policy directives issued by the highest levels in Washington. However, orders which emanated from the middle-level agencies, that should have given specific details of how to implement the higher directives, were often faulty or nonexistent. For example, during the Italian campaign instructions were received to close all fascist institutions. Carrying out this sweeping mandate would have halted the operations of most hospitals. Obviously, a middle-level body should have foreseen this problem and accommodated Washington's wishes to the practical need to maintain local health services. But since this was not done, individual officers were forced to use their own judgment and decide either to obey or to disregard the order.[55]

Another illustration of a middle-level agency's failure to assume responsibility involved the denazification program pursued in postwar Germany. John Gimbel indicated that the wholesale purging of low ranking German civil service personnel was both ill-advised and ineffective. In one case he reported that a specialist in municipal government was able to continue his duties even though he had been officially removed by American authorities. To circumvent his dismissal the city appointed his wife as a clerk in his former office, where she merely functioned as a courier. Thus, the purged official worked on the city's files and correspondence at home, while an inexperienced administrator chosen by MG authorities filled a chair at the office. Eventually, this American appointee gained courage and hired the purged official back into the office as a minor employee. Unexpectedly, the approved politician died, whereupon the commander of the U. S. unit ordered the purged official dismissed again. The city council then voted to give him six months retroactive salary for his services. Similar instances were apparently not unusual and Gimbel concluded that "Numerous examples testify to the fact that long friendships and loyalties . . . were not broken up by military government directives which divided Germans into 'Nazis' and 'non-Nazis.'"[56] Again, recognition of human predispositions by the middle-level groups would have prevented much trouble.

Although the Army has on occasions had difficulty with the Post Office Department, the Mutual Security Administration, and with almost all middle-level agencies, its most persistent quarrel has been with the Department of State. Records abound with illustrations, some of which should be recounted to show the bitterness between the two, the different approach each adopted, and the ultimate harm their friction caused occupation efforts. An instance of the serious nature of interdepartmental bickering occurred in 1943 and 1944 during the meetings of the Washington coordinating group referred to as the Supply Subcommittee. While the structure of this group seems confused, it contained representatives from the War Department, the State Department, and the independent wartime agency. To be specific, this organ was a subordinate part of the Combined Civil Affairs Committee (CCAC), which was itself a part of the War Department's Civil Affairs Division (CAD). Supply Subcommittee (CCAC(S)) included representatives from (1) the State Department, (2) from the Army's Civil Affairs Division, and (3) from an independent agency titled the Foreign Economic Administration (FEA). The latter being a part of the Office of Emergency Management (OEM). These conferees attempted to solve major substantive civil affairs issues.

A prolonged controversy in this committee concerned the purchase, transportation, and distribution of relief supplies which would be needed in France and the Low Countries after the D-Day invasion. Agricultural items, especially those needed for planting, became a severe bottleneck. Army spokesmen contended that its facilities could only handle those supplies most urgently needed to prevent disease and unrest, and that seeds and fertilizers were not included in this category. The State Department disagreed. It, along with FEA, held that farmers had to obtain these materials to support the local population. Obviously convinced that its position was correct, the military imposed an additional obstacle by vaguely alluding to transportation priorities. Should the FEA purchase agricultural items of relief supplies in question from its own budget the War Department would not guarantee shipping space. Since all cargo vessels were under military control, the implication for the civilian agency was that the consignments purchased by FEA might remain on the docks for an indefinite period.

At this point the Army did make a gesture toward compromise by suggesting that it might consent to buy, with its own money, some seed and fertilizer and ship them to Europe. However, it insisted that these items were to be sold on a strictly cash basis to the receiving nations. State Department people protested again, arguing that the European countries were bankrupt and that it was ridiculous to attach a pay-as-you-go condition to the program. While the negotiators bickered in Washington over this one point, occupation officials overseas individually had to find creative ways to prevent starvation.[57]

Another illustration of the disagreements between the War and State Departments occurred during the Dumbarton Oaks Conference of 1944. In this instance, the State Department wanted the conferees to begin discussion on the question of postwar boundaries for the yet to be occupied countries. However, the Joint Chiefs of Staff brought sufficient pressure to bear to block such talks for fear that Allied unity in the war effort might be weakened.[58] Again, a long and costly delay ensued. When the time should have been used for cooperative planning, it was consumed by sparring agencies unable to find a compromise.

The Combined Committee for North Africa (CCNA) was one more noteworthy body which tried to perform a policy making role while dissension reigned. This episode started when American forces occupied Algiers and civil affairs officers attached to General Eisenhower's headquarters arrived on the scene. They took up their posts and began functioning in accordance with the theater commander's directives but immediately encountered a complication. It seemed that Washington and Algiers could not settle upon a mutually satisfactory policy. Yet, the administration of Algiers was officially the responsibility of the CCNA, which was headed by a Special Assistant to the Secretary of State. Situated in Washington, this Combined Committee of civilian officials was in the impossible position of directing an occupation by remote control. The civil affairs officers from Eisenhower's staff were also in the awkward predicament of having their authority constantly questioned.

Communications quickly became a primary complaint of the field representatives and the home office of the CCNA. This was not surprising since all dispatches had to be channeled through military message centers. As a result, officials who perhaps wished to insure that the military's staff had as much policy making power as possible were in a manipulative position. A suggestion that the Army deliberately tampered with the transmission of information and instructions between CCNA Headquarters in Washington and its field office in North Africa has never been confirmed. However, Professor Walter Millis implies as much when he notes that the Army had what amounted to a veto power over all dispatches sent and received in Algiers.[59]

In addition to CCNA, several other agencies with headquarters in Washington sent delegations to Algiers. Their function was to proffer advice and counsel to Eisenhower's staff and sometimes to play a part in the actual implementation of specific programs. They represented bodies as diverse as the State Department, Lend-Lease Administration, Board of Economic Warfare, Treasury Department, and the Office of Economic Relief and Rehabilitation. Some staff members brought with them brief cases filled with data and instructions, while others arrived without any clear notion as to what they were supposed to accomplish. Most, however, appeared to have the attitude that Army civil affairs personnel should be responsive to their suggestions.

Their sincerity and dedication cannot be questioned; yet, it was difficult for them to argue that their judgment was superior to that of the military governors who had been handling civilians since the invasion. Instances of overeagerness and tactlessness prompted a defensive and resentful reaction among CAMG officials. The result was a series of unpleasant altercations which served to confuse an already complicated situation.

When civilian officials held influential posts in Washington, it was questionable as to whether the theater commander had any effective jurisdiction over their activities. Walter Millis suggests that the North African operation became so congested and fragmented that something had to be done to enforce a reasonable degree of coordination.[60] Robert D. Murphy, who had previously gained a firsthand knowledge of the region as a career Foreign Service Officer, headed Eisenhower's Civil Affairs Section in Algiers. Though he had the confidence of the military leaders, he lacked the authority to curb the excessive intrusions.

The problem was thought to be alleviated when on December 18, 1942, Roosevelt appointed Murphy as his personal representative in North Africa with the rank of Minister. In this capacity he had unquestioned supervisory authority over the field operations of all civilian agencies. Unfortunately, Murphy's ability to deal with the situation was hampered by the multiplicity of roles which had been assigned to him. Besides being the President's personal representative for civil affairs, he was also the political advisor to Eisenhower, the President's emissary to the French leaders, and an officer in the State Department's Foreign Service. His difficulties were worsened when the British decided to bring along their own political and economic missions. And the final blow fell when FDR made a number of personal and unrecorded commitments to the French at the Casablanca Conference regarding relief measures for Northern Africa.[61]

From a policy standpoint it is instructive to observe the next step taken by U.S. Government officials as they attempted to untangle the North African civil affairs muddle. They adopted an approach which was repeated on later occasions when problems in other regions demanded action. Using typical Washington know-how, the corrective device resorted to was the creation of a new and additional agency to coordinate and integrate the work of the existing bodies. Following an appeal from Eisenhower's headquarters, John J. McCloy was sent to Algiers for the specific purpose of analyzing the situation and recommending a workable solution.

McCloy was in a commanding position since he was an Assistant Secretary of War and had the personal confidence of the President. He recommended the establishment of a North African Economic Board which was to be headed by the multidutied Murphy. This coordinating group was to be assigned the task of integrating the relief efforts of American military and civilian agencies with those of the French and the British. Unfortunately, the efforts of this new organ were essentially unproductive. While helping to alleviate minor frictions, the Board was unable to find satisfactory answers in cases where conflicting policy guidance came from different offices in Washington.[62]

Inter-agency feuds had been a common occurrence in past occupations, and better advanced planning for North Africa might have been expected. As the first major civil affairs operation of the war, it was certain to be a closely watched proving ground. Secrecy surrounding the choice of the region to be invaded doubtless made posthostility planning more difficult. However, this alone cannot be used as the excuse for the prolonged confusion and indecision. Agencies must share in the blame.

A larger task, of course, was charting relief and rehabilitation programs on a global basis. Characteristically, the War Department and civilian agencies in the nation's capital claimed primacy. In June 1943 the Office of Foreign Economic Coordination (OFEC) was established. Operating under the direction of the Department of State, it was to cooperate with the War, Navy, and Treasury Departments in economic assistance matters. It also was to bring together representatives of the Board of Foreign Relief, the Lend-Lease Administration, and the Office of Foreign Relief and Rehabilitation Operations. The OFEC, besides, was to appoint to each combat theater a single delegate who would represent all the various groups which were directly concerned. However, the OFEC was dissolved by Executive Order in September of the same year after little had actually been accomplished.[63]

Displaying no discouragement, the Executive Order which dissolved the OFEC created in its stead the Office of Foreign Economic Administration (FEA) which also was placed under the guidance of the State Department. This order formally merged the Board of Economic Warfare, the Lend-Lease Administration, and the Office of

Foreign Relief and Rehabilitation Operations. Clarity in coordination had triumphed, but only two months later in November 1943 FDR sent a letter to the Secretary of War which once again muddled efficiency. The President shifted the direction of the entire civilian relief effort from the State Department to the Army. Further evidencing his confidence in the War Department, Roosevelt extended its authority over reconstruction activities to include the first six months after the close of the conflict.[64]

As the war progressed, coordinated policy planning by Washington agencies improved somewhat. In March 1943 the Army's Civil Affairs Division (CAD) was created, and its powers were gradually increased until it became the undisputed joint Army-Navy body for policy.[65] Simultaneously, the Department of State established the Special Office for Occupied Areas and gave to it responsibility for coordinating the activities of civilian groups involved in civil affairs programs. Still, the most important decisions were typically reached outside the coordinated agencies. The only sure instance where basic policy was developed by a coordinated body was in the case of the initial post-surrender policy for Japan. This came from the Subcommittee for the Far East of the State-War-Navy Coordinating Committee (SWNCC (FE)).

Coordinated agencies were given two equally important duties. One was to develop a single integrated civil affairs effort, and the other was to translate the basic national goals into workable directives. They did an average job in the first area, but their record in furnishing meaningful guidance to the field was a dismal failure. The standard quip in postwar Europe that the *New York Times* was a more up-to-date and accurate source for directives than the official communications from Washington agencies was frequently true.

To this point we have been concerned primarily with instances in which administrative organs played a role in civil affairs operations which were characterized by decentralized leadership. Professor Ernest R. May's succinct comment that "Coordination is no substitute for thought," [66] is cuttingly descriptive of the underlying cause of agency failure.

An examination of U. S. occupations suggests that agency problems were less conspicuous when a system of centralized control was established. While the administrative structures were not inherently superior, they had less opportunity to obstruct policy. Certainly, they committed their share of blunders, but when centralized control was utilized the policy vacuum was filled by a strong leader. For example, it is difficult to imagine General MacArthur being intimidated by even the most complex of bureaucratic arrangements.

Also, in the Siberian Intervention centralization eliminated much of the agency bungling in policy matters. Here General Graves refused to be hamstrung when higher authorities could not reach an agreement concerning the question of the official recognition of the Kolchak government. He ordered his forces to remain neutral and refused to support the new regime. Justifying his independent attitude as a policy issue, he pointed in his autobiography to a key passage in Wilson's *Aide Memoire*.

"The following part of the policy will bear repeating as it governed the American troops during their entire nineteen months in Siberia; viz., the solemn assurance to the people of Russia, in the most public and solemn manner that none of the Governments uniting in action in either Siberia or in Northern Russia contemplates any interference of any kind with the political sovereignty of Russia, any interference in the internal affairs [of that country]." [67] To Graves the assurance of noninterference was explicit and irrevocable, except upon the direct order of the President.

The Kolchak controversy posed a direct challenge to Graves when the State Department attempted to dictate and change overall policy. At the time, State Department representation in Siberia was exercised through Roland S. Morris, who received his instructions directly from his superiors in Washington. On one occasion the State Department sent Morris a wire stating that the Kolchak Government was to be accorded diplomatic recognition. When Morris approached Graves with this policy order, the general not only refused to apply the new directive, but also succinctly brushed the entire State Department aside with the following retort:

Morris: "The State Department is running this, not the War Department."

Graves: "The State Department is not running me." [68]

Whenever the agency question is involved, it is difficult to assess whether the centralized or decentralized pattern of leadership is the most desirable. A significant advantage of central control is that a decision, be it right or wrong, is made and there is no doubt who made it. If a general goes too far in establishing his own policy in isolation from Washington authorities, the White House can remove him. In a decentralized situation it is hard to get a decision as well as trace down the originating official. There are always heroes willing to step forward if the policy is successful, but when failure ensues cubbyholes are available in most agencies where villians can hide. On the other side of the coin, centralized direction loses some of its appeal because of its authoritarian and arbitrary character. The policy decision can be just as wrong when made by one person as when made through the interaction of several bodies. Besides, a danger exists that when the complex process of discussion of alternatives is minimized or neglected the best course of action is often missed.

Problems of agency malfunctions could be minimized by specifically allocating the policy making function to a clearly identified group. Unfortunately, a precise pinpointing of responsibility would be as difficult to sustain as to establish. Competing groups can always put forth arguments justifying their right to share in formulating decisions. Another critical factor is often overlooked when disputes over policy jurisdiction erupt. Officials who deal directly with local populations need assurance that it is practical to place their faith in the organizations which are presumed to be capable of providing prompt and knowledgeable guidance.

TRAINING AND THE POLICY QUESTION

A systematic technique for adequately preparing personnel is a principal requisite for improving the quality of America's civil affairs effort. Thoroughly trained professionals are a must item for commanders who work with foreign nationals. In turn, it is obligatory that combat leaders recognize that these specialists can make a substantial contribution, and that they deserve maximum administrative support. When these two conditions are realized a new generation of modernized and streamlined occupation agencies can be envisioned.

How easy it is to prescribe a simple treatment for a complex malady. Yet without exploring the questions involved, such suggestions offer little more help than numerous other timeworn clichês. They are in the same category as "provide better teachers for school systems and education will improve," and "elect better officials and state legislatures will be more effective."

Numerous writers cited earlier, as well as officials who have discussed the situation with us, hold firm opinions about civil affairs training. Occupation posts, some suggest, should be filled by people from public service professions, men such as city managers, mayors, and social workers. But it is difficult enough to put these specialists into uniform during a major war, let alone when lesser emergencies

arise. The more experienced municipal employees and elected officials are usually older men who have such essential positions that their
home communities would suffer because of their prolonged absence.
Other than during a declared major conflict it is impractical for the
Army now to rely heavily upon these individuals, although it has done
so in the past.

Increasingly, the Army has found it advisable to maintain on active
duty a wider array of specialists, including some for civil affairs. The
Korean Conflict caught the military unprepared on this score and
forced the conscription of reserve units and individual experts. The
year 1961 ushered in the Berlin Crisis, which again necessitated calling
up the reserves for additional manpower; but Pentagon leaders were
beginning to realize that too much dependence had been placed upon
the inactive CA forces. Congressional legislation and Executive
Orders imposed an additional restriction upon recruitment by limiting
the recall of reservists during small wars. New requirements for countering the communist wars of national liberation have demanded the
expanded use of the professional soldier.

The traditional role of the CAMG reserves may have changed
unalterably. In the light of the current situation, the procedures for
procuring specialists by mobilizing reserve units seems obsolete and
unrealistic. This is a strong assertion, but we believe it to be the
unavoidable meaning behind the changing personnel picture of the
past decade. A possible exception exists in the case of a small number
of highly trained men whose professions make it possible for them
to accept assignments as small war mobilization designees. These
reserve officers must be in a position to move into and out of uniform
without disrupting unduly their personal careers. It will be difficult
to locate competent specialists willing to leave their homes and
jobs for periodic active duty tours. Members of this new citizens'
auxiliary must henceforth assume that they will be called during
lesser crises. Hopefully, these people can be drawn primarily from
the federal civil service, research institutions, and foundations which
specialize in foreign affairs.

Experiences from previous mobilizations have pointed up the many
problems and difficulties encountered in using civilian leaders as military governors during national emergencies. Rigorous requirements
of health and physical stamina present a continuing perplexity, especially since there is an insistence that these temporary officers must
be trained first as soldiers and second as functional specialists. The
question of what constituted the proper emphasis upon physical

conditioning generated some of the more heated criticisms of the World War II training programs.

Having an average age of about forty-five, many likely candidates who were highly skilled experts in civilian life had not engaged in strenuous physical activity for several years. Sergeants from the combat branches, who were frequently placed in charge of physical training classes, had little sensitivity regarding the background of the individuals or the nature of the specialized mission they were to perform. Many officers were sent home from Europe because of heart conditions which probably had been aggravated through overexertion in training.[69] And undoubtedly others were left with physical scars which became serious only after a latent period. To accuse those in charge of having had a callous attitude would be unfair, but the prevading climate of near hysteria which surrounded the development of training programs does warrant censure.

Hopefully, this will not happen again, since more practical knowledge is now available. Training experiences of new organizations, such as the Agency for International Development and the Peace Corps, provide fresh ideas which have applicability to civil affairs. Consequently, the repetition of past mistakes by the Army would be inexcusable. Whether the future need concerns supplying personnel for a small war or a world war, training centers possess the potential for achieving a new level of effectiveness in their programs.

Highlights of previous civil affairs experiences can portray the relationship between the training predicament and military occupation policy. Though assigned MG duties as early as the Mexican War, the Army did not acknowledge the need for a special instructional program until the Second World War. In 1942 a School for Military Government was established, but its facilities soon proved inadequate.[70] Originally it was estimated that about six thousand officers would be trained, yet by 1946 over twelve thousand had graduated from its courses.

The primary burden for preparing most of the officers was assumed by the Civil Affairs Training Programs inaugurated during the summer and fall of 1943 on ten university campuses.[71] Headed by civilian directors chosen by the university officials, the Civil Affairs Training Schools (CATS) proved quite successful except for the insufficient number of men trained. Although coordination between the soldiers and the educators sometimes presented difficulty, a general atmosphere of cooperation prevailed.

These programs had many elements in common with the original

Peace Corps's system for preparing Volunteers; both involved the need for close cooperation between the university and federal agencies. Being temporary, they were designed to insure the continued autonomy of the college. Another similarity was that budgeting and administration were under the control of a non-academic branch of the university which had a direct channel to the campus president. Parallel reasons for disagreements between federal officials and university administrators also developed in both programs and discord often centered around the question of the instructional approach which should be utilized and the competence of professors chosen by the university to conduct the courses.

As mentioned earlier, the Army started its own School for Military Government. Situated on the campus of the University of Virginia in Charlottesville, it functioned directly under the control of the military and inevitably retained the distinct flavor of a traditional Army school. Unlike the CATS centers, its goal was to train officers to fill high level staff positions on the theater level and in other major commands. Emphasis was placed upon the subjects of military organization and procedures which were believed applicable to any theater where the student might eventually be assigned. By the nature of its program, therefore, the Charlottesville school did not represent a major departure from the Army's standard technique for officer training.

In contrast, the programs conducted by the universities stressed language and area studies. The subject matter closely resembled courses which were part of the normal academic curriculum, and instruction was designed to prepare students for specific assignments in Europe and the Far East. Prior to reporting to the university, the CATS student received one month of instruction at Fort Custer, Michigan. This consisted of military indoctrination, physical training, and a survey of general military government problems. The university programs for the European theater were ended in early 1944, while those for the Far East continued for another year. In August 1945, all major training centers, including Charlottesville, were closed. During 1946, however, the shortage of occupation officers became sufficiently acute that the Army was forced to open a temporary School for Government of Occupied Areas at Carlisle Barracks, Pennsylvania.

Shortcomings can be cited showing instances where training could have been more effective. However, there is agreement that the officers who received formal training performed more ably than those who were assigned directly to CA units without having had such instruction. Professor Zink indicated that most military leaders who had earlier doubted the value of specialized education came to appreciate it.[72]

The single most serious training deficiency was the graduates' weakness in the knowledge of language, customs, and behavior patterns of foreign populations. Officers frequently had a good start toward mastering a language when they finished the formal course of training, but through failure to continue practicing while awaiting overseas assignments much was forgotten. This situation could have been overcome by closer attention to the student's needs. However, little could have been done to counter the private jokes which were repeated everywhere that those taught Japanese would surely be sent to Germany, and *vice versa.*

Language instruction provided in the CATS programs could not be judged totally adequate when compared with the caliber available during the 1960's because instructional techniques have been improved substantially during the intervening years. Neither the Army nor universities had developed by World War II a standardized system for mass training in linguistics. Individual teachers sometimes followed their own personal whims without fully appreciating the practical overseas requirements. Where more obscure tongues and dialects had to be taught, few qualified instructors were available anywhere within the United States. And the extent to which the language phase was inadequate could be traced directly to the pre-World War II university curriculum in America. The academic community had neglected its responsibility to modernize the teaching of foreign languages.

In the field of area studies, however, the responsibility for shortcomings in training stemmed principally from Army bungling. It is common knowledge today that civil affairs specialists sent overseas frequently lacked sufficient information concerning the political, economic, and social conditions of the regions to which they were assigned. Needless bureaucratic tangles and red tape caused by the Army and other governmental bodies created many problems. Coordination between military agencies broke down with the result that valuable training materials were wasted and misused. For example, the University of Michigan conducted an extensive study of conditions which might be anticipated upon the occupation of several of the German states. Somehow this valuable data was not made available to civil affairs students destined to serve in those states.[73] This mistake might have been forgiven had the materials eventually been sent overseas. Unfortunately, research data, including portions of the Michigan study, were often never forwarded.

Professors teaching the area studies courses were severely handicapped by the scarcity of information on current happenings overseas. Much of their material was based upon prewar sources and therefore outdated. While the Army was preparing officers for difficult assignments, it seemed unwilling or unable to take action to remedy the situation. On occasions, instructors were forced to rely upon journalistic accounts appearing in popular magazines for resource data.[74] This created an extremely frustrating predicament for faculty and students alike; and these difficulties were compounded since many of the most able professors who were experts in foreign affairs were in uniform elsewhere and unavailable for classes.

Gradually the situation improved. Beginning in 1943, CAMG officers who had gained experience in the early phases of the North African, Sicilian, and Italian campaigns were returned to act as instructors in the various training centers.[75] They contributed firsthand accounts of common situations which the students might later meet, as well as imparting an informal working knowledge of the current situation in specific occupied regions. With these added insights, the graduates were leaving the schools with much more information at their disposal. Paralleling the improvement in the caliber of lectures, worthwhile research was being conducted in conjunction with the preparation of MG specialists. Scholars were preparing a series of occupation handbooks which described each country where significant operations were anticipated. Seventeen handbooks were issued for each region likely to be overrun; and they contained current data on a wide range of political and social problems.[76] They were invaluable as teaching aids and later as operational guides overseas.

As the occupations were terminated, formal training programs passed into oblivion. The Provost Marshal General's School (PMGS) was given the obligation of maintaining the nation's capability in civil affairs, but it took only a minimal interest until 1950, when it reinstituted a specific course which was offered by its Military Government Department. The end of this dormant period coincided with the new demands created by the Korean Conflict.

In addition, formal training was provided from 1950 through 1953 at various temporary centers which were activated on military installations. While the Korean War was in progress, Washington leaders recognized that special preparation for civil affairs personnel was desirable. But as the combat situation stabilized, the number of men needed diminished and the temporary training facilities, which were supplementing the PMGS, were closed.

Following the end of hostilities in 1953, the training picture remained bleak for two years. Then, in 1955, a major change took place when the Military Government Department was divorced from its parent agency, accorded autonomy, and designated the U.S. Army Civil Affairs and Military Government School. When it welcomed its first class, its staff consisted of only a handful of instructors and its few officers and classrooms were located on the same post where the School had previously functioned as a subordinate organ. Relations between the fledgling facility and the large and proud PMGS organization were exceedingly cordial and cooperative. In fact, it was suspected that the PM people were as pleased to be rid of their maverick stepchild as the civil affairs people were delighted with their new independence.

A Pentagon reorganization ordered in 1958 resulted in the upgrading of the training facility's status from a Class II to a Class I type activity, and provided for substantial expansion of both its staff and physical plant. The next year a further advance was made when its name was changed to U. S. Army Civil Affairs School (USACAS), the title it still retains.[77] These significant moves were undertaken by top leadership in response to a number of pressures, not the least of which was the influence of domestic politics. Powerful interest groups and politically influential reserve officers were lobbying in both the Pentagon and Congress on behalf of a strong civil affairs branch.[78]

However, it is impossible to know what would have happened to the USACAS had not the communists launched their campaign of insurgency in the late 1950's. It might eventually have been reabsorbed into a larger center, probably the PMGS or the Judge Advocate General's School. Perhaps it would have been abolished quietly when its civilian patrons retired from the Army Reserve and the National Guard. Certainly, the 1958 strengthening of civil affairs training was a reversal of the historic pattern of peacetime neglect and was the signal for a reappraisal of the cold war potential of the CAMG function. Since that date about seven thousand American officers, in addition to several hundred representatives of some twenty-four foreign nations, have attended the CA School.

Alterations in the organization of civil affairs training schools have made possible a greater flexibility in the subjects taught. But of even greater importance, changes in the content of training programs have reflected a process of maturing. When formal instruction was revived in 1950, it closely resembled the World War II concept. The new curriculum constituted an attempt to embody the better features of both the Charlottesville program and the CATS projects. An emphasis upon teaching civil affairs staff procedures was favored. Nevertheless, efforts were made to include area studies segments within broader courses. While the Korean War was in progress, special consideration was given to familiarizing officers with the more important characteristics of that country.

The limited ability and experience of the instructional staff made the operation of an effective area studies program exceedingly difficult. While some instructors had excellent credentials, others were career combat officers who were assigned to the School as a "broadening" experience in their career pattern. It was not unusual for the latter to lack both background and interest in civil affairs. During this period in which they were gaining on-the-job training, they were ill-prepared to conduct classes for students.

Lesson plans and instructional materials, particularly those relating to area studies and academic subjects, were often researched and written by reserve officers who were on active duty with the School for two week tours each year. While differences in points of view between the full-time instructors and the part-time reservists occurred occasionally, a practical working relationship and a feeling of mutual respect generally prevailed. At that juncture in the School's history, both groups were equally vital to its continued existence. The informal and impromptu attitude at the School did have advantages, and the atmosphere was uninhibiting, fostering a free exchange of ideas. This afforded the authors an invaluable opportunity for discussion and study of training and its relationship to overall policy.

Our conclusion was that civil affairs training centers of the future would probably adopt one of two basic approaches, or perhaps a combination of both. Under the first, training would be organized along rather conventional lines. This shall be termed the Generalist View. Representing a plan which has long been accepted and promoted by the military academies and leadership schools for higher ranking officers, it is based upon the premise that all Army officers require the ability to deal with the maximum number and type of different situations. These leaders should be combat officers first but also possess the experience to serve effectively in a variety of administrative positions. For example, the infantry officer should be able to perform well as a commander of troops, administrator of a supply depot, professor of military science, manager of a post exchange, or commander of a civil affairs unit. Ideally, the generalist is a man of all talents. Generalists often see themselves as a pipeline for transmitting policy directives from the combat commander to the civilian population. This scheme for developing skills has been championed by career officers.

The second approach to training can be called the Specialist View. This opinion generally found favor among reserve officers and those career officers who intermittently had been assigned to civil affairs. As might be expected, the reservists thought of training in terms of their own civilian career requisites. This part-time contingent included a substantial number of educators and governmental officials who had had World War II occupation experience. Physicians, engineers, attorneys, police officers, and business executives naturally saw themselves as specialists. Typically, they believed it possible to make the greatest contribution by performing civil affairs functions which paralleled their civilian professions.

They urged that training should be technically oriented and patterned after the approach followed by the specialized branches of the Army. Taking their cue from organizations such as the Medical Corps, Corps of Engineers, Chemical Corps, and Judge Advocate General's Branch, some of the reserve people considered the traditional generalist to be an outmoded relic unable to face technological advances. An ideal CA unit was considered to be a loosely knit structure existing for the purpose of helping assigned experts perform their professional tasks. Combat commanders were expected to permit them wide individual latitude with a minimum of interference.

While the large issue has been the policy role of the individual officer, it has usually been debated circumspectly in other realms, especially training. In part, its implications extend to the future practicability of civilian supremacy in policy matters. The arguments, cloaked in the debate over training, can be examined by probing the generalist and specialist concepts. Generalists held that civil affairs functions were the responsibility of all officers, regardless of branch. The specialists have instead emphasized the capabilities of those people who understand the politics of government.

Those who argue for specialization point out that the experience of past occupations clearly demonstrates the need for skilled practitioners. Managing or overseeing of a civilian society is inherently different from the execution of a military campaign. While admittedly the latter demands a high degree of professionalism, it is expecting too much to assume that the typical soldier will understand the intricacies of complex civilian problems unless he has had intensive advance preparation. Whether the career officer wishes it or not, by merely being assigned to this type of unit he takes on the role of an expert.

To be effective, his level of technical competence must be on a par with that of his professional counterpart in the occupied country. For example, if he is dealing with the mayor of a small village, it is essential that he have an equivalent political knowledge. This skill may be developed through formal school courses. The officer working with civilian leaders and populations requires a minimum competence in one or more areas which relate directly to the health, welfare, and progress of the local community.

University sponsored training projects of World War II concentrated upon governmental problems which would be encountered overseas. According to the argument for specialization, these were pointed in the right dirction. However, in recent efforts to prepare personnel for civic action duty, both school facilities and on-the-job training have been used instead of limiting education to course work offered at training centers. Apparently each has complemented and reinforced the other to the general benefit of the operation. The USACAS has inaugurated a series of courses to meet the personnel requirements; and after it became apparent that the civic action duties would extend over a prolonged period, several officers with field experience were assigned as instructors. It is still too early to know whether the current emphasis upon specialization is a temporary expedient or whether it reflects something more permanent.

Those trained in the traditional military pattern find objection to the specialist approach. They believe it would be a mistake to encourage the development of an independent-minded, self-styled corps of specialists, an elite. Barring a major war and a call-up of reserve experts, career officers will be the ones having to deal with foreign civilians. Consequently, training should be keyed primarily to their needs. They conclude that the World War II Charlottesville program with its emphasis upon staff problems and general considerations, such as the requirements of international law, would best prepare the Army for its work.

Students of national security who have been associated with civil affairs over the years or have otherwise taken a special interest in the field were perturbed by events of the early 1960's which involved the Special Forces question. Officials in civil affairs and related Army agencies had expended time and effort on basic studies aimed at finding ways for better utilizing the military's resources in dealing with civilians in underdeveloped nations. Though often imperfect and quite speculative, their work did represent a fundamental contribution. New ground was broken in areas which had hitherto been neglected. The development of the civic action concept was one such advance. Special Forces leaders liberally borrowed these CA ideas and techniques, which in time became the characteristics which set these units apart from the standard Army structure. The drive and ingenuity demonstrated here merits compliment. However, it was inevitable that grumbling, jealously, and hostility would result when Special Forces public relations exponents began capitalizing upon techniques such as civic action and counterinsurgency.

Senior commanders and their subordinates in the conventional combat arms suspected that a concerted and improper propaganda campaign had been set in motion by a handful of middle-level officers who somehow felt themselves superior to the rest of the officer corps. Bucking the system from the inside was one thing. But an attempt to reach directly the President, civilian leaders, and the general public and to persuade them that Special Forces represented an *avant-garde* which had the answer to winning the war in Vietnam and similar conflicts was quite a different matter. Recrimination was bound to follow when the Special Forces people were unable to live up to the impossible claims which had been made on their behalf. If the new units had been able to solve the problem of insurgency, perhaps many of the Army's specialized agencies including civil affairs would have been absorbed into an enlarged Special Forces structure. But when it became obvious that success in Vietnam would require a much wider commitment of conventional ground troops, the Green Beret lost much of its prestige and influence.

The reaction in military circles seemed to be directed as much against the idea of elitism itself as it was against the individuals who had championed the Special Forces concept. As related to civil affairs, the reaction meant that many officers and civilian officials who had been outspoken advocates of specialization and of their own separate branch became less vocal and in several cases actually reversed their positions.

This series of events is likely to have a subtle though profound impact upon any decisions made by top leadership regarding the future role played by CA people in overall military policy. If the idea becomes widely accepted that the creation of a corps of professional administrators will cause threat to the established military leadership pattern, the type of hostility once directed against Special Forces could be focused upon civil affairs. While they are basically different in concept, both possess the potential of development into major specialties. When specialists become elitists, a threat emerges which cannot be ignored.

The root of the concern for policy may actually lie in the implications of the question of political education. It can be argued that the political ability of the official is the single most important skill required by the civil administrator. In any case, it ranks in significance with technical competence. The specialist in agronomy or public health may be expert in his narrow field yet be as naive politically as the ancient cavalry officer. Political judgment and acumen are exceedingly difficult qualities to define or measure except by observing the relative success or failure of the practitioners. America's record of military occupations demonstrates aptly the value of civil affairs officials being sensitive to subtle forces both overseas and at home which affect policy.

However, to accept the idea that political power on the part of officers is desirable is in itself a controversial matter. To countless citizens and numerous governmental leaders the thought of the Army launching a program openly involving political education of officers raises the specter of an insidious threat to the hallowed principle of civilian supremacy.

Americans quake a bit when they face the possibility of large contingents of the military professionals being taught the art of power manipulation in government. The question of whether this reaction is reasonable or irrational is complex. Louis Smith has traced the evolution of the American tradition of civil dominance to forces which have been a part of the national scene since the period before the Revolution.⁷⁹ And there has developed an ingrained popular distrust of the military establishment *per se*.

Army leaders have always been wary of any actions which stimulated suspicion that they were promoting programs containing distinct political elements. This hesitancy has included training. For example, during the late 1950's and early 1960's the Fort Gordon School devoted attention to the area of political education for civil affairs personnel. A Cold War Course was developed and incorporated into the curriculum in order to provide systematic instruction in world problems, especially the tactics and strategy of the international communist movement. It was difficult to dispute the suggestion that officers in both the active and reserve components could profit from a better understanding of these current issues. Yet the task of organizing and presenting a meaningful course in this politically charged and academically complex area posed serious difficulties.

Many authorities on military policy believe that political education must be introduced into the Army curriculum if the U. S. wishes to achieve maximum effectiveness from its participation in occupations and civil affairs. It would be unfair if this side of the issue were not recounted. The reasonableness of this position is aptly demonstated through a recitation of past experiences where officers lacked knowledge of political situations. Instances of naivete have taken several typical forms in occupations.

Observers have pointed to the inept use of propaganda materials aimed at regions to be occupied or already occupied. The highly respected Robert W. Komer reported, for example, that pre-invasion propaganda for Sicily contained exaggerated claims that the Americans would immediately remedy the serious food shortage. Inability to deliver on this implied promise left the inhabitants disappointed and angry and stirred resentment and resistance against the Allies.[80]

Propaganda failures were often the result of errors of omission as well as the consequences of unwise actions. Even when made-to-order issues were present, occupation officials frequently did not appreciate their value and captilize on them in time. For example, James P. Pappas noted that in the public health field definite steps were taken to improve local conditions. Though this was far in excess of the expectations of the civilians, few serious attempts were made to publicize these contributions.[81] Another illustration can be drawn from postwar Japan. Robert B. Textor charges that at one point books sufficient to stock eight libraries were resting unused in warehouses while trained librarians were marking time in Tokyo eagerly awaiting the opportunity to serve the American effort.[82] And thus the propaganda effect of these books was needlessly lost. Perhaps the U.S. Information Service will assume part of the propaganda function of civilian administrators.

Political immaturity led to other mistakes. Since officials generally chose to adopt a hands-off attitude they offered little counsel to labor unions, political parties, and other vital local organizations. In occupied Italy, for example, the political parties and the labor unions, whose cooperation was essential, were infiltrated with communists to the point where it was nearly impossible to operate the government without acceding to their demands. Yet, U. S. authorities often were unwilling or unable to recognize that their own failure to play a strong hand was helping neither America nor Italy.[83]

Opportunities among youth were also missed. The new generation of Japanese was desperately in need of information as to how the principles of democracy could be applied effectively to the economic and social problems that faced their country. When the youth saw that the Americans seemed much more interested in organizing sports, recreation, and similar "campfire" activities, many probably wondered if the occupiers themselves felt that democracy was worth talking about.[84]

Again, when occupation officials spoke before gatherings of sophisticated Japanese or European leaders, the Americans could not begin to compete with the best local politicians in the audience. Too often U. S. spokesmen failed to have the information and background necessary to make a knowledgeable presentation. Their embarrassment was especially acute when pointed questions from the floor revealed their ignorance of the workings of America's own political system. Such performances were probably very comforting to local leaders who naturally surmised that the U. S. had little intention of enforcing basic changes in their way of doing things. Otherwise, Washington certainly would have assigned occupation officials who were political professionals.

Carl Dreher, among others, found it appalling that American occupying forces actually did not understand the intricacies of democracy any better than they did the subtleties of communism. It never occurred "to them that communist organization, zeal, planning and willingness to sacrifice individual interests for collective ends" was a major factor to be reckoned with. And it could be "countered only by a corresponding constructive passion on the part of the citizens of the democracies, and specifically themselves." [85]

Dealing with leaders of political institutions overseas continues to be a vital part of the Army's present activities. If the record of previous operations can provide insight into the future, it demonstrates that the individual officer in the field will be forced to assume substantial burdens as a policy agent. In the various Vietnamese programs as well as in civic action projects underway in other countries, evidence corroborates this.

But do Americans want their soldiers to become expert in the techniques and mechanics of politics? Our governmental system relies heavily upon the assumption that civilian supremacy is successful largely because the generals have been isolated and insulated from the political life of the state. Have our views changed so that we are now willing to encourage uniformed personnel to involve themselves in a wider spectrum of public affairs? Obviously, the issue transcends the problems of the civil affairs phase of military policy. Yet the manner in which the question is ultimately resolved will play a major role in determining the future course of this aspect of American foreign policy.

CHAPTER V

SUMMARY AND POSTLUDE

The issue of military occupation is not outdated. To the contrary, it is as current as the American involvement in Korea, the Dominican Republic, and Vietnam. As long as the U. S. has a military or national security policy, the problem of occupation will be present. Forms, definitions, and styles may change, but the need to deal effectively with foreign civilians will remain, and the ingredients of foreign policy can definitely be identified within civil affairs/military government actions. Though these experiences have been a relatively small part of the entire foreign policy spectrum, they provide convincing evidence that CAMG records deserve careful study by those charged with planning and implementing any type of overseas activities.

This survey was designed to discover whether a common thread of reason has existed in the occupation policies which have been applied from 1846 to the present day. The aim in this chapter is neither to predict nor advise, but rather to summarize the present pattern and to evaluate some alternatives. First, it was necessary to recognize and set aside those factors which were not consistently present in occupations. For instance, little proof indicated that all occupations were conducted either with unusual kindness or extraordinary brutality. Not all were directed by a single top authority nor did they all utilize the same type of administrative structure. Some operations occurred on the territory of friendly states, while others took place in hostile countries. The competence of Army personnel assigned to civil affairs could not be judged as a fundamental element in policy because history suggests that in each case leaders were neither wholly able nor completely ineffectual. Ventures were not based exclusively upon the principles of international law, nor restricted totally to military and diplomatic motives and goals. Finally, the use of the Army in handling civilian populations overseas has not been uniformly successful or unsuccessful from the standpoint of long-range results.

At this point it is also important to recognize the growing involvement of the United States in small wars. Barring a return to a policy of isolationism, it is necessary to accept the conclusion that the present trend in world military strategy appears increasingly to emphasize the intermingling of occupation type civil affairs programs with limited war conflicts. However, to terminate the discussion here would be to neglect the requirement of applying past experiences to contemporary problems. New forces in policy must be considered, whether they represent the product of the natural evolution of American society or stem from the deliberate manipulation of leadership.

The theoretical level of policy, where consistent elements or ingredients could be found, is an abstract conceptual framework depicting the policy formulation process. On this plane the various components and forces within policy are broad and inclusive in both their source and application. A survey of America's various occupation policies reveals the continual relevance of the following factors: national interest, national principles, national mood, and individual leadership. Each of these has stood as a primary element in the process whereby policy was laid down.

However, policy also contains a number of secondary or lesser ingredients. While not on the same level as the primary elements listed above, they are sufficiently important to merit attention. Occupation agencies are considered as an extended element of individual leadership. Allied cooperation is a facet closely associated with the idea of national interest. And under the heading of principles and mood are found international law, the journalists, political interest groups, and Congressional influence.

In summarizing some of the ideas brought to light, greatest clarity can be achieved by dealing with each primary ingredient separately. Each must be analyzed to its final conclusion, which means that combined with the summary will be a series of speculations concerning the possible course each will take in the future. Radical alteration or lesser modification of the existing policy ingredients could present either promising or frightening possibilities.

In order to see the evolution of occupation policy, the historical stages of national interest become the essential backdrop. During the early history of America the drive for manifest destiny and territorial expansion were explicit goals. Gradually, during the course of the second half of the nineteenth century, the interest of economic growth reached a predominant position. Then by World War I the idea of maintaining the *status quo* had moved into the forefront. Not until the World War II occupations were under way did the next shift take place. National self-preservation and survival then became the paramount interest. From the middle of the postwar occupations until apparently the present the U. S. has been operating on the level of national security, a level which some have suggested assumes an importance above most other values.

This stage in the evolution of national interest is where many theorists and practitioners in foreign affairs believe America stands today. However, the authors suggest that security has progressed or degenerated into the next phase of national interest, which stage they label Aggressive Democratization. Superficially, the term aggressive democratization appears to indicate a race between the West and the communist bloc to determine which side can mold the world into its ideological image. For our purposes, however, the question is really whether U. S. foreign policy has taken the lead in expressing not only a new level of interest but also a new goal: the democratization of all pliable regions of the globe. This definition does eliminate the connotation of colonialism with its various trappings of sovereign domination and economic exploitation since the pursuance of this course may well exploit the economy of the United States itself.

It is recognized that those who will disagree with the above evolution or definition have persuasive arguments on their side. Among the more notable of these is the assertion that policies such as counterinsurgency represent merely diversionary strategies designed to insure national self-preservation. In this line of reasoning, both the Korean and Vietnamese Conflicts are seen as traditional limited wars with the related attempts at democratization judged simply as ready and expedient tools for insuring American survival. If this is the correct interpretation of the progression of events during the past two decades, then the prime national interest of survival remains unchanged.

However, if the idea of aggressive democratization has validity, a new national interest is emerging through subtle and scarcely perceptible changes; and the historic pattern of national interest could be amended as follows: territorial expansion, economic growth, maintenance of the status quo, national survival, and now aggressive democratization. Aggressive democratization in this context has developed in the process of defensive measures undertaken to contain hostile moves by the Soviet bloc.

The implications for military planners, should aggressive democratization have emerged, reach shocking proportions. Debate over the political training of officers is no longer pertinent, for the obligation to train an elite military force to help establish Western style governments in foreign areas must be recognized and accepted. If the world is to accept democracy, an instrument such as the armed forces becomes indispensable. The relatively successful utilization of the Army for this purpose in recent occupations, for example in Japan, may serve as a prototype in the minds of policy makers.

Certainly, an espousal of aggressive democratization would have far reaching consequences. Yet, only twice to date has the question received so much as an indirect examination by a major governmental forum. The Senate Foreign Relations Committee's hearings in 1966 and 1968, which had the stated purpose of ascertaining the present and future bases of the Vietnamese policy, brought the issue into the open. Though an effort to explore all competent points of view was sincere, the difficulty of facing the foreign policy quandary revealed itself. Discovery of the national purpose was continually sidetracked by emotional tirades which belabored peripheral problems. Concern for devising new means whereby military policy could more effectively satisfy overseas needs without violating domestic values was largely absent from public discussion.

Had the idea that America possessed a set of inviolable national principles been introduced, clarity might have ensued. This traditional element makes the thought of aggressive democratization repugnant to Americans. As recounted earlier, national principles included such altruistic heights as humanitarianism, individualism, civilian supremacy, and above all political self-determination. This last ideal is at the core of the current accommodation dilemma. As early as the nation's founding, can be seen an American reluctance to inflict a new form of government, even democracy, upon any people. Certainly, this was illustrated through the historic distaste for administering occupations following wars. And consciously or unconsciously, the ideal of self-government for all countries was expressed through specific statements, proclamations, and operational directives.

Inevitably, the shrinking of the world through modern technology, coupled with the protracted threat of the international communist movement, placed new stresses upon national values. In World War II, the time-honored abhorrence and rejection of a policy of inflicting new political systems upon foreign peoples was ignored in the name of a higher purpose. Perhaps the American citizenry convinced itself that the only humane course was to bestow democracy upon states plagued by tyranny. The real problem is that America has continued in this attitude through Korea and Vietnam apparently without identifying the violation of national principles. Should no national conscience develop, the next step will probably be the establishment of new regimes through occupation in emerging nations living under previously non-democratic systems.

If the events of the post-World War II period heralded a significant shift in policy direction, the influence of another element, the public mood, must be appreciated. This primary ingredient in policy was traced in earlier chapters and pinpointed as a force in each occupation. Popular sentiment was seen to fluctuate from extremes of vengeance to humanitarian sympathy, and from apathy to concern. When it was reflected, for example, in the denazification program for postwar Germany, the policy direction was quite clear and definable. However, when the mood was absent or failed to crystallize into a definite pattern, such as during the Vietnamese and Korean ventures, the policy has appeared less precise.

To facilitate an analysis of this phenomenon, it was useful in this book to consider jointly the policy ingredients of mood and principles. This device also provided a convenient vehicle for categorizing and defining the various types of U. S. wars and occupations. The headings chosen for the groupings were in line with the above primary policy ingredients. For example, a conflict waged within national boundaries is designated as a War of Opposition when it describes a situation wherein national ideals and public temper worked in diverse and competing directions within policy. The American Civil War occupation illustrates the confusion occurring when these two fundamental forces collide.

This problem was not as evident in major international wars where the indication was that American higher aspirations and immediate sentiments were consistent and reinforced each other, though usually without design. These conflicts and their consequent civil affairs aspects are classified as Wars of Unintentional Support. Policy characteristics of both World Wars, the Mexican War, and the Spanish-American War reflect this compatibility.

A third category seems best described by the phrase, Wars of Public Indifference, and includes the Siberian Intervention, the Korean Conflict, and the Vietnamese venture. In this type of limited military engagement, wars and occupations occur simultaneously. While resembling other forms of warfare, they are noteworthy because the policy ultimately decided upon embodies a mixture of mood and principles.

Special significance is attached to the national mood because in these wars the American people failed to develop a consensus on the ends sought. The most concrete and immediate consequence of this has been that the other primary elements within policy gained over-riding influence and achieved special emphasis in cases where the local citizens did not themselves hold a unified attitude toward the occupier.

TRENDS TOWARD AGGRESSIVE DEMOCRATIZATION

On the assumption that it could be true that under the guise of humanitarianism or under the cover of the cold war the U. S. might have embarked upon a policy of aggressive democratization, several questions must be posed. Is it inevitable and/or desirable that the present trend toward aggressive democratization continue? Is it feasible or even possible that reversal of this foreign policy direction can be accomplished? The first question will be explored in this section.

In discussing the implications of national interest as manifested through aggressive democratization, we are dealing with the small wars wherein occupation and combat are undertaken jointly. Because of its contemporary importance and since it illustrates the point well, the involvement in Vietnam will be used often as an example. However, should a similar set of circumstances arise and the U. S. intervene or attempt to intervene in Latin America, Africa, or in other Southeast Asian countries, the same policy considerations theoretically would apply.

Many indicators point toward the inevitability of continued aggressive democratization, especially when some of this nation's foreign policy instruments are observed dispassionately. For example, in this context foreign aid measures constitute an attempt to purchase influence in a share of the world. The Alliance For Progress is particularly suspect because of restrictions which withhold assistance until democratic reforms are initiated. Programs such as the Peace Corps, Agency for International Development technical teams, Voice of America, cultural broadcasts and the USIS can be construed as propagandizing efforts used for exporting democratic institutions. More blatant attempts through small wars and interventions such as in Vietnam and the Dominican Republic can hardly be labeled more definitely than instances of overt coercion. These policies should not automatically be condemned. After all, the American system is based in no small part upon a trust in the judgment of the citizenry to make the correct decision on basic issues. If changing the world into the American image is a desirable course in the mind of the people, why not continue without fuss? A logical assertion can be advanced that there are few forms of government as worthy of exporting as democracy.

Since altering the natural evolutionary process appears difficult or undesirable, one must consider the military future if the tendency persists. Perhaps the outcome of the Vietnamese war will indicate whether democratization is to continue. A negotiated final settlement which divided Vietnam into zones of influence would be consistent with the democratization pattern. This could be accomplished under the auspices of the United Nations or through bilateral meetings with Hanoi officials. While completely satisfying few segments of American opinion, national prestige could thus be saved and both the hawks and doves placated.

Certainly, a negotiated agreement would harmonize with the public sentiment to end the human and material cost of the war. The same approach has already been followed in Berlin and Korea, and experience suggests that settlement through division of territory with the communists is both practical and expedient. Once a definite zone has been declared to be within the Western orbit, democratization has moved forward with a quickened pace, and the U. S. has acquired one more piece of the world to mold in its image.

If the device of settlement by means of a territorial division should prove unworkable, another option appears open to foreign policy planners and national security strategists. A prolonged war could serve American ambitions for world change. Three qualifications are contained in our definition of a prolonged war. First, it entails participation in a land action spanning a minimum of a decade. The duration feature is a prime characteristic, and while the criterion cannot hinge upon a precise number of years it does imply a protracted military presence. Second, the prolonged war may be confined to a relatively small area such as Vietnam, or it may be enlarged to encompass an entire region such as Southeast Asia. No geographic restriction is implicit in the definition, which also means that there is no limit to the number of nation states which could be overrun in the process. A final qualification is that atomic weapons would not be used. If the conflict escalated to the point of a nuclear exchange, then the military action would no longer be in the category of a prolonged war.

As seen here, the central theme of prolonged war is that recognizable bounds are placed upon the combat strategy applied. The reason that this form of conflict must be considered is that it constitutes a feasible form of war for the United States to wage. Arguments can be advanced that it is an effective means for furthering aggressive democratization since the more inclusive it becomes the more fruitful are the prospects. Occupation forces will continue civic action, pacification, revolutionary development, and similar programs while fighting is in progress. Conducted by the United States, such constructive projects will help build the host countries economically, educationally, and politically.

Britain played its part earlier, but there also military power was accepted as a long term investment in the areas being developed. Political and social leadership throughout its former Asian colonies was to a degree Westernized through the educational policy introduced by London. But always the British Army remained in the wings, prepared to act if political instability became excessive. That epoch has obviously closed; however, the plea is often heard that for America today to settle for anything less than a favorable division of the Asian land mass between East and West would mean sacrificing past successes and precipitating future failures.

Should a prolonged land war require years and a substantial investment in economic and human resources, these costs in themselves would not invalidate the basic aims of the policy. From this standpoint, these goals should not be scrapped now because of discomfort or inconvenience. Persistence hopefully will lead to a time when the emerging independent and powerful states of the region will assume a greater share of the burden.

Ample reason also exists for an examination of the negative consequences of embarking upon a prolonged war. The initial resistance stems from the domestic popular mood because such a conflict is not appealing to the many people who impatiently await an early and decisive outcome. These Americans can hardly be expected to accommondate themselves to a seemingly endless military venture.

Certainly, popular sentiment could be colored by the economic and human cost and by the fear of seeing the Soviet Union forge ahead in wealth while America waged a costly war to save the underdeveloped world from itself. Aside from the purely domestic economic question, the price of honoring global commitments must also be considered. Insurgency or other serious trouble may erupt in different places concurrently, and perhaps it would be economically unfeasible for even a wealthy world power to fight more than one war at a time.

The conclusion can be drawn that if this country favors participating in small wars to further democracy, it should pragmatically choose one of two different types of conflicts: (1) a short engagement where a land division with the communists can be achieved and occupation forces readily moved into the area, or (2) a prolonged war where democratization can be carried on by civil affairs units while the fighting continues.

REVERSAL POSSIBILITIES

The next question is this: what are some of the forces and events which could bring about a reversal of the trend toward aggressive democratization? Certainly the most effective device would be dropping the atomic bomb. Such a course could, at least, be depended upon to produce a complete change in foreign policy. Admittedly, this is an exceeding dangerous method to employ in order to avoid the infliction of an ideology.

Once nuclear weapons are used, it may be impossible to halt the process of regression through the various stages of national interest. Instead of moving back to the self-preservation phase and neatly stopping, the all-out conflict could degenerate into a race for annihilation. Or the results of the war could cause American society to revert to the level of the cave man's civilization, where personal survival would re-emerge as the consuming ambition of mankind.

Unfortunately, this could happen because Americans are not a notably patient people and they seem to prefer fighting a short decisive war. They might be propelled into an atomic conflict, for example in Vietnam, should they become enraged over atrocities or some other developments. On the other hand, they could bungle themselves into a nuclear war by permitting the fighting to escalate to the point where the bomb had to be used. Occupation troops, if any were still on the scene after such a holocaust, would hardly be available for furthering aggressive democratization. They would be far too busy helping in the personal survival of man.

A second and more palatable alternative to the impending wave of aggressive democratization would be total withdrawal from conflict already precipitated, or nonintervention in a potentially threatening situation. This solution, which is termed here total withdrawal, has won support for several reasons. First, the legal position of the U. S. in these operations has been shaky. Many Americans are unwilling to forget, for example, that Congress failed to declare a state of war concerning Vietnam, though a major conflict was undertaken.

Another argument for total withdrawal is that, according to the revered principles of individualism and self-determination, the U. S. has little business injecting itself into the affairs of other states. This mandate precludes any attempt to impose a governmental system alien to the local people. In the Vietnamese case, the long-range issue goes beyond the problem of reaching a settlement with Hanoi. Inescapably it concerns the right of the United States to use force in democratizing any foreign country, particularly when that state has never posed a direct or indirect threat to this nation. In addition, the specter of protracted land wars conjures up disquieting feelings in the popular mind. Thoughtful citizens demand to know the reasons why youth must be sacrificed for ventures which continually appear unprincipled, purposeless, and unwinnable.

Arguments can also be advanced that these wars, which appear to be increasing in frequency and intensity, create an excessive drain on the domestic economy. Of course, the elimination of training armies and occupation forces would most particularly alleviate the monetary costs.

While one can see the logic of total withdrawal or noninvolvement, a complete refusal to participate in small wars would also have its drawbacks. Primarily it would appear to the rest of the world that America was pursuing a policy of isolationism and had decided that the maintenance of the *status quo* was once again its prime objective. By totally withdrawing from Vietnam the U. S. would certainly be charged with abandoning Asian nations that have looked toward the West for help in modernization. In the light of this revised approach, emerging Asian states could be expected to strengthen their ties with Red China and the Soviet Union, and the position of Japan, the Philippines, and South Korea would be especially tenuous.

Latin America would also have many questions. Would the new isolationism take a less absolute form within the Western Hemisphere? Would the Monroe Doctrine concept continue to prevail? Under a new policy of noninvolvement what could Latin American states expect from the U. S. in terms of military forces, including advisory groups, which might be made available to them in emergencies? Without assurance of U. S. aid, would the sole course open to these countries be expansion of their own military establishments? From the standpoint of Washington's hope for a comprehensive foreign policy for the future, evaluation would also be demanded. Could withdrawal from Asia and Africa while engaging in selective interventions in Latin America succeed? Could this country afford total noninvolvement in Central and South America?

Public opinion, it is true, could compel a return to traditional isolationism through the election of a new administration in Washington. However, suppose that the citizenry had no desire to establish an American stronghold in the world or to isolate itself, but instead chose to initiate a positive action. This leads to the third suggestion for accomplishing a reversal of aggressive democratization and concerns expanding relationships with the United Nations. Hopefully, this proposal would then balance the negative results of withdrawal against the positive benefits of a new and creative idea.

Following this plan, the United States would substitute a commitment to the international organization in place of its previous promises to individual emerging states. Washington might agree as an initial overture to invest a sum of money in the UN which was roughly equivalent to the cost of waging limited war. An immediate advantage would be the acceptability of a withdrawal from Southeast Asia. If sufficiently frustrated by the slow progress of the fighting, Americans might decide to retire, provided they were able to convince themselves that the decision was motivated by altruistic aims for world peace. By delegating to the UN the authority for resolving disputes which have the potential of becoming small wars, a desirable image would be projected to the world. The policy would then stand as a reaffirmation of confidence in the international body, which is patterned largely after the political institutions of Western liberalism. Principles and idealism would assume a revived emphasis in policy. Under the new guidelines, the world apparatus assumes the responsibility for determining democratically the criteria for justified and legal intervention in the internal affairs of sovereign states. No longer could this country be accused of forcing its form of government upon others or determining world policy solely on the basis of the interests of the United States.

With this act, America could take an additional step by furthering its dedication to the idea that people of all nations possess the right to a direct voice in their own destiny. The United States Ambassador or chief representative to the United Nations could be elected on a popular basis. It is difficult to speculate with any degree of certitude upon the international reaction to such a departure. Certainly, responses by other UN members could be expected. Governments of the advanced democratic states might soon be forced to grant their citizens a similar direct voice and the more developed communist countries, which have incorporated at least the illusion of popular suffrage, would be hard pressed to ignore the prospect. But it is in the uncommitted nations where the effect of the popular election of the UN delegate would be most beneficial for the United States. They could scarcely avoid re-examining the nature of their relations with the major power blocs and with the United Nations itself. A form of international rivalry along more peaceful lines might ensue. Ideally, the zeal of the East-West race would be channeled into new avenues. Unlike the present political antagonism, the future criteria for national prestige would reflect the volume of resources contributed by each side to achieve world peace and modernization.

America's accelerated participation in the UN would offer a vehicle not only for terminating the Vietnamese dilemma but also for defining policy regarding future small war involvements. Responsibility for insuring the peace and spreading democratic institutions would be passed from Washington to UN headquarters. Such a clear declaration would mean that the U. S. has no intention of defending the world community from communism or dictatorships of any other hue, unless other nations share the concern and the burden. By allocating to the UN the money it would spend on small wars, America would be contributing a substantial share of the organization's operating budget; therefore, it could count on having a major voice in policy decisions. The long-range contributions to world stability and progress would be less than the cost of waging unilaterally a series of small wars.

From the perspective of national security planners and civil affairs policy makers, the task of working within international machinery is not novel. World War II established solid precedents, which were subsequently expanded in the cold war regional security organizations. Korea and Vietnam were further instances where the armed forces gained experience in joint combat efforts. However, Army relations with civilians could be more effective if the soldiers better coordinated their activities with international welfare agencies. Civil affairs then would embody a force higher than purely American ambitions. World principles, world interests, world opinions, and world leadership would then be included within national policy ingredients. The result could be a mutual reinforcement as well as a reciprocal compromise on the means and goals of military action.

Unavoidably, the negative aspects of this plan must be taken into account. The most obvious disadvantage would be a partial loss of national identity and sovereignty. Bringing the UN so directly into American foreign policy would alarm many citizens. While policy theorists may argue that such feelings are irrational, they still exist.

A serious doubt would arise about the ability of the UN to solve international problems better than the United States government. Laymen and leaders alike would wonder if meshing American military policy with that of a world organization could lead to participation in a war contrary to our own national interest. Admittedly, this is a possibility since democracy has a way of never completely pleasing any individual or group.

There is no assurance that if the Vietnamese question, for example, were turned over *in toto* to the UN that the settlement would be satisfactory for the United States. The world body might decide to declare all of Asia a region of nonintervention, the results of which mandate could be devastating for this country's position in the Pacific. Through penetration and intimidation, the entire Orient might ultimately be incorporated into the communist orbit. Washington might belatedly realize that parts of the Middle East and Africa had been also unalterably subverted. Perhaps this country would find itself in a situation where its high ideals of international cooperation and self-determination had seemingly been betrayed by the United Nations. Consequently, the reaction might be more striking than if national interests had merely been defeated in the game of power politics.

Professed economic objections would also be raised domestically, though the expenditures for the UN would be less than those required for small wars. Many would doubtless look at the appropriations as unwelcome symbols of a needless abandonment of our own right to economic self-determination. And perversely, success of the new policy in quelling further conflicts might eventually foster apathy and renew demands that international spending must stop because resources are needed for internal development. The proposal perhaps expects the American citizenry to display a degree of financial foresight which is beyond their present capacity.

Also, perhaps too much can be expected from an international organization at this stage in world history, because should it take the risk and fail, the negative reaction would be catastrophic. Thus far the world body has had a fair record of success, but the impact of both its accomplishments and failures has been measured largely in terms of national interests. Under the plan being suggested, the United States would also be placing in jeopardy its national principles. If UN actions fall short of the American notion of adequacy, deep popular disillusionment would ensue. This feeling could spark a demand for withdrawal from all types of international peace keeping machinery. Certainly, the destruction of the United Nations system would then be imminent.

In summary, prospects for halting or reversing the trend toward aggressive democratization do not seem hopeful insofar as America's small war policy is concerned. Drastic escalation into nuclear conflict would not improve the situation, and total withdrawal or non-involvement accomplishes little more than pre-World War II isolationism. If the United Nations could be used courageously, the outlook might be more promising. In that case, if democratization continued it would not be the version espoused and recommended by this country alone. One could at least expect more extensive debate before future unilateral interventions were undertaken.

All these alternatives, for promoting or reversing aggressive democratization, re-emphasize the scope and dimension of the civil affairs problem. Therefore, it is impractical for the Army to develop a plan for dealing with foreign civilians solely upon the basis of combat strategy, and in isolation from the broader goals of international policy.

High level policy makers also need to realize that within each alternative there are devices which while generally thought to be beyond their control are sometimes subject to manipulation. For example, in the modern small war the relationship between public mood and propaganda is especially significant. Propaganda can be employed for swaying the public mood if used efficiently. However, the danger to democracy posed by leaders making such an attempt is serious and the results can be more fearful than the public indifference it seeks to by-pass or eradicate.

To digress into a discussion of the numerous techniques available to the policy maker would be inappropriate here. However, it is worthwhile to consider one insight into this capacity which was furnished quite unintentionally by President Kennedy. Unlike Truman's actions at the outbreak of the Korean Conflict, JFK did not make a running start, leaving public opinion behind, when the Cuban missile crisis broke. He brought the entire citizenry to their television sets on a twenty-four hour vigil as he explained the implications of the situation and the threat of attack upon the American mainland. The popular sentiment was a near consensus supporting his actions and commands. Had he ordered an invasion, the protests would probably have been minor.

Admittedly, the threat was close to the Florida coast and involved a country about which most citizens had some knowledge. A fair assumption is that the White House was sincere in its dedication to national principles, as well as being quite desperate. Yet the effectiveness of the mobilization and manipulation of public sentiment during this period may have established an imposing precedent. A gradual intensification in propaganda, reinforced by contrived military incidents, might be used expediently to gain popular support for wars of public indifference. Even during such a conflict, the national mood could be changed by a propaganda build-up. It could become a powerful instrument in jarring the lethargy which characterizes this type of war.

INDIVIDUAL LEADERSHIP AND EXTENDED ELEMENTS

A fourth major policy ingredient traced in this book was the role of the Army officer. It was seen that the individual made important contributions on a very high plane throughout occupation experiences. Recapitulating briefly, evidence indicates that two typical command patterns emerged; these were termed decentralized and centralized control. World War II was a primary source of illustrations because the size of its occupations placed the leadership question into sharp perspective.

General Eisenhower stands as the prototype of the theater commander who utilized a decentralized approach. This system can be defined as a form of administration wherein the commanding general delegates substantial policy making power to his major subordinates. They, in turn, conduct the various phases of the civil affairs program within their geographic areas. As a result, in some regions an enlightened policy is followed, while in others little is done to achieve Washington's long-range aims. Decentralization is often instituted when the supreme commander does not personally believe that the Army should be involved in civilian questions other than those necessary for combat operations. The existence of administrative dissension and duplication often undermines the potential value of this system and typically creates or perpetuates an inconsistent and sometimes indiscernible policy. In its favor is the fact that decentralization usually operates in a nonarbitrary fashion, allowing lower ranking officers great latitude in using their own initiative and ability.

Under centralized control, as exemplified by MacArthur's occupation of Japan, an unimpeachable chain-of-command radiates from the top headquarters. However, the individual who chooses this approach, being exceedingly strong willed, may surround himself with subordinates of a lesser ability. Also, a danger exists that a general deficient in political judgment attempting centralized direction could misuse his prerogative and become a satrap. The chief arguments in its favor are the uniformity and efficiency with which policy is implemented throughout the occupied nation. Preconditions must be met for this system to operate properly. First, the White House and the Joint Chiefs must delegate adequate decision making power to the single military representative, and second, he personally must understand the nature of America's overall foreign policy goals.

It is not difficult to evaluate both centralized and decentralized control in the light of aggressive democratization. The latter is more democratic yet it is less useful as a tool to democratize. A loose knit structure should probably be favored if a foreign policy is adopted whereby small wars or interventions are dropped, and simultaneously, only a small contingency force of civil affairs experts is to be maintained. But if world democratization becomes the avowed theme of national policy, the Army must create a greatly expanded corps of civil administrators. It will need the services of highly trained professional officers who can be expected to remain in a troubled overseas area for an indefinite period. And the best assurance for their individual success as leaders rests upon the type of training they have received.

The training concept adopted should parallel the administrative structure to be employed in the field. A centralized structure for managing civil affairs there could be tied closely to a training program based upon the Project Manager concept. This plan is preferred because, while most advantageously used under centralized control, it does embody some of the best characteristics of the decentralized pattern.

The project manager system has emerged since World War II, and has become a vehicle whereby federal agencies can quickly tap outside resources and thereby accomplish highly specialized tasks. While used for a variety of programs, it has proved especially invaluable to training. Most recently, the Peace Corps built its entire training structure around this idea, and the Agency for International Development used the device on a limited scale in preparing civic action personnel for Vietnam.

A unique organizational concept is at the core of the project manager system, whereby responsibility for developing and operating the entire program is delegated to a single official. He has a free hand in shaping his administrative structure, recruiting instructors, determining the curriculum, and arranging for facilities such as housing, classrooms, and transportation. In the planning and contracting phase, a training site must be chosen to which eminently qualified instructors can be attracted. This is not an easy selection. If training takes place on a military installation, obtaining the services of experts is a problem. On the other hand, if the Army moves into a university in peacetime and insists upon complete control over its own educational project, the result is likely to be serious friction with campus administrators. The service academies may offer the best settings. West Point, Annapolis, and Colorado Springs possess the convenience of being recognized elements of American higher education while simultaneously they are accustomed to the military's special idiosyncrasies.

After the site is chosen, the manager must decide upon the content of the course. For instance, if the program's aim is to train thirty-five civic action specialists for assignment among three contiguous Latin American states the instruction must include topics common to the three nations as well as detailed insights into conditions in each particular country. Intensive training in language and survival skills must be included in the program, and scheduling of classes becomes exceedingly complex. Initially, the project manager will need several weeks for advanced planning, and his progress during this phase must be monitored closely by the Army. It would have the opportunity to accept or reject his plan, depending upon its adequacy and the overseas situation. Should the military decide to retain the manager to direct the actual training cycle, additional requirements come into play. Instruction must be conducted at an accelerated pace and rarely should exceed twelve weeks duration. Otherwise, costs per student become prohibitive and the value of quickly placing trained officers into a troubled region is lost. To further the development of a successful project manager system, the director should accompany the graduates overseas and exercise a direct role in coordinating their field activities. Then he would be able to appreciate the strengths and weaknesses of the program which he devised.

While civil affairs has been a distasteful assignment in the eyes of most professional officers, the opportunity to assume a responsibility of this dimension would affect the career standing of the man in charge. He would be under extreme pressure to submit an adequate training proposal which he, subsequently, would be asked to conduct. He would be expected to receive the praise for his ability to operate the project, or the blame for his incompetence. His skill in working with others and his astuteness in handling subordinates would be severely tested. Consequently, the caliber of personnel wishing to be associated with civil affairs could be expected to rise dramatically.

But the application of the project manager approach to training represents only limited advantages; it does not in itself improve the efficiency of the administrative system within the theater. This benefit can be accomplished, however, if the manager concept is applied to all CA operations within the theater. In effect, the entire occupation program for a country would have to be considered a single project under the command of one official. As in the case of training programs, the civil affairs manager would receive his power from the highest authorities, presumably the Joint Chiefs. Occupation policy would be administered through a command chain distinct from that employed for combat purposes.

However, if the project manager concept is too controversial for the Army, Congress, or the public to accept, a more moderate alternative might be adopted; a substitution is the creation of a new CA agency. Though made with understandable hesitancy, this suggestion may offer an appropriate solution. The new agency's sole *raison d'etre* would be the responsibility for working directly with governmental leaders in countries where a civil affairs policy was being applied. Potential situations might include traditional belligerent occupation, civil affairs and pacification in small wars, and civic action projects in nations desiring only limited American military support. One of its major functions would be training and supporting the military officers assigned to the country teams.

The country team concept, evolving as a consequence of modern small wars, indicates a positive step in the direction of enhancing policy coordination. However, its publicly debated shortcomings in Vietnam point up the necessity for further refinement. Correlative to the establishment of a new agency is the problem of its continuity. Traditionally, machinery erected during periods of crisis was disbanded when the emergency passed. This waste is especially inexcusable if an extended series of military interventions is in the offing.

Another alternative which merits consideration is the incorporating of the existing civil affairs structure into the Judge Advocate General's Branch. This highly regarded contingent insures that statutory and constitutional procedures are followed by military authorities. Logically, its function could be expanded to include more direct control over civil affairs operations. Reinforcing the shift to the Judge Advocate's office is the fact that the problem of the political content of training could be more easily resolved. Furnishing political education to the military professionals might not be so repugnant to the public if the instruction took place under the control of a school dedicated to the law.

To this point the summary and speculations have been confined to the four basic ingredients of national security policy: interests, principles, public mood, and individual leadership. However, other elements must be included in order to complete the framework. Because of their dependent relationship, these constitute the next lower level of generalization within the conceptual system, and their significance hinges upon their being the extended aspects or overt expressions of the fundamental ingredients of policy.

Reviewing these secondary or extended elements, we see that Congress, the journalists, and political interest groups historically have been important in the formulation of overseas efforts. Yet their influence was primarily a reflection and manifestation of the basic ingredient of the prevailing mood-of-the-day. International military alliances with friendly states, as well as participation in multilateral organizations concerned with civil affairs, can be viewed as devices for furthering American national interests.

International law has long been a consideration in policy. Its seeming preeminence however, has sometimes led to an exaggerated estimation of its significance. International codes governing military conduct have represented the common denominator of civilized behavior, and these legal restraints evolved as a law among nations rather than a law above nations. Provisions applying to occupation mirror the individual states' standards of morality and ideals. Thus, it appears valid to interpret international law as an extended element of the basic policy ingredient of national principles.

Ostensibly the legal factor within policy is increasing. The Nuremberg Doctrine, the Geneva Conventions of 1949, and the Universal Declaration of Human Rights place greater stress upon defining the jurisdiction which a governmental official can rightly exercise over private citizens; and the movement toward clearer and stricter rules could culminate in the emergence of a distinct legal morality standing above the particular ideals of individual states.

However, processes and machinery of law have a habit of developing very slowly, and presently, the American policy for small wars has created an unprecedented challenge to the traditional definitions. Evidence justifies the thesis that the current civil affairs practices have yet to be incorporated fully into the framework of world law.

In a military operation such as that in Vietnam a gap in international law can be discerned. This is the problem of providing effective protection for civilians and military personnel on both sides.

The record of past wars reveals that in most instances the combatants were forced to rely upon codes written to cover the conduct of previous conflicts. Perhaps once each decade, an international conclave ought to be called in order to provide a systematic procedure for evaluating and revamping codes. Regardless of whether serious hostilities are in progress at the time, these deliberations would be valuable because they could serve as a forum for articulating the world conscience. Hopefully, the twentieth anniversary of the adoption of the Universal Declaration of Human Rights (1968) will generate a revived interest in its application to civil military legal questions.

Recent generations have witnessed the replacement of traditional peace treaties by military occupations. The present generation seems to be observing the replacement of major wars by unconventional limited conflicts within which military civil affairs plays a leading role. It may occur that a modernized hybrid version of military occupation will become a standard vehicle of foreign policy. This prospect is distasteful, but the goals sought in Korea, Vietnam, and the Dominican Republic have already forced the American people to accept new forms of military challenges.

Undoubtedly, the best solution is the elimination of war itself. If mankind fails in this, America must at least approach war and occupation policy with a clear, unemotional logic. The sole recourse immediately open and practicable is the development of a correspondingly modernized national security policy.

REFERENCES

CHAPTER I

1. Malcolm S. MacLean, "Military Government — Fact And Fancy," *Public Administration Review*, 7:275, Autumn, 1947.

2. U.S. Army Field Manual 27-10. *The Law of Land Warfare*, 1956, p. 141.

3. U.S. Army Field Manual 41-5, *Joint Manual of Civil Affairs/Military Government*, 1958, p. 4., U.S. Army Field Manual 41-10, *Civil Affairs Operations*, 1962, p. 5.

4. Field Manual 41-5, *op. cit.*, p. 4.

5. For an excellent discussion see William V. O'Brien, "Legitimate Military Necessity in Nuclear War," in *World Polity II* (Washington, Georgetown Univ. Press, 1960), pp. 35-120.

6. Field Manual 27-10, *op. cit.*, p. 138.

7. Morris Greenspan, *The Modern Law of Land Warfare* (Berkeley: Univ. of California Press, 1959), p. 219.

8. U.S. Department of the Army Publication 27-1, *Treaties Governing Land Warfare*, 1956, p. 152.

9. Gerhard von Glahn, *The Occupation of Enemy Territory* (Minneapolis: Univ. of Minnesota Press, 1957), p. 21.

10. DA Publication 27-1, *op. cit.*, p. 137.   11. Greenspan, *op. cit.*, p. 215.

12. "Geneva Convention Relative to the Protection of Civilian Persons in Time of War," 1949, DA Publication 27-1, *op. cit.*, p. 155.

13. Greenspan, *op. cit.*, p. 223.   14. Field Manual 27-10, *op. cit.*, p. 139.

15. Edward H. Litchfield, (ed.), *Governing Postwar Germany* (Ithaca: Cornell University Press, 1953), p. 14.

16. *Ibid.*, p. 15.

17. "Hague Convention III Relative to the Opening of Hostilities, Art. I, 1907," DA Publication 27-1, *op. cit.*, p. 2.

18. Geneva Convention, Art. 3, DA Publication 27-1, *op. cit.*, pp. 24-25.

19. Harry L. Coles and Albert K. Weinberg, *Civil Affairs: Soldiers Become Governors*, Special Studies, United States Army in World War II (Washington: Office of the Chief of Military History, Department of the Army, 1964), p. 654. This fine volume was an outgrowth of an earlier unpublished collection of documents compiled by Albert K. Weinberg.

20. Hardy C. Dillard, "Power and Persuasion: The Role of Military Government," *The Yale Review*, 42:212, December, 1952.

21. *Ibid.*

22. President's Committee to Study the United States Military Assistance Program, *Supplement to the Composite Report*, Vol. II (Washington: Government Printing Office, 1959), p. 95.

23. *Ibid.*, p. 114.

24. For a more extensive examination of respective views on this point see Coles & Weinberg, *op. cit.*, Chapter I.

25. Hanson W. Baldwin in Lester Markel and others, *Public Opinion and Foreign Policy* (New York: Harper & Brothers for the Council on Foreign Relations, 1949),

p. 118. For another study of militarism which deals with this question at length see Alfred Vagts, *A History of Militarism* (New York: Meridian Books Inc., rev. ed., 1959).

26. For further elaboration see Carl J. Friedrich and associates, *American Experiences in Military Government in World War II* (New York: Rhinehart & Company, 1948), pp. 10-17.

27. Hajo Holborn, *American Military Government* (Washington: Infantry Journal Press, 1947), p. 107.

28. *Ibid.*

29. Harold Zink, *American Military Government in Germany* (New York: The Macmillan Company, 1947), p. 39.

30. Coles and Weinberg, *op. cit.*, p. 94. Numerous references to this problem are included under other headings in the same work.

31. The Marquet Memorial Library for Civil Affairs Research was named in honor of the late Major General William F. Marquet. Serving as the Army's first Chief of Civil Affairs Military Government from 1952-1955, he had been instrumental in persuading both congressional and Pentagon leadership that the Army should undertake a major civil affairs role in rebuilding Korea. The library's collection includes over eight thousand volumes of scholarly studies and bound government documents, plus a reasonably complete and current selection of pertinent periodicals. Administered by a professional civilian librarian, it operates under the command control of the Civil Affairs School at Fort Gordon, Georgia.

32. For further evidence that civil affairs policy has become increasingly divorced from the traditional idea of military government see Philip H. Taylor and Ralph J. Braibanti, *Administration of Occupied Areas* (Syracuse: Syracuse Univ. Press, 1948), p. 4. For excellent historical and contemporary analysis of the impact of limited war upon this question see Robert E. Osgood, *Limited War: The Challenge of American Strategy* (Chicago: Univ. of Chicago Press, 1957), and Michael Halperin, *Limited Warfare in the Nuclear Age* (New York: John Wiley & Sons, Inc., 1963).

33. Marshall Knappen, *And Call It Peace* (Chicago: Univ. of Chicago Press, 1947), pp. 15-16.

34. Zink, *op. cit.*, pp. 14-15.

35. Thomas R. Fisher, "Allied Military Government in Italy," *The Annals of the American Academy of Political and Social Science*, 267:116, January, 1950.

36. Robert B. Textor, *Failure in Japan* (New York: The John Day Company, 1951), pp. 187-188.

37. *Ibid.*, p. 188.   38. Zink, *op. cit.*, pp. 14-15.   39. *Ibid.*, pp. 36-37.

40. James P. Pappas, "A Review of United States Civil Affairs Military Government, 1787-1955: An Analysis of the Development of Concepts," (unpublished study prepared for the Army War College, Carlisle Barracks, Pennsylvania, p. 20.)

41. Clellen S. Ford, "Occupation Experiences on Okinawa," *The Annals*, 267:177, January, 1950.

42. Dillard, *op. cit.*, p. 212.

43. Ralph H. Gabriel, "American Experiences with Military Government," *American Political Science Review*, 37:438, June, 1943.

44. Harvey C. Mansfield with Harold Stein in Walter Millis (ed.), *Arms and the State* (New York: The Twentieth Century Fund, 1958), p. 124.

45. Fisher, *op. cit.*, p. 116. 46. Pappas, *op. cit.*, p. 29.

47. Robert Komer, "Civil Affairs and Military Government in the Mediterranean

Theater," (an unpublished study prepared for the Office of the Chief of Military History, United States Army, 1952), Ch. 11, p. 43.

48. Quoted in Morris O. Edwards, "A Case Study of Military Government in Germany During and After World War II," (unpublished Ph.D. dissertation, Georgetown Univ., Washington, 1957), pp. 76-77.

49. James L. McCamy, *The Administration of Foreign Policy* (New York: Alfred A. Knopf, 1952), p. 270.

50. For a revealing expression of Congressional sentiment on the hemispheric implication of the U.S. policy toward Cuba see Senator Hubert H. Humphrey, *A Report on the Alliance for Progress, 1963*, Committee on Appropriations and Foreign Relations (Washington: Government Printing Office, 1963,) p. 37.

51. The Joint Resolution of Congress, Oct. 3, 1962, stated that immediate steps should be taken by the United States "to prevent by whatever means may be necessary, including the use of arms, the Marxist-Leninist regime in Cuba from extending, by force or the threat of force, its aggressive or subversive activities to any part of the hemisphere." On October 22, 1962, President Kennedy responded to the Congressional resolution and reaffirmed U. S. determination "to prevent in Cuba the creation or use of an externally supported military capability endangering the interests of the United States and all the nations of the Western Hemisphere." For additional statements indicating the temper of Congress during the debate on the desirability of a strong stand on the question of American intervention see Subcommittee on Inter-American Affairs of the Committee on Foreign Affairs, House of Representatives, Hearings, *Castro-Communist Subversion in the Western Hemisphere*, February 18-March 6, 1963, 88th Congress (Washington: Government Printing Office, 1963). The subsequent intervention in the Dominican Republic during the Johnson Administration further evidenced the long-range significance of the 1963 policy decision.

CHAPTER II

1. Benjamin Akzin, *Data on Military Government in Occupied Areas: With Special Reference to the United States and Great Britain*, Public Affairs Bulletin No. 16, Library of Congress (Washington: Government Printing Office, 1942), pp. 18-19. Consult also Earl S. Pomeroy, "The American Colonial Office," *Mississippi Valley Historical Review*, 30: 521-32, March, 1944. For further description of early occupations see U.S. Army Civil Affairs School. *History of Civil Affairs* (Fort Gordon, Georgia: U.S. Army CA School, Special Text ST 41-170, 1959), pp.27-33. A succinct analysis of the relationship of domestic growth and development to overseas expansion is included in Thomas A. Bailey, *A Diplomatic History of the American People* (New York: Appleton-Century Crofts, Inc., 4th edition, 1950), p. 458.

2. Akzin, *op. cit.* For details concerning the precedent setting Siberian intervention see the autobiography of William S. Graves, *America's Siberian Adventure* (New York: Peter Smith, 1941). For a critical analysis of this occupation see Clarence A. Manning, *The Siberian Fiasco* (New York: Literary Publishers, 1932). Probably the most complete official source regarding the Army's World War I occupation of the Rhineland is Colonel Irvin L. Hunt, *American Military Government of Occupied Germany, 1918-1920*. Report of the Officer in Charge of Civil Affairs, Third Army and American Forces in Germany (4 vol. mimeographed ed., Coblenz, 1920; Printed ed.,

Washington: Government Printing Office, 1943). A useful chronology of the establishment of the military command headquarters for post-World War I Germany is contained in Provost Marshal General's School, Military Government Department, *Military Government: An Historical Approach* (Fort Gordon: Georgia: PMG School, 1951), p. 105.

3. See especially the five rules framed for the guidance of occupation personnel in the *Handbook for Military Government in Germany* (Issued by Supreme Headquarters Allied Expeditionary Force, Office of the Chief of Staff, December, 1944), p. ii. These and other directives are compiled in Beate Ruhm von Oppen (ed.), *Documents on Germany Under Occupation, 1945-1954* (New York: Issued under the auspices of the Royal Institute of International Affairs by Oxford University Press, 1955), pp. 15-16. This collection does not include the large number of additional directives of lesser importance which were issued by the various military and civilian agencies in the field.

4. Kenneth W. Thompson gives specific credit to these four in *Political Realism and the Crisis of World Politics* (Princeton University Press, 1960), pp. 22-38. For a readily available summary discussion of the Realist theory by the same author see "American Approaches to International Politics," reprinted in George A. Lanyi and Wilson C. McWilliams, (ed.), *Crisis and Continuity in World Politics* (New York: Random House, 1966), pp. 20-33.

5. For further reference to this and other aspects of the Realist approach see the following basic works: Hans J. Morgenthau, *In Defense of the National Interest* (New York: Knopf, 1951); *Politics Among Nations,* 4th ed. (New York: Knopf, 1966); *Scientific Man Versus Power Politics* (Chicago: University of Chicago Press, 1946); Reinhold Niebuhr, *Christian Realism and Political Problems* (New York: Charles Scribner's Sons, 1953); *The Children of Light and the Children of Darkness* (New York: Charles Scribner's Sons, 1950); Nicholas J. Spykman, *America's Strategy in World Politics: The United States and the Balance of Power* (New York: Harcourt Brace & Co., 1942); and Edward Hallett Carr, *The Twenty Years Crisis 1919-1939* (London: Macmillan & Co., Ltd., 1946).

6. Hans J. Morgenthau, *In Defense of the National Interest, op. cit.,* p. 88.

7. Among their better known works stand the following: Walter Lippmann, *U.S. Foreign Policy: Shield of the Republic* (New York: Pocket Books, Inc., 1943); George F. Kennan, *Realities of American Foreign Policy* (Princeton: Princeton University Press, 1954); Robert E. Osgood, *Ideals and Self-Interest in America's Foreign Relations* (Chicago: University of Chicago Press, 1953); J. William Fulbright, *The Arrogance of Power* (New York: Random House, Vintage Books, 1966); Charles O. Lerche, Jr., *Foreign Policy of the American People* (Englewood Cliffs, N.J.: Prentice-Hall, Inc., 1958).

8. Robert E. Osgood, *Ideals and Self-Interest, op. cit.,* p. 5.

9. For analyses which explore the various sides of these questions see among others Inis L. Claude, Jr., *Power and International Relations* (New York: Random House, 1962); Arthur A. Ekirch, Jr., *Ideas, Ideals, and American Diplomacy* (New York: Appleton-Century Crofts, 1966); Stanley H. Hoffmann (ed.), *Contemporary Theory in International Relations* (Englewood Cliffs, N. J.: Prentice-Hall, Inc., 1960); Paul Seabury (ed.), *Balance of Power* (San Francisco: Chandler Publishing Co., 1965); and Frederick H. Gareau, *The Balance of Power and Nuclear Deterrence* (Boston: Houghton Mifflin Co., 1962).

10. Hans J. Morgenthau, *Politics Among Nations, op. cit.,* p. 202.

11. Robert E. Osgood, *Ideals and Self-Interest, op. cit.,* p. 5.

12. The categorization for the three initial occupations in this listing are taken from Akzin, *op. cit.* An official compilation of more recent operations in which the U.S. Army has played an administrative role is not available. An apology is therefore made in advance should the list be incomplete or in some instances inaccurate. No attempt was made to classify or include the U.S. Navy occupations which were undertaken for varying durations on the Pacific islands during World War II, other than the Ryukyu Islands operation where the Army quickly assumed the major role.

13. For an authoritative account by the American delegate on the scene in Berlin at the time see Jack Bennett, "The German Currency Reform," *The Annals,* 267:43-54, January, 1950.

14. For an authoritative treatment see Harry L. Coles, Jr., "Civil Affairs Agreements for Liberated Territories," *The Annals,* 267:131-139, January, 1950.

15. For a most comprehensive and detailed account of Army civil affairs field operations during the initial period see E. Grant Meade, *American Military Government in Korea* (New York: King's Crown Press of Columbia Universty, 1951).

16. U.S. Army Civil Affairs School, *History of Civil Affairs, op. cit.,* pp. 80-81; and Department of State, *United States Policy in the Korean Crisis* (Washington: Government Printing Office, 1950) p. 18.

17. The following are questions which might eventually be dealt with in SOLOG Agreements: "(1) Military necessity, (2) Benefits of the governed, (3) Economy of trained personnel, (4) Humanity, (5) Support of the commander's mission, (6) Reciprocal responsibilities, (7) Continuity of policy and command, (8) Continuity of plans and operations, (9) Command responsibility, (10) Integration of personnel in operations, (11) Integration of occupation, and (12) Timely transference of authority." Provost Marshal General, "Preliminary Reports SOLOG," *Civil Affairs Military Government Studies, 1951-1953,* (unpublished series of miscellaneous studies and reports, Provost Marshal General's School, Fort Gordon, Georgia, 1953), Section IV, N. P. (Mimeographed).

18. In most instances SOLOG and STANAG Agreements duplicate each other. The principal pertinent SOLOGs are: No. 29, "Civil Affairs/Military Government Principles of Operations," and No. 39, 40, and 41, "Standard Civil Affairs/Military Government Documents."

CHAPTER III

1. Osgood, *op cit.,* p. 442.

2. William Reitzel, Morton A. Kaplan, and Constance G. Coblenz, *United States Foreign Policy, 1945-1955* (Washington: The Brookings Institution, 1956), pp. 472-473.

3. For an excellent concise statement on the importance of the concept "humanitarianism" in democratic thought see Crane Brinton, Humanitarianism," *Encyclopedia of the Social Sciences,* pp. 544-548.

4. For a well documented study of propaganda statements see Hans Speier, "War Aims in Political Warfare," *Social Research,* 12:157-180, May, 1945.

5. A useful and authoritative source is Doris Appel Graber, *The Development of*

the Law of Belligerent Occupation: 1863-1914 (New York: Columbia University Press, 1949), p. 18.

6. *The War of the Rebellion, a Compilation of the Official Records of the Union and Confederate Armies,* Series III, Vol. III. U. S. House of Representatives Document No. 287, 56th Congress, 1st Session (Washington: Government Printing Office, 1899), p. 146.

7. Department of State, *A Decade of American Foreign Policy, Basic Documents, 1941-1949.* (Washington: Government Printing Office, 1950), pp. 1-2.

8. Thomas A. Bailey, *A Diplomatic History of the American People, op. cit.,* p. 270.

9. For a succinct account of Taylor's civil affairs failures see Ralph H. Gabriel, "American Experience with Military Government," *The American Historical Review,* 49:631, July, 1944.

10. For the text of General Order No. 20 see U. S. Army Civil Affairs School, *History of Civil Affairs, op. cit.,* pp. 17-19. The question of the meaning of the concept *law of nations* was the subject of a noteworthy statement by the influential Congressman Seddon. To him, it was the ". . . code of law to govern all international relations, founded in part on the practices of nations but more correctly binding as deduced from the . . . principles of justice and the higher ethics of morality and humanity." Quoted in Gabriel, *American Historical Review, op. cit.,* p. 643.

11. Gabriel, *Ibid.,* pp. 635-638. 12. *New York Journal,* March 22, 1898.

13. Thomas A. Bailey, *op. cit.,* p. 498. 14. *Ibid.*

15. David F. Healy, *The United States in Cuba* (Madison: The University of Wisconsin Press, 1963), p. 10. This important study pieces together the major factors involved in American civil affairs policy in Cuba.

16. *Ibid.,* p. 44. For primary sources see Robert P. Porter, *Industrial Cuba* (New York: G. P. Putnam's Sons, 1899), and Robert P. Porter, "The Future of Cuba," *North American Review,* 148:418-423, April, 1898.

17. Healy, *op. cit.,* p. 24. 18. *Ibid.* 19. *Ibid.,* p. 34.

20. *Ibid.,* p. 36. 21. *Ibid.,* p. 37. 22. *Ibid.* 23. *Ibid.,* p. 38.

24. Human Relations Area Files, *Philippines* (New Haven: Human Relations Area Files, 4 vols., 1955), Vol. I, p. 89.

25. Healy, *op. cit.,* p. 139.

26. See David Bernstein, *The Philippine Story* (New York: Farrar, Straus & Co., 1947), p. 53.

27. Area Files, *Philippines, op. cit.,* p. 86.

28. Healy, *op. cit.,* p. 210. 29. *Ibid.*

30. From a letter written by Elihu Root to Philip C. Jessup quoted in Jessup, *Eilhu Root* (New York: Dodd, Meade & Co. 1938), Vol. I, p. 345.

31. For Wood's personal account of the calling of the Cuban Constitutional Convention see War Department, *Civil Report of Brigadier General Leonard Wood, Military Governor of Cuba, for the period from December 20, 1899 to December 31, 1900* (Washington: Superintendent of Public Documents, 12 vols., 1901), Vol. I, pp. 9-10.

32. See Pierrepont B. Noyes, *While Europe Waits for Peace* (New York: The Macmillan Co., 1921). For selected documents see Coles and Weinberg, *op. cit.,* pp. 6-7.

33. For interesting insights by the American General on the scene see Henry T. Allen, *The Rhineland Occupation* (Indianapolis: Bobbs-Merrill Co., 1927).

34. Ernst Fraenkel, *Military Occupation and the Rule of Law: Occupation Govern-*

ment in the Rhineland, 1918-1923 (New York: Oxford University Press, 1944), p. 106.

35. Robert W. Komer, *The Other War in Vietnam — A Progress Report* (Washington: Agency for International Development, 1966), Pamphlet. For a well documented and perceptive analysis of the historical evolution of limited war see Robert Endicott Osgood, *Limited War: The Challenge to American Strategy, op. cit.*

36. Bailey, *Diplomatic History, op. cit.*, p. 592.

37. Richard D. Snyder & Edgar S. Furniss, Jr., *American Foreign Policy* (New York: Rinehart & Co., 1954), p. 15.

38. Graves, *op. cit.*, pp. 5-10.

39. Department of State, *American Foreign Policy 1950-1955.* Pub. No. 6446 (Washington: Government Printing Office, 1957), Vol. II, p. 2556.

40. Department of State, *Viet-Nam: The Struggle to be Free.* Pub. No. 8048 (Washington: Government Printing Office, 1966), pp. 10-11.

41. For excellent studies of the role played by journalists in policy questions see Dan Nimmo, *Newsgathering in Washington* (New York: Atherton, 1964), and Lester Merkel & others, *Public Opinion and Foreign Policy, op. cit.*

42. Bernard C. Cohen, *The Press and Foreign Policy* (Princeton: Princeton University Press, 1963), pp. 209-213.

43. *Ibid.*, p. 233.   44. *Ibid.*, p. 234.   45. *Ibid.*, pp. 245-246.

46. For an interesting account of the impact of the journalists on the questions of fraternization and denazification, see respectively Harold Zink, *American Military Government in Germany, op. cit.*, pp. 238-239: and John D. Montgomery, *Forced to be Free* (Chicago: University of Chicago Press, 1957), pp. 191-192.

47. Textor, *op. cit.*, pp. 40-42. This is an excellent source for accounts of specific problems which the journalists faced in Japan.

48. *Ibid.*, p. 40.

49. Harry E. Wildes, *Typhoon in Tokyo* (New York: The Macmillan Co., 1954).

50. Franklin L. Burdette, "Influence of Noncongressional Pressures on Foreign Policy," *The Annals*, 289:92-99, September, 1953.

51. E. Pendleton Herring, *Group Representation Before Congress.* (Baltimore: The Johns Hopkins Press, 1929), pp. 230-238. This early study contains an interesting approach to the classification problem. For the 1955 list see Brooks Emery, "Non-Governmental Organizations in International Affairs," *Social Science*, 30:239-243, October, 1955.

52. For a comprehensive listing see Subcommittee on International Organizations and Movements, Committee on Foreign Affairs, U. S. House of Representatives, Hearings, *Overseas Programs of Private Nonprofit American Organizations, Report No. 3* (Washington: Government Printing Office, May 25, 1965).

53. Richard W. Gable, "Interest Groups as Policy Shapers," *The Annals*, 319:85, September, 1958. For further insights into the question of the Army functioning as a political interest group see Samuel P. Huntington, "Interservice Competition and the Political Roles of the Armed Forces," *American Political Science Review*, 55: 40-52, March, 1961.

54. Gable, *op. cit.*, p. 90.

55. Donald C. Blaisdell, "Pressure Groups, Foreign Policies and International Politics," *The Annals*, 319:149-157, September, 1958.

56. U. S. Government Historical Reports on War Administration, *Report of the American Commission for the Protection and Salvage of Artistic and Historic Monuments in War Areas* (Washington: Government Printing Office, 1946), p. 1. The entire

report merits serious examination.

57. United Nations Command, *Civil Assistance and Economic Affairs, Korea, 1 July 1954-30 June 1955* (Seoul: Headquarters, Korean Civil Assistance Command, 1955), p. 150. For illustrations of the problem in the World War II German occupation see Lucius D. Clay, *Decision in Germany* (Garden City: Doubleday & Co., 1950).

58. This case was summarized from Stephen K. Bailey and Howard Samuel, *Congress at Work* (New York: Henry Holt & Co., 1952), pp. 239-248.

59. Similar state organizations were created later to handle Hungarian and then Cuban refugees.

60. Abraham Holtzman, *Interest Groups and Lobbying* (New York: The Macmillan Co., 1966), pp. 133-138.

61. Clement E. Vose, "Litigation as a Form of Pressure Group Activity," *The Annals*, 319:20, September, 1958.

62. Holtzman, *op. cit.*, p. 139 includes a list of valuable sources relating to direct legislative efforts by pressure groups.

63. Divergent viewpoints exist between the *positivist* and *Grotius* schools as to whether custom and usage or abstract principles should be the starting point for the development of specific rules of international law. However, since war and occupation relate directly to the treatment accorded individuals by states, the idea that a law of humanity plays a role is widely accepted. For thoughtful discussions on this question see Charles G. Fenwick, *International Law* (New York: Appleton-Century-Crofts, 3rd ed., 1948); Kurt von Schuschnigg, *International Law* (Milwaukee: The Bruce Publishing Co., 1959); C. Wilfred Jenks, *The Common Law of Mankind* (New York: Frederick A. Praeger, 1958); Hans Kelsen, *Principles of International Law* (New York: Rinehart & Co., 1952); Arthur Nussbaum, *A Concise History of the Law of Nations* (New York: The Macmillan Co., 1947); Percy E. Corbett, *Law in Diplomacy* (Princeton: Princeton University Press, 1959); Quincy Wright, *The Study of International Relations* (New York: Appleton-Century-Crofts, Inc., 1955). For an excellent selection of references see Jean-Robert Leguey-Feilleux, "The Law of War: A Bibliography, 1945-1958," *World Polity*, Vol. II, *op. cit.*, pp. 319-413.

64. Graber, *op. cit.*, p. 291.   65. *Ibid.*

66. Quoted from J. L. Brierly, *The Law of Nations* (New York: Oxford University Press, 6th ed., 1963), p. 29.

67. *Ibid.*, p. 31.   68. *Ibid.*, pp. 37-40.   69. Graber, *op. cit.*, p. 26.

70. Between the 1874 *Declaration of Brussels* and the 1899 *Convention with Respect to the Laws and Customs of War on Land*, the private Institute of International Law published in 1880 a *Manual of the Laws of War on Land*. Also, from 1864 to 1899 the International Red Cross worked for measures to insure the humane treatment of victims of war.

71. Inis L. Claude, Jr., *Swords into Plowshares* (New York: Random House, 1959), pp. 28-34. See also J. B. Scott, ed., *The Reports to the Hague Conferences of 1899 and 1907* (Oxford: Humphrey Milford, 1917).

72. 1. Hague Convention No. III of October 18, 1907, Relative to the Opening of Hostilities. 2. Hague Convention No. IV of October 18, 1907, Respecting the Laws and Customs of War on Land, and Annex thereto, embodying the Regulations Respecting the Laws and Customs of War on Land. 3. Hague Convention No. V of October 18, 1907, Respecting the Rights and Duties of Neutral Powers and Persons in Case of War on Land. 4. Hague Convention No. IX of October 18, 1907, Concern-

ing Bombardment of Naval Forces in Time of War. 5. Hague Convention No. X of October 18, 1907, for the Adaptation of Maritime Warfare to the Principles of the Geneva Convention. See Department of the Army, *The Law of Land Warfare, op. cit.*, and Department of the Army, *Treaties Governing Land Warfare, op. cit.*

73. Graber, *op. cit.*, p. 287.

74. Various attempts were made to codify the law of war between World War I and II; see Fenwick, *op. cit.*, pp. 82-84. The U. S. is currently a party to three such conventions. 1. Geneva Convention Relative to the Treatment of Prisoners of War of July 27, 1929. 2. Geneva Convention for the Amelioration of the Condition of the Wounded and Sick in Armies in the Field of July 27, 1929. 3. Treaty on the Protection of Artistic and Scientific Institutions and Historic Monuments of April 15, 1934; known as the Roerich Pact, only the U. S. and several American Republics are parties to this treaty.

75. For the text of the Declaration of Berlin see U. S. Senate, *A Decade of American Foreign Policy, 1941-1949*, Senate Document 123, 81st Congress, 1st Session (Washington: Government Printing Office, 1950), pp. 62-70.

76. See Hans Kelson, "The Legal Status of Germany According to the Declaration of Berlin," *American Journal of International Law*, 34:518-526, 1945.

77. Litchfield, *op. cit.*, pp. 14-15.   78. *Ibid.*, p. 15.

79. For further discussion of the 1949 Geneva Conventions see Gerhard von Glahn, *The Occupation of Enemy Territory, op. cit.*, and Morris Greenspan, *The Modern Law of Land Warfare, op. cit.*

80. They are: 1. Geneva Convention for the Amelioration of the Conditions of the Wounded, Sick, and Shipwrecked Members of the Armed Forces at Sea of August 12, 1949. 2. Geneva Convention Relative to the Treatment of Prisoners of War of August 12, 1949. 3. Geneva Convention for the Amelioration of the Condition of the Wounded and Sick in Armed Forces in the Field of August 12, 1949. 4. Geneva Convention Relative to the Protection of Civilians in Time of War of August 12, 1949.

81. Guenter Lewy, "Superior Orders, Nuclear Warfare, and the Dictates of Conscience," *American Political Science Review*, 55:7, March, 1961. The idea of military necessity is an important factor inherent in modern war law codes. For a pertinent analysis see William V. O'Brien, "Military Necessity," *World Polity, op. cit.*

82. Address of July 25, 1951. Quoted in Frederick L. Schuman, *International Politics* (New York: McGraw-Hill, 1948), p. 132.

83. Much of the data in this section relating to U. S. participation in human rights activities in the UN were drawn from L. K. Hyde, Jr., *The United States and the United Nations* (New York: Manhattan Publishing Co., Prepared for the Carnegie Endowment for International Peace, 1960), pp. 153-194.

84. Cited in *Ibid.*, p. 159.

85. For a discussion of the Soviet view toward international law see Oliver J. Lissitzyn, "International Law in a Divided World," *International Conciliation*, No. 542, March, 1963.

86. Hyde, *op. cit.*, p. 166.   87. Hyde, *Ibid.*, p. 170.   88. *Ibid.*, p. 181.

CHAPTER IV

1. Harold Zink, "The Political Scientist Looks at Military Government in the European Theater of Operations," *American Political Science Review*, 40:1109, December, 1946. Several views presented in this chapter were expressed earlier in a study prepared by the primary author for the Army Civil Affairs School. See, "An Approach to United States Army Civil Affairs Policy" (unpublished study, U.S. Army Civil Affairs School, Fort Gordon, Georgia, 1960).

2. George C. S. Benson & Maurice Neufeld, "American Military Government in Italy," in Carl J. Friedrich & Associates, *American Experiences in Military Government in World War II, op. cit.,* p. 122. However, by November, 1943, some directives began to appear.

3. Thomas R. Fisher, "Allied Military Government in Italy," *op. cit.,* p. 115.

4. For further accounts of decentralized control in North Africa, Italy, and Sicily see Francis Wray, *Military Government with Combat Troops* (original study prepared in typescript was later printed as Special Text 41-150 by the Provost Marshal General's School, Fort Gordon, Georgia, 1950).

5. John A. Hearst, Jr., "The Evolution of Allied Military Government in Italy," (unpublished Ph.D. dissertation, Columbia University, New York, 1960), p. 275

6. Because of his outstanding contribution as a member of the Civil Affairs Section, Allied Forces Headquarters, which handled the operation in North Africa, Spoffard was subsequently promoted to the rank of Brigadier General. In a succession of posts in AMGOT (Allied Military Government of Occupied Territory) he continued to play an important role in framing joint American British plans for the occupation of Sicily and Italy.

7. For a more thorough discussion of Poletti's questionnaire and categories see Hearst, *op. cit.,* pp. 155-156.

8. For a collection of memos, reports, and directives issued by Poletti in Sicily and Italy see Coles and Weinberg, *op. cit.,* Part II, "Soldiers Learn Politics in Italy," pp. 157-649.

9. Robert W. Komer, "Civil Affairs and Military Government in the Mediterranean Theater," *op. cit.,* Section XIX-14, "Epuration."

10. We owe special appreciation to Professor Ned Holsten of Augusta College for many of the observations and insights regarding the role of Colonel Poletti. Professor Holsten whose book on the reconstruction of the Italian Government is pending release by the University of South Carolina Press, was an active duty Army civil affairs officer for twenty years. For one of the few published background sketches of Poletti see: Charles Poletti in collaboration with George Tucker, "Scrubbing Up After the Dictators," *The American Magazine,* 138:17, November, 1944.

11. Fisher, *op. cit.,* p. 121.

12. Harold Zink, *American Military Government in Germany, op. cit.,* pp. 23-24.

13. Dwight D. Eisenhower, *Crusade in Europe* (Garden City: Doubleday & Co., 1952), p. 441.

14. Harold Zink, *American Military Government in Germany, op. cit.,* p. 26.

15. *Ibid.*

16. For a generally sympathetic biography of Butler see Hans L. Trefousse, *Ben Butler: The South Called Him the Beast* (New York: Twayne Publishers, 1957), p. 123.

17. *Ibid.,* p. 110.   18. *Ibid.,* pp. 117-118.

19. Walter L. Fleming, *The Sequel of Appomattox* (New Haven: Chronicles of America Series, Yale University Press, Vol. 32, 1919), pp. 140-141.

20. For a vivid account of Littlefield's actions see Jonathan Daniels, *Prince of Carpetbaggers* (Philadelphia: J. B. Lippincott, 1958).

21. Fleming, *op. cit.*, p. 206.

22. For a highly critical evaluation of MacArthur see Walter Millis with Harvey C. Mansfield and Harold Stein, *Arms and the State*, *op. cit.*, p. 266.

23. Russell Brines, *MacArthur's Japan* (New York: J. B. Lippincott, 1948), p. 63.

24. Charles A. Willoughby, *Maneuver in War* (Harrisburg: Military Service Publishing Co., 1939), p. 235.

25. For a more complete account of the Sorianos affair see Frank Kluckhohn, "Heidelberg to Madrid—The Story of General Willoughby," *The Reporter Magazine*, 7:26-29, August 19, 1952.

26. *Ibid.*, p. 29.

27. *Ibid.*, p. 26, as quoted from Gunther's book *The Riddle of MacArthur*.

28. *Ibid.*, p. 25.   29. *Ibid.*, p. 26.

30. Committee on Foreign Affairs, House of Representatives, *Mutual Security Act of 1960*, Hearings, 86th Congress Washington: Government Printing Office, 1960), Part V, p. 745. It is interesting to note that Willoughby was preceded as a witness before the committee by another ex-member of MacArthur's staff, Brig. General Bonner Fellers (Ret.), who testified as Vice Chairman and National Director of the Citizens' Foreign Aid Committee. His enthusiasm for the "Fortress America" concept presents a revealing picture of where this wing of the military has stood on foreign policy matters.

31. *Ibid.*, p. 741.   32. *Ibid.*, p. 743.   33. *Ibid.*, p. 752.

34. For an authoritative account see Harry E. Wildes, *Typhoon in Tokyo*, *op. cit.*, p. 306.

35. Kluckhohn, *op. cit.*, p. 28.   36. Wildes, *op. cit.*

37. *Ibid.*, p. 307.   38. Kluckhohn, *op. cit.*   39. *Ibid.*

40. Jerome Forrest and Clarke H. Kawakami, "General MacArthur and His Vanishing War History," *The Reporter Magazine*, 7:21, October 14, 1952.

41. Kluckhohn, *op. cit.*   42. Forrest and Kawakami, *op. cit.*, p. 22.

43. Kluckhohn, *op. cit.*   44. Forrest and Kawakami, *op. cit.*, p. 21

45. Wildes, *op. cit.*, p. 307.   46. Kluckhohn, *op. cit.*   47. *Ibid.*

48. Kazuo Kawai, *Japan's American Interlude* (Chicago: University of Chicago Press, 1960), p. 18. Numerous other accounts describing the centralized nature of the Japanese occupation are available. Among the most authoritative and informative of these are the following: Edwin M. Martin, *The Allied Occupation of Japan* (Stanford: Stanford University Press, 1948); Robert A. Fearey, *The Occupation of Japan, Second Phase: 1948-1950* (New York: Macmillan Co., 1950); Robert B. Textor, *Failure in Japan*, *op. cit.*, R. P. Dore, *Land Reform in Japan* (New York: Oxford University Press, 1959); and Ralph J. D. Braibanti, "Administration of Military Government in Japan at the Perfectual Level," *American Political Science Review*, 43:250-274, April, 1949.

49. Manning, *op. cit.*, p. 90.   50. Graves, *op. cit.*, pp. 10-11.

51. For an able treatment see Gene M. Lyons, *Military Policy and Economic Aid: The Korean Case, 1950-1953* (Columbus: The Ohio State University Press, 1961), Ch. V, "The Failure of American Policy," is especially relevant, pp. 109-130.

52. Ralph H. Gabriel, "American Experience with Military Government," *Ameri-*

can Political Science Review, op. cit., pp. 430-431.

53. *Ibid.,* 432-433.   54. Millis, *op. cit.,* pp. 44-45.

55. Fisher, *op. cit.,* p. 119.

56. John Gimbel, "American Denazification and German Local Politics, 1945-1949," *American Political Science Review,* 54:88-89, March, 1960. For a comprehensive account of the World War II problems of policy coordination on the Washington scene see Paul Y. Hammond, "Directives for the Occupation of Germany; The Washington Controversy," in Harold Stein (ed.), *American Civil-Military Decisions* (New York: The Twentieth Century Fund, 1963), pp. 311-464.

57. Millis, *op. cit.,* pp. 126-127.

58. For elaboration see Ernest R. May, "The Development of Political-Military Consultation in the United States," *Political Science Quarterly,* 70:175, June, 1955.

59. Millis, *op. cit.,* p. 125.   60. *Ibid.,* p. 172.   61. *Ibid.,* p. 125.

62. *Ibid.*   63. Holborn, *op. cit.,* p. 12.   64. *Ibid.,* p. 13.

65. For a thorough and authoritative study of the agency question within the military during World War II consult Ray S. Cline, *Washington Command Post* (Washington: Department of the Army, Office of The Chief of Military History, 1951).

66. May, *op. cit.,* p. 180. For numerous references to the problem of coordination among agencies see Morris O. Edwards, *op. cit.;* and James P. Pappas, *op. cit.*

67. Graves, *op. cit.,* pp. 10-11.   68. *Ibid.,* p. 217.

69. Harold Zink, *American Military Government in Germany, op. cit.,* p. 8.

70. For data concerning World War II training programs, see the following authoritative accounts: Robert J. Matthew, *Language and Area Studies in the Armed Forces* (Washington: American Council on Education, 1947), Ch. VI, "The Civil Affairs Training Schools Program," pp. 91-102; and John B. Mason, "Lessons of Wartime Military Government Training," *The Annals,* 267:183-192, January, 1950; and Coles and Weinberg, *op. cit., pp.* 10-13.

71. Training programs for the European and Mediterranean theaters were conducted at Harvard, Yale, Pittsburgh, Michigan, Stanford, Chicago, Boston, Northwestern, Wisconsin, and Western Reserve. Asiatic programs were established at Harvard, Yale, Michigan, Chicago, Northwestern, and Stanford.

72. Harold Zink, *American Military Government in Germany, op. cit.,* pp. 16-17.

73. *Ibid.,* p. 17.

74. For example, an article appearing in the February 1943 issue of *Fortune Magazine* written by Ray C. Evans titled "Prepare to Occupy," was reproduced in pamphlet form by the School for Government of Occupied Areas at Carlisle Barracks. The following notation was inserted on the inside cover: "The subject material is considered to be very valuable in any study of civil affairs or military government." Yet the article contained little more than a summary description of the civil affairs training program already in progress.

75. Notable among these was Charles M. Spofford who had played a key role on planning staffs in the Mediterranean Theater. When reassigned to the Charlottesville School, he brought along his personal collection of papers and documents. These were reproduced and widely circulated among the various civil affairs training centers. Being the first readily available and documented account of World War II occupation experiences, the "Spofford Papers" contributed a needed dimension of realism to instruction.

76. These covered the following topics: geographical and social background, gov-

ernment and administration, legal affairs, government finance, money and banking, natural resources, utilities, transportation systems, communications, public health and sanitation, agriculture, industry and commerce, labor, public works, public safety, education, public welfare, and cultural institutions. Professor Zink believed, however, that the single most valuable source of information for planning the German occupation was the *Basic German Handbook* prepared by the British Combined Intelligence Department; Zink, *American Military Government in Germany, op. cit.,* p. 18.

77. Many of the judgments concerning postwar civil affairs training are drawn from the personal experiences of the primary author.

78. The Military Government Association has been a major vehicle through which active and reserve officers mobilized political interest group pressure. Its active and honorary members have included influential figures from the military agencies, civilian officers, Congress, state governments, universities, and informational media. Figures such as Adm. Ben Morell, Gen. Mark Clark, Gen. Lucius D. Clay, Lt. Gen. C. W. Wickersham, Sen. Strom Thurmond, Hon. John J. McCloy and Amb. W. J. Sebald, have held prominent offices.

79. Louis Smith, *American Democracy and Military Power* (Chicago: The University of Chicago Press, 1951). See especially Ch. II, "The American Tradition of Civil Dominance."

80. Robert W. Komer, "Civil Affairs and Military Government in the Mediterranean Theater," *op. cit.,* Ch. 11, p. 44.

81. Pappas, *op. cit.,* p. 34.   82. Textor, *op. cit.,* p. 159.

83. Fisher, *op. cit.,* p. 120.   84. Textor, *op. cit.,* p. 153.

85. Carl Dreher, "Close-Up of Democracy," *The Virginia Quarterly Review,* 23:106, Winter, 1947. For illustrations of Army efforts to raise the level of political education of its officers see John W. Masland and Laurence I. Radway, *Soldiers and Scholars* (Princeton: Princeton University Press, 1957).

GENERAL ORDER 20, ISSUED BY GENERAL WINFIELD
SCOTT ON FEBRUARY 19, 1847 [EXCERPTS]

1. It may well be apprehended that many grave offenses not provided for in the act of congress establishing rules and articles for
the armies of the United States, approved April 10, 1806, may be
again committed—by, or upon, individuals of those armies, in Mexico, ending the existing war between the two Republics. Allusion
is here made to atrocities, any one of which, if committed within the
United States or their organized territories, would, of course, be tried
and severely punished by the ordinary or civil courts of the land.

2. Assassination; murder, malicious stabbing or maiming; rape;
malicious assault and battery; robbery; theft; the wanton desecra-
tion of churches, cemeteries or other religious edifices and fixtures,
and the destruction, except by order of superior officer, of public or
private property are such offenses.

3. The good of the service, the honor of the United States and the
interest of humanity, imperiously demand that every crime, enumerated above, should be severely punished.

4. But the written code, as above, commonly called the Rules and
Articles of War, provides for the punishment of not one of those
crimes, even when committed by individuals of the Army upon the
persons or property of other individuals of the same, except in the
very restricted case in the 9th of these articles; nor for like outrages,
committed by the same individuals, upon the persons or property of
a hostile country, except very partially, in the 51st, 52nd, and 55th
articles; and the same code is absolutely silent as to all injuries which
may be inflicted upon individuals of the Army, or their property
against the laws of war, by individuals of a hostile country.

        *   *   *   *   *   *

6. For all the offenses, therefore, enumerated in the second paragraph above, which may be committed abroad—in, by or upon the
Army, a supplemental code is absolutely needed.

7.That unwritten code is Martial Law, as an addition to the written military code, prescribed by Congress in the Rules and Articles

of War, and which unwritten code, all armies, in hostile countries, are forced to adopt—not only for their own safety, but for the protection of the unoffending inhabitants and their property, about the theaters of military operations, against injuries contrary to the laws of war.

8. From the same supreme necessity, martial law is hereby declared, as a supplement code in and about, all camps, posts, and hospitals which may be occupied by any part of the forces of the United States, in Mexico, and in and about all columns, escorts, convoys, guards and detachments, of the said forces, while engaged in prosecuting the existing war in and against the said republic.

9. Accordingly, every crime, enumerated in paragraph 2 above, whether committed — 1. By any inhabitant of Mexico, sojourner or traveler therein, upon the person or property of any individual of the United States forces, retainer or follower of the same; 2. By any individual of the said forces, retainer or follower of the same, upon the person or property of any inhabitant of Mexico, sojourner or traveler therein; or 3. By any individual of the said forces, retainer or follower of the same, upon the person or property of any other individual of the said forces, retainer or follower of the same—shall be duly tried and punished under the said supplemental code.

10. For this purpose it is ordered, that all offenders, on the matters aforesaid, shall be promptly seized and confined and reported, for trial, before commissions to be duly appointed as follows:

11. Every military commission, under this order will be appointed, governed and limited, as prescribed by 65th, 66th, 67th, and 97th of the said Rules and Articles of War . . . and provided also that no sentence of a military commission shall be put in execution against any individual, whatsoever, which may not be, according to the nature and degree of the offense, as established by evidence, in conformity with known punishments, in like cases, in some one of the States of the United States of America.

12. This order will be read at the head of every company of the United States forces, serving in Mexico, or about to enter that theater of war. (United States Army Civil Affairs School, *History of Civil Affairs, op. cit.,* pp. 17-19).

GENERAL ORDER 100, "INSTRUCTIONS FOR THE GOVERNMENT OF ARMIES OF THE UNITED STATES IN THE FIELD," APRIL 24, 1863, PREPARED BY FRANCIS LIEBER [Excerpts]

Section I. Martial law—Military jurisdiction—Military necessity—Retaliation.

1. A place, district, or country occupied by an enemy stands, in consequence of the occupation, under the martial law of the invading or occupying army, whether any proclamation declaring martial law, or any public warning to the inhabitants, has been issued or not. Martial law is the immediate and direct effect and consequence of occupation or conquest.

The presence of a hostile army proclaims its martial law.

2. Martial law does not cease during the hostile occupation, except by special proclamation, ordered by the commander-in-chief, or by special mention in the treaty of peace concluding the war, when the occupation of a place or territory continues beyond the conclusion of peace as one of the conditions of the same.

3. Martial law in a hostile country consists in the suspension by the occupying military authority of the criminal and civil law, and of the domestic administration and government in the occupied place or territory, and in the substitution of military rule and force for the same, as well as in the dictation of general laws, as far as military necessity requires this suspension, substitution, or dictation.

The commander of the forces may proclaim that the administration of all civil and penal law shall continue either wholly or in part, as in times of peace, unless otherwise ordered by the military authority.

4. Martial law is simply military authority exercised in accordance with the laws and usages of war. Military oppression is not marital law; it is the abuse of the power which that law confers. As martial law is executed by military force, it is incumbent upon those who administer it to be strictly guided by the principles of justice, honor, and humanity-virtues adorning a soldier even more than other men,

for the very reason that he possesses the power of his arms against the unarmed.

5. Martial law should be less stringent in places and countries fully occupied and fairly conquered. Much greater severity may be exercised in places or regions where actual hostilities exist or are expected and must be prepared for. Its most complete sway is allowed—even in the commander's own country—when face to face with the enemy, because of the absolute necessities of the case, and of the paramount duty to defend the country against invasion.

To save the country is paramount to all other considerations.

6. All civil and penal law shall continue to take its usual course in the enemy's places and territories under martial law, unless interrupted or stopped by order of the occupying military power; but all the functions of the hostile government—legislative, executive, or administrative—whether of a general, provincial, or local character, cease under martial law, or continue only with the sanction, or, if deemed necessary, the participation of the occupier or invader.

*   *   *   *   *   *

11. The law of war does not only disclaim all cruelty and bad faith concerning engagements concluded with the enemy during the war, but also the breaking of stipulations solemnly contracted by the belligerents in time of peace, and avowedly intended to remain in force in case of war between the contracting powers.

It disclaims all extortions and other transactions for individual gain; all acts of private revenge, or connivance at such acts.

Offenses to the contrary shall be severely punished, and especially so if committed by officers.

*   *   *   *   *   *

13. Military jurisdiction is of two kinds: First, that which is conferred and defined by statute; second, that which is derived from the common law of war. Military offenses under the statute law must be tried in the manner therein directed; but military offense which does not come within the statute must be tried and punished under the common law of war. The character of the courts which exercise these jurisdictions depends upon the local laws of each particular country.

*   *   *   *   *   *

14. Military necessity does not admit of cruelty—that is, the infliction of suffering for the sake of suffering or for revenge, nor of

maiming or wounding except in fight, nor of torture to extort confessions. It does not admit to the use of poison in any way, nor of the wanton devastation of a district. It admits of deception, but disclaims acts of perfidy; and, in general, military necessity does not include any act of hostility which makes the return to peace unnecessarily difficult.

*   *   *   *   *   *

21. The citizen or native of a hostile country is thus an enemy, as one of the constituents of the hostile state or nation, and as such is subjected to the hardships of the war.

22. Nevertheless, as civilization has advanced during the last centuries, so has likewise steadily advanced, especially in war on land, the distinction between the private individual belonging to a hostile country and the hostile country itself, with its men in arms. The principle has been more and more acknowledged that the unarmed citizen is to be spared in person, and honor as much as the exigencies of war will admit.

23. Private citizens are no longer murdered, enslaved, or carried off to distant parts, and the inoffensive individual is as little disturbed in his private relations as the commander of the hostile troops can afford to grant in the overruling demands of a vigorous war.

24. The almost universal rule in remote times was, and continues to be with barbarous armies, that the private individual of a hostile country is destined to suffer every privation of liberty and protection and every disruption of family ties. Protection was, and still is with uncivilized people, the exception.

*   *   *   *   *   *

Unjust or inconsiderate retaliation removes the belligerents farther and farther from the mitigating rules of regular war, and by rapid steps leads them nearer to the internecine wars of savages.

29. Modern times are distinguished from earlier ages by the existence at one and the same time of many nations and great governments related to one another in close intercourse.

Peace is their normal condition; war is the exception. The ultimate object of all modern war is a renewed state of peace.

The more vigorously wars are pursued the better it is for humanity. Sharp wars are brief.

30. Ever since the formation and coexistence of modern nations,

and ever since wars have become great national wars, war has come to be acknowledged not to be its own end, but the means to obtain great ends of state, or to consist in defense against wrong; and no conventional restriction of the modes adopted to injure the enemy is any longer admitted; the law of war imposes many limitations and restrictions on principles of justice, faith, and honor. (*The War of the Rebellion,* A Compilation of the Official Records of the Union and Confederate Armies, Series III, Vol. III, House of Representatives Document No. 287, 56th Congress, 1st Session (Washington: Government Printing Office, 1899), pp. 146-164).

APPENDIX C

PRESIDENT WILSON'S AIDE MEMOIRE

The whole heart of the United States is in the winning of this war. The controlling purpose of the Government of the United States is to do everything that is necessary and effective to win it. It wishes to cooperate in every practicable way with the allied governments, and to cooperate ungrudgingly; for it has no ends of its own to serve and believes that the war can be won only by common council and intimate concert of action. It has sought to study every proposed policy or action in which its cooperation has been asked in this spirit, and states the following conclusions in the confidence, that if it finds itself obligated to decline participation in any undertaking or course of action, it will be understood that it does so only because it deems itself precluded from participating by imperative considerations either of policy or fact.

In full agreement with the allied governments and upon the unanimous advice of the Supreme War Council, the Government of the United States adopted, upon its entrance into the war, a plan for taking part in the fighting on the western front into which all its resources of men and material were to be put, and put as rapidly as possible, and it has carried out this plan with energy and success, pressing its execution more and more rapidly forward and literally putting into it the entire energy and executive force of the nation. This was its response, its very willing and hearty response, to what was the unhesitating judgment alike of its own military advisors and of the advisors of the allied governments. It is now considering, at the suggestion of the Supreme War Council, the possibility of making very considerable additions even to this immense programme which, if they should prove feasible at all, will tax the industrial processes of the United States and the shipping facilities of the whole group of associated nations to the utmost. It has thus concentrated all its plans and all its resources upon this single absolutely necessary object.

In such circumstances it feels it to be its duty to say that it cannot, so long as the military situation on the western front remains critical, consent to break or slaken the force of its present effort by

189

diverting any part of its military force to other points or objectives.
The United States military force is at a much greater distance from
any other field of action. The instrumentalities by which it is to
handle its armies and its stores have at a great cost and with great
difficulty been created in France. They do not exist elsewhere. It is
practical for her to do a great deal in France; it is not practicable
for her to do anything of importance or on a large scale upon any
other field. The American Government, therefore, very respectfully
requested its Associates to accept its deliberate judgment that it
should not dissipate its force by attempting important operations
elsewhere.

It regards the Italian front as closely coordinated with the western
front, however, and it willing to divert a portion of its military forces
from France to Italy if it is the judgment and wish of the Supreme
Command that it should do so. It wishes to defer to the decision of
the Commander-in-Chief in this matter, as it would wish to defer
in all other matters particularly because it considers these two fronts
so related as to be practically but separate parts of a single line and
because it would be necessary that any American troops sent to
Italy should be subtracted from the number used in France and be
actually transported across French territory from the ports now used
by armies of the United States.

It is the clear and fixed judgment of the Government of the
United States, arrived at after repeated and very searching recon-
siderations of the whole situation in Russia, that military intervention there would add to the present sad confusion in Russia rather
than cure it, injure her rather than help her, and that it would be
of no advantage in the prosecution of our main design, to win the
war against Germany. It cannot, therefore, take part in such intervention or sanction it in principle. Military intervention would, in
its judgment, even supposing it to be efficacious in its immediate
avowed object of delivering an attack upon Germany from the east,
be merely a method of making use of Russia, not a method of serving her. Her people could not profit by it, if they profited by it at
all, in time to save them from their present distresses, and their substance would be used to maintain foreign armies, not to reconstitute
their own. Military action is admissible in Russia, as the Government of the United States sees the circumstances, only to help the
Czecho-Slovaks consolidate their forces and get into successful cooperation with their Slavik kinsmen and to steady any efforts at

self-government or self-defense in which the Russians themselves may be willing to accept assistance. Whether from Vladivostok or from Murmansk and Archangel, the only legitimate object for which American or allied troops can be employed, it submits, is to guard military stores which may subsequently be needed by Russian forces and to render such aid as may be acceptable to the Russians in the organization of their own self-defense. For helping the Czecho-Slovaks there is immediate necessity and sufficient justification. Recent developments have made it evident that that is in the interest of what the Russian people themselves desire, and the Government of the United States is glad to contribute the small force at its disposal for that purpose. It yields, also, to the judgment of the Supreme Command in the matter of establishing a small force at Murmansk, to guard the military stores at Kola and to make it safe for Russian forces to come together in organized bodies in the north. But it owes it to frank counsel to say that it can go no further than those modest and experimental plans. It is not in a position, and has no expectation of being in a position, to take part in organized intervention in adequate force from either Vladivostok or Murmansk and Archangel. It feels that it ought to add, also, that it will feel at liberty to use the few troops it can spare only for the purposes here stated and shall feel obligated to withdraw these forces, in order to add them to the forces at the western front, if the plans in whose execution it is now intended that they should develop into others inconsistent with the policy to which the Government of the United States feels constrained to restrict itself.

At the same time the Government of the United States wishes to say with the utmost cordiality and good will that none of the conclusions here stated is meant to wear the least color of criticism of what the other governments associated against Germany may think it wise to undertake. It wishes in no way to embarrass their choices of policy. All that is intended here is a perfectly frank and definite statement of the policy which the United States feels obligated to adopt for herself in the use of her own military forces. The Government of the United States does not wish it to be understood that in so restricting its own activities it is seeking, even by implication, to set limits to the action or to define the policies of its Associates.

It hopes to carry out the plans for safeguarding the rear of the Czecho-Slovaks operating from Vladivostok in a way that will place it and keep it in close cooperation with a small military force like its own from Japan, and if necessary from the other Allies, and that will assure it of the cordial accord of all the allied powers; and it proposes to ask all associated in this course of action to unite in assuring the people of Russia in the most public and solemn manner that none of the governments uniting in action either in Siberia or in northern Russia contemplates any interference of any kind with the political sovereignty of Russia, any intervention in her internal affairs, or any impairment of her territorial integrity either now or hereafter, but that each of the associated powers has the single object of affording such aid as shall be acceptable, and only such aid as shall be acceptable, to the Russian people in their endeavor to regain control of their own affairs, their own territory, and their own destiny.

It is the hope and purpose of the Government of the United States to take advantage of the earliest opportunity to send to Siberia a commission of merchants, agricultural experts, labour advisers, Red Cross Representatives, and agents of the Young Men's Christian Association accustomed to organizing the best methods of spreading useful information and rendering educational help of a modest sort, in order in some systematic manner to relieve the immediate economic necessities of the people there in every way of which opportunity may open. The execution of this plan will follow and will not be permitted to embarrass the military assistance rendered in the rear of the westwardmoving forces of the Czecho-Slovaks. (Department of State, Washington, July 17, 1918.)

INDEX

Agency for International Development
(AID), 19, 25, 70, 72, 137, 155, 165
Aggressive democratization, 152-165
Aide Memoire, 64, 134
Air Force, U.S., 72
Airlift, Berlin, 37
Akzin, Benjamin, 31
Alaska *(See* Annexation).
Algiers *(See* North Africa).
Alliance for Progress, 155
Allied Commission, theater-wide direc-
tive, 106
Allied Control Council (ACC), 39, 40,
109
American Coalition of Patriotic
Societies, 118
American Law Institute, 95
American Protective Association, 58
American Society of International Law,
95
Amicus Curiae, 82
Annapolis, U.S. Naval Academy, 166
Annexation and annexed territories, 31
Archaeological Institute of America, 79
Army Civil Affairs School (USACAS),
14, 19, 141, 144, 146
Army Reserve, 19, 20, 22, 141
Artillery Branch, 21
Atlantic Charter, 49, 50, 89
Australia, 117
Austria, 36

Bailey, Stephen K., 81
Baldwin, Hanson W., 17
Balkans, 12
Belgium, 36, 41
Berlin, 36-39, 88, 97, 156
Beveridge, Senator Albert J., 57
Bill of Rights, 59, 94
Black Friday, 114
Blockade, Berlin, 97
Board of Economic Warfare, 130, 132
Board of Foreign Relief, 132
Bolshevik *(See* Siberian Intervention).

Bricker, Senator John, 97
Brines, Russell, 116
Britain, 1, 35, 41, 43-44, 58-59, 102,
107-108, 118, 157
Brooke, General John R., 56
Brussels Code of 1874, 86, 87
Buddhists *(See* Religious questions).
Butler, General Ben, 111-113

Caesar, 23
Cairo Declaration of 1943, 42
California *(See* Annexation).
Canada, 43-44
Caribbean, 2
Carlisle Barracks School, 138
Carnegie Endowment, 96
Carr, E. H., 34
Cartels, German, 82
Casablanca Conference, 131
Castro's Cuba, 25-27
Catholic Church *(See* Religious ques-
tions).
Cavalry Branch, 21
Central America, 72
Chafee, General Adna R., 56
Charleston, occupation, 114
Charlottesville Training Center *(See*
Virginia, University).
Chemical Corps, 143
Chicago Sun, 77
China, Red, 159
Christian Science Monitor, 76
Churchill, Winston, 49, 107
Citizens' Committee for Displaced Per-
sons, 81
Civic Action, 8-9, 14, 19, 39, 63, 70, 72-
73, 148, 157
Civil Affairs Branch, USAR, 19
Civil Affairs Committee (CCAC), 129
Civil Affairs, definition, 4, 10, 15, 16
Civil Affairs Division, Army (CAD),
79, 129, 133
Civil Affairs Training Schools (CATS),
137-139, 142